Exploring Southern California Beaches

David Crowell

FALCON®
HELENA, MONTANA

A FALCON GUIDE ®

Falcon® Publishing is continually expanding its list of recreational guidebooks. All books include detailed descriptions, accurate maps, and all information necessary for enjoyable trips. You can order extra copies of this book and get information and prices for other Falcon® books by writing Falcon, P.O. Box 1718, Helena, MT 59624, or by calling toll-free 1-800-582-2665. Also, please ask for a copy of our current catalog. Visit our website at www.FalconOutdoors.com or contact us by e-mail at falcon@falcon.com.

All black-and-white photos by the author unless otherwise noted.

Cataloging-in-Publication Data is on file at the Library of Congress.

CAUTION

Outdoor recreational activities are by their very nature potentially hazardous. All participants in such activities must assume responsibility for their own actions and safety. The information contained in this guidebook cannot replace sound judgment and good decision-making skills, which help reduce exposure, nor does the scope of this book allow for the disclosure of all the potential hazards and risks involved in such activities.

Learn as much as possible about the outdoor recreational activities in which you participate, prepare for the unexpected, and be cautious. The reward will be a safer and more enjoyable experience.

 Text pages printed on recycled paper.

CONTENTS

APPENDICES

ABOUT THE AUTHOR

ACKNOWLEDGMENTS

Mother Ocean . . . for everything.

San Miguel Island . . . for connecting my soles to the earth.

The falcon in the night . . . for your guidance and stirring my animal spirits.

Dad . . . for providing me with eyes that see the world as it is.

Mum . . . for providing me with eyes that see the world as it can be.

Clint . . . for Ventura, surfing, food, friendship, love . . . I'm proud to be your brother.

Debbie . . . for going first . . . I'm proud you're my sister.

John . . . for the reassurance.

Marie . . . for bringing Heidi to the coffee shop.

Bill . . . for sharing your journey.

Lara . . . for reawakening the ocean in my soul.

Will Harmon . . . for giving me the confidence to continue writing.

Glenn Law . . . for grabbing the manuscript by the horns and getting it to press.

Bill Schneider . . . for hiring me to do the job.

Heidi . . . for being patient while I slugged it out with this beast. Your faith in me gives me strength, your friendship provides sanity, and your love makes everything worthwhile.

LIFE'S A BEACH

The sun, rising slowly above the coastal mountains, casts its rays upon the shore-line of Southern California. The Pacific Ocean is "glassy" and reflects the pink sky of dawn. A group of surfers is already in the water enjoying another successful dawn patrol. Shorebirds dart around in the foam of the receding tide in search of food in the sand.

As the sun climbs up into the sky, human activity increases. The thumping of volleyballs is heard as they are passed and spiked in friendly and heated competi-tion alike. The asphalt paths that border the sands begin to fill up with in-line skaters, bikers, joggers, and others out for a stroll by the sea where dolphins are visible playing offshore, their fins gently arcing above the water's surface as they wander the coast.

As the sun climbs still higher, the air temperature heats up. It is now well into the PTH, Peak Tanning Hours. Groups of people stake out territory with blankets and towels. Their portable audio systems create an eclectic mix of sounds as one strolls the beach. Yet it all is dwarfed by the rhythm of the ocean.

The wind begins to pick up and the sky fills with bright colors as kites dart and weave in the onshore breeze. The same wind, creating a choppy ocean, sends the surfers to shore to be replaced by their sailing cousins, windsurfers. Farther out to sea, sailboats tack and jibe en route to offshore islands where many will don scuba equipment to view the world of wonder that exists beneath the ocean's surface.

Now, the sun is finishing its day's journey through the Southern California sky. A kayaker can be seen returning from a fishing trip at a nearby kelp bed. A spout of water spits skyward, revealing the location of a migrating gray whale. The wind is breathing its last breaths and the Pacific looks like molten mercury reflect-ing the oranges, yellows, and reds of the setting sun. A surfer shares a last wave during this glass-off with a squadron of pelicans that glide effortlessly on a cushion of air above the wave. Reaching shore, the surfer grabs the board and looks back to sea. The sun has dropped beneath the horizon and the sky is alight in neon-pink fire as the day's last light hits clouds high overhead. The surfer heads back home to the sound of a quiet beach, just the slow building and release of noise from the waves.

The sound of the ocean . . . breathing.

Welcome, Explorers

All explorers share a thirst for discovery. Some have a specific something they're looking for while others can't quite put their fingers on it. Juan Rodriguez Cabrillo, the first European known to explore Southern California, had the stars guide him. *Exploring Southern California Beaches* provides a navigational tool for modern-day explorers' use in their discovery of the same jewel, the California coast.

The fun of exploration *is* the discovery, like finding the little coffee shop that nobody else knows about or the secluded cove just around the corner that lacks footprints of past travelers. This guide's aim is to give you a jumping-off point, a ground zero for your explorations, a place to start your journeys and to wander back to when feeling overwhelmed. This guide provides the framework to build the memories upon which future tales will be based.

The guide's maps are useful in the field, helping you stay on track and prompting the explorer within.

So grab the sunscreen and your sunglasses. We've got discoveries to make!

How to Use This Guide

Exploring Southern California Beaches will help you find the beach experience you are looking for. Whether it's a rousing game of volleyball, a lazy day in the sun, a wave to surf, shells to find, crowds, or solitude, this tome can help you find it. The book has been arranged to give you information that will help you differentiate among the plethora of places to play along Southern California's shore. Your perfect beach experience differs from anyone else's. That's a good thing! If the information you desire isn't here, then a phone number or website that can get you that info will be listed.

Exploring Southern California Beaches describes beaches that extend from the United States border with Mexico at the Pacific Ocean northward to the San Luis Obispo County line. This area has been divided into 19 regions, which have been subdivided into each of that region's beaches. The regions are shown on the California state map, which also includes major thoroughfares of significance to coastal travel. Regional maps are keyed to the beaches and sites discussed in the region's description.

Each regional chapter begins with a brief description of the area and shares some local flavor. This is followed by directions via major highway to reach the region. Next is a listing of the beaches along with activities and amenities associated with the beach. Camping areas are listed with a brief description of cost and available amenities.

Finally, other sites of interest are listed with a contact number if appropriate. These are a mix of natural and manmade sites that may be of interest to explorers. Museums and zoos, along with areas of shopping and amusement, are placed here.

Between the regions you will find essays with enlightening information on a variety of beach-related activities and phenomena.

Overview Map

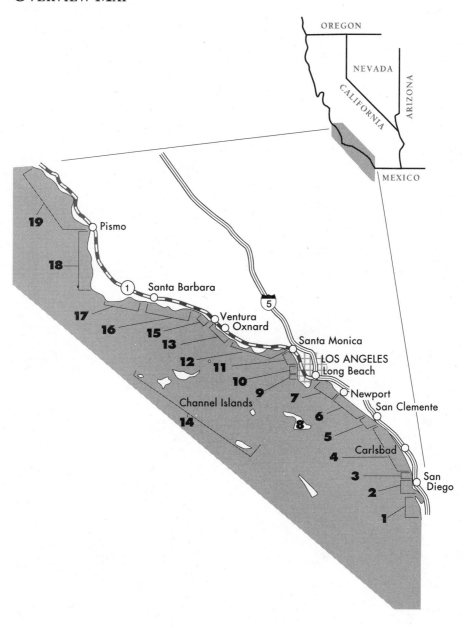

OREGON

NEVADA

CALIFORNIA

ARIZONA

MEXICO

19

Pismo

18

① Santa Barbara

⑤

17

16

15

Ventura
Oxnard

13

Santa Monica

12

11

LOS ANGELES
Long Beach

10

9

7

Newport

Channel Islands

8

6

San Clemente

14

5

4

Carlsbad

3

San
Diego

2

1

REGION 1

U.S.–MEXICO BORDER TO CORONADO

A wide expanse of sand spans the border of the United States and Mexico. On the surface, things couldn't look better. However, Tijuana's sewage often taints the water, making it unsafe for human contact. This is an unfortunate sign of the times. Mexico has made a commitment to clean things up, but that will take time. The soft, white, sandy shoreline continues northward up the coast past the towns of Imperial Beach and Coronado. The water quality improves as well. San Diego County conducts rigorous testing and posts signs when water quality is low.

Border Field State Park, California's southernmost beach, makes the best of things, offering horseback and hiking trails within a well-preserved estuary, home to a number of birds and other wildlife.

Imperial Beach has been a beach hangout since a ferry began carrying beachgoers here from San Diego in the early 1900s. It is now struggling with its beach-bum past, striving to put some shine on its image. These white sands are the location of the world's longest-running sandcastle competition.

Coronado claims a colorful recreational history. In addition to its 2 miles of wide, sandy shoreline, it boasts the largest wooden structure west of the Mississippi, the Hotel del Coronado. The classic Victorian structure, circa 1887, was the first hotel equipped with electric lights whose installation Thomas Edison directed. The couple who built the hotel bought the island in 1885. They used to boat to the brush-covered expanse and hunt rabbits. Coronado maintains pride in its tourism past, which visitors appreciate.

The sheltered side of San Diego Bay, known as South Bay, includes the towns of Chula Vista and National City. Chula Vista offers coastal visitors access to San Diego Bay via the Chula Vista Launching Ramp. This connects with Marina View Park, which offers a plethora of recreation opportunities. Sweetwater Marsh gives wildlife watchers a natural treat. National City is home to L. M. "Pep" Pepper Park. On the bay, this is a popular put-in for boaters.

For general beach weather conditions in the region, call 619-221-8884.

Access

From the south—Take I-5 from its beginning at the Mexican border. This also marks the southern border of the region. Dairy Mart Rd. is the southernmost coastal access road.

From the north—Take I-5 southbound. The San Diego Coronado Bridge marks the region's northern border and the quickest route to Coronado.

U.S.–Mexico Border to Coronado

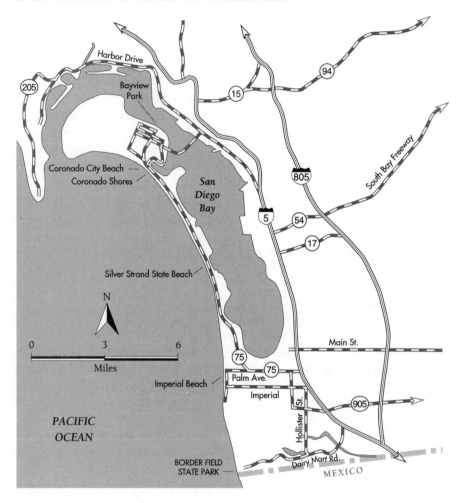

Beaches

Border Field State Park

Imperial Beach

Silver Strand State Beach

Coronado Shores Beach

Coronado City Beach

Camping

Sweetwater Summit Regional Park—County Parks Dept., 619-565-3600, $16, 60 sites, tent and RV sites with partial hookups at Otay Lake.

San Diego KOA—619-427-3601, $30, 270 tent and RV sites, full hookups available.

Chula Vista Marina and RV Park—619-422-0111, $25 to $40, 237 RV sites with full hookups.

International Motor Inn RV Park—619-428-4486, $22, 42 RV sites with full hookups.

Silver Strand State Beach—800-444-7275, $18, 124 sites for self-contained RVs.

Other points of interest

Tijuana River National Estuarine Research Reserve—619-575-3613 or 619-435-5184, 301 Caspian Way, Imperial Beach. This is a great bird-watching spot with limited beach access. 10:00 A.M. to 6:00 P.M., Wednesday to Sunday.

Sweetwater Marsh National Wildlife Reserve—619-575-1290, 1000 Gunpowder Point Dr., Chula Vista. Located at the end of E St. in Chula Vista, this is the largest salt marsh in the bay area. A favorite for numerous birds, some endangered, and the site of the Chula Vista Nature Interpretive Center. A shuttle ride is required. Call for current information.

L. M. "Pep" Pepper Park—619-686-6200. Public boat ramp, dock, fishing platform, and picnic area at the southern terminus of Tideland Ave. in National City.

Glorietta Bay—On the southern, bay side of Coronado lies a friendly little park and marina. Take Strand Way off Strand Blvd. (CA 75).

Chula Vista Launching Ramp—619-686-6200, ten lanes of concrete, a hoist, docks, and picnic areas with barbecue grills. A popular way to access the bay. Take the Marina Parkway Exit from I-5 and head for the water.

Coronado's Parks

Bay View, Harbor View, Centennial, and Coronado Tidelands Regional Park offer views and play along San Diego Bay.

BORDER FIELD STATE PARK

This 2-mile stretch of sandy beach is smack dab on the U.S.–Mexico border. While a wide variety of water-related activities occur here, the water is frequently polluted. Surfers often risk exposure to unsanitary water to surf the Sloughs, a big wave break off the park's shore. Look for warning signs that alert beachgoers to water conditions. The Mexican city of Tijuana lies a stone's throw away. Visitors to Border Field are sure to see U.S. Border Patrol agents keeping everyone on their respective sides of the fence. The contrast is stark. The Mexico side of the beach is crowded while the U.S. side is deserted as if taunting the southern neighbor with its open space. The park's trails for hiking and horseback riding weave a course through the Tijuana River Estuary, affording up-close wildlife views along with educational signs. The park lies within the Tijuana River National Estuarine Research Reserve, which offers additional beach and wildlife habitat. Trails that enter the dunes are closed from April to August to protect endangered seabirds. The reserve's visitor center at 301 Caspian Way in Imperial Beach is an interactive, natural history museum with a picnic area with restrooms.

The Dairy Mart Ponds give equestrians and hikers another batch of trails. They're located just off Interstate 5 on Dairy Mart Road and are visible on the way to the park.

ACCESS: From the north—Take I-5 southbound, exit on Dairy Mart Rd., and turn right. After 1 mile, keep right as the road joins Monument Rd. and follow this road into the park.

From the south—Cross over from Mexico into the United States and continue north on I-5. Exit on Dairy Mart Rd. and turn left. After 1 mile, keep right as the road joins Monument Rd. and follow this road into the park.

To reach the reserve's visitor center, turn left (south) off Imperial onto 3rd St. Turn left on Auto Rd., then right into the lot on Caspian Way.

PARKING/ENTRANCE FEES: The lot at the end of Monument Rd. is free as is park usage. If you have a horse, corrals are available outside of the park. The research reserve's visitor center is also free of charge.

HOURS: State Park—9:30 A.M. to 7:00 P.M., Thursday to Sunday. Reserve Visitor Center—10:00 A.M. to 4:00 P.M., Wednesday to Sunday.

AMENITIES: Wheelchair-accessible restrooms, picnic tables, barbecue pits.

ACTIVITIES: Biking, horseback riding, swimming, surfing, fishing, wildlife viewing.

FOR MORE INFORMATION: 619-575-3613 or 619-435-5184.

Water-quality Hotline—619-338-2073.

Surf/weather Report—619-221-8884.

IMPERIAL BEACH

Imperial Beach, formed when the South San Diego Investment Company decided to capitalize on the area's sunny disposition by touting it as a cure for lung ailments, became a beach destination in 1906 when the ferry/train combination brought weekend guests over from San Diego. This swath of sand seems to come straight from Southern California beach lore. The surf here is powerful with the low tide often creating hollow waves. Surfers line up (wait in the water) on either side of the municipal pier. The pier, located at the end of Evergreen Avenue, has a cafe and a place for anglers to clean their catch. Imperial Beach is also home to Sand Castle Days in August, the world's longest-running sandcastle competition. The city provides lifeguards for the designated swimming area between Palm Avenue and Imperial Beach Boulevard. There's a comforting lack of pretense at IB—as it's known to locals—just ordinary folks enjoying life by the sea. The buildings have been spruced up in the last few years. Luckily, some rugged beach shacks are still stuffed with surfers. IB offers the essentials, like fast food and cheap shelter, on the city's main commercial strips, Palm Avenue and Imperial Beach Boulevard.

ACCESS: From I-5, exit onto Palm Ave. (Hwy 75) and head west toward the ocean. That's a right if heading away from San Diego or a left if Mexico is behind. Palm Ave. leads straight to the beach. Keep left where Hwy 75 bears right going to Silver Strand State Beach. Turn onto Seacoast Dr., Ocean Ln., or 1st St. to get to parking.

PARKING: There is a parking lot at Seacoast and Elm, near the pier. If that's full, drive along Seacoast, checking the small lots on the ocean side of the street and then try again one block farther inland. If really desperate, continue south on Seacoast past Imperial Beach Blvd. and continue the search. Check the signs before you park.

HOURS/FEES: The beach is free and always open. The parking lot at Seacoast and Elm is $2. The rest are free.

AMENITIES: Beach, restrooms, showers, volleyball nets, lifeguard.

PIER: Wheelchair-accessible restrooms, fish cleaning area, plaza, cafe.

ACTIVITIES: Fishing, surfing, volleyball, sunbathing.

FOR MORE INFORMATION:

Imperial Beach Lifeguard Station—619-423-0208; urgent, 619-423-8322; business, 619-423-8328; www.ci.imperial-beach.ca.us.

Water-quality Hotline—619-338-2073.

Surf/weather Report—619-221-8884.

Current Wave Height—cdip.ucsd.edu/models/san_diego.gif.

SILVER STRAND STATE BEACH

Silver Strand State Beach sits on a narrow spine of land separating San Diego Bay and the Pacific Ocean, allowing access to both. The two sides are connected by tunnels, which allows pedestrians to cross safely under Highway 75 to access either body of water. The Pacific side offers up some temperamental beach-break for surfers, but shell-hunting beachcombers will enjoy the wide, white strand of sand. Fishing is also popular at this full-service state park, which includes nature trails among the dunes and wetlands. When the RV camping lot is full, it looks like a can of oversized sardines, but this is still a nice place to recreate.

ACCESS: From the south—From I-5, cross the bay via the Coronado Bridge. There is a toll of $1 for the bridge if traveling alone. Remain on Hwy 75 by following the signs as it joins 3rd St. then turns left on Orange Ave., which turns southward becoming Silver Strand Blvd. It's another 5 miles to the beach.

The only parking is in the pay lot. Day use is $4.

HOURS/FEES: Sunrise to sunset. The park suggests calling ahead for hours of operation. Day use fee is $4; Camping fee is $18.

AMENITIES: Wheelchair-accessible restrooms, showers, lifeguard, covered picnic area, grills, RV camping (125 sites), first aid.

ACTIVITIES: Wildlife viewing, swimming, surfing, shell collecting.

FOR MORE INFORMATION: 619-435-5184 or 619-755-2063.

Camping reservations—800-444-PARKS.

Water-quality Hotline—619-338-2073.

Surf/weather Report—619-221-8884.

Wave model—cdip.ucsd.edu/models/san_diego.gif.

CORONADO SHORES BEACH

Coronado Shores Beach has the basic beach ingredients: surf and wide sands set against a cement seawall-promenade. There are no facilities beyond the promenade that overlooks the shore activities. The beach is narrower than Coronado City Beach. The exclusive condominium properties that line the inland side of this shore help keep the strand relatively secluded.

ACCESS: Exit from I-5 onto Hwy 75 (San Diego–Coronado Bridge) and cross the bay. Traveling on this road costs $1 if only one person is in the vehicle. Remain on Hwy 75 following the flow of traffic. When the highway completes a turn to the

THE CLASSY AND HISTORICAL HOTEL DEL CORONADO PRESIDES OVER CORONADO CITY BEACH.

south and becomes Orange Ave., turn right on Avenida del Sol (just over a mile from the bridge). Turn right on Avenida de las Arenas, pass to the left of the gatehouse, and park in the lot.

From Imperial Beach—Follow Hwy 75 north. Pass Silver Strand State Beach and enter Coronado. Turn left on Avenida de las Arenas, pass to the left of the gatehouse, and park in the lot.

PARKING: The lot described is free. If the hundred or so spaces are filled, park at Coronado City Beach or across Hwy 75 on Strand Way in Glorieta Bay Park.

HOURS/FEES: This free beach keeps hours of 5:00 A.M. to 11:00 P.M.

AMENITIES: A cement seawall and adjoining promenade.

ACTIVITIES: Surfing, swimming, strolling, fishing, shell collecting, sunbathing.

FOR MORE INFORMATION:

Coronado Parks and Recreation—619-435-4179.

Surf/weather Report—619-226-9492.

CORONADO CITY BEACH

The historic Hotel del Coronado gives an ambiance of class to the wide, sandy, easily accessible Coronado City Beach, which may explain why it's the most popular beach in Coronado. The melodic thumping of volleyballs harmonizes with the Pacific's rhythm for a most pleasant tune. An area for canines and picnickers occupies the beach's north end, and Sunset Park at the north end of Ocean Boulevard offers its grassy expanse for similar uses.

ACCESS: From I-5, take Hwy 75 across the bay to Coronado. Crossing this bridge costs $1 for vehicles with only one occupant. Remain on Hwy 75 as it turns left and becomes Orange Ave. Just under a mile from the bridge, the road forks. Stay left on Isabella Ave. and follow it to Ocean (don't turn left onto 10th). Ocean runs the length of the beach.

PARKING: On-street parking is plentiful by the beach. If full, look inland on the residential streets.

HOURS/FEES: 5:00 A.M.to 11:00 P.M. are the hours for this free beach.

AMENITIES: Picnic area with barbecue, lifeguard, restrooms, volleyball nets, dog run.

ACTIVITIES: Swimming, volleyball, surfing, fishing, sunbathing.

FOR MORE INFORMATION:

Coronado Parks and Recreation—619-435-4179.

Surf/weather Report—619-226-9492.

SAN DIEGO AND SAN DIEGO BAY

San Diego, the sixth largest city in the United States, claims to have perfect weather with a small-town feel. While that may be a stretch, San Diego is a tourist delight with everything a traveler could need in a resort destination: Five-star dining, theater, sporting events, theme parks, zoological gardens, and museums are within easy reach.

The 17-mile-long San Diego Bay, one of the best natural harbors in the world, is home to a variety of entertaining and educational sites. The three-masted *Star of India,* home of the floating Maritime Museum, sets a sailing tone for a day on the bay. Seaport Village and downtown's Horton Plaza are popular area icons. The San Diego Trolley offers an inexpensive way to check it all out.

Those interested in the realms of yachting will want to stop by Shelter and Harbor Islands, both of which are reachable via car. Spanish Landing Park in Harbor Island's cove commemorates the landing of Sebastian Vizcaino. He's the guy who named the bay back in 1602.

SAN DIEGO HAS IT ALL, INCLUDING SUNNY BEACHES, GLITZY MALLS, INTRIGUING MUSEUMS, FINE RESTAURANTS AND HOTELS, AND THE WORLD-FAMOUS SEA WORLD AND SAN DIEGO ZOO.

A stop at the San Diego visitor center (2688 East Mission Bay Dr., 619-276-8200) will help you orient to the inland treasures here.

To keep things manageable, this book separates the San Diego area into three regions: U.S.–Mexico Border to Coronado, Point Loma to Pacific Beach, and La Jolla to Torrey Pines.

Following are some of the "must see" sites to keep in mind if the beaches aren't calling:

Sea World—619-226-3901, 1720 South Shores Rd. Mission Bay Park's 150-acre entertainment and marine life park, where world famous "Shamu" lives.

San Diego Zoo—619-234-2153, 2920 Zoo Dr.—www.sandiegozoo.org. More than 4,000 animals and 6,500 plants all neatly organized for viewing pleasure.

Balboa Park (see listings below).

Following are some important points of contact for Balboa Park:

House of Hospitality—619-239-0512—1549 El Prado.

Park Administration—619-235-1100.

You will also find a vast selection of museums, theaters, and gardens, all within a park setting. A full day won't scratch the surface here. Each museum has a separate entry fee with Tuesdays free at some museums.

A sampling of the museums and theaters in Balboa Park:

Centro Cultural de la Raza (Latino, Chicano Culture)—619-235-6135.

Natural History Museum—619-276-8200 or 619-232-3821.

Museum of Photographic Arts—619-239-5262.

Old Globe Theatre—619-239-2255.

Reuben H. Fleet Space Theater and Science Center—619-238-1233.

San Diego Aerospace Museum—619-234-8291.

San Diego Automotive Museum—619-231-2886.

San Diego Museum of Art—619-232-7931.

San Diego Museum of Man—619-239-2001.

Spanish Village Arts and Crafts Center—619-233-9050.

Timken Art Gallery—619-239-5548.

Padres (NL) and Chargers (NFL)—619-283-4494 and 619-280-2111, 9499 Friars Rd. The sporting teams of Jack Murphy Stadium.

Old Town San Diego State Historic Park—619-220-5422—4002 Wallace St. Historic San Diego (1821–1872) is preserved in this state park. Souvenirs, restaurants, and history lessons are presented in a re-creation that includes five original adobe buildings. Corner of San Diego Ave. and Twiggs St.

Old Town Trolley—619-298-8687. Connects to most of downtown's tourist centers. Look for the yellow circle marking its stops.

Maritime Museum—619-234-9153, 1306 North Harbor Dr. A floating, hands-on exhibit of three old ships paired with models and artifacts of a bygone era. The three-masted windjammer, *Star of India*, brings the sights and sounds of history to life.

Seaport Village—619-235-4014, West Harbor Dr. at Kettner Blvd. Shops and dining on a bayside promenade.

Gaslamp Quarter—619-233-5227, 410 Island Ave., www.gaslamp.com. Theaters and galleries in historic downtown San Diego.

Tijuana—888-775-2417 or 800-522-1516. Go south of the border. Bring your driver's license but leave your rental car behind.

Mission Basílica San Diego de Alcala—619-298-3317, 2510 Juan St. The first in the chain of twenty-one missions where the Spanish began "settling" what they called Alta California. This mission dates back to 1769.

San Diego Convention Center—619-525-5000.

CASTLES MADE OF SAND

Sitting in the sand. Just sitting in the sand. What a glorious feeling. Happy as a clam. Ever been on the beach and wondered where the sand between your toes comes from?

Basically it comes from upstream and up the coast. Rivers, creeks, and even small trickles of rain runoff all carry a sediment load. This sediment eventually makes it to the ocean, where it is picked up and moved along the coast before finally being dumped in a submarine canyon.

This is a slow cycle, and the sand spends lots of time moving on and off the shore on its journey. The sand is constantly moving like a slow conveyer belt with waves and currents driving the engine. In the winter, storms churn up big waves that speed up beach erosion, kicking up the sand and allowing the currents to move it along. The sand then settles into sandbars from where it is slowly pushed back to shore until the next big waves send it back to the currents. The longshore current, which basically flows southward along the beach at varying rates due to waves that hit the coast at an angle, is responsible for the sand's migration. The whole process is called the littoral drift.

The river deposits sand in the ocean and it is moved along by the waves and currents. How nice and harmonious, eh? Well, it used to be, but Californians can't live on bread alone. Even if they could it still takes water to make bread. So to that end, the rivers that feed sand to the ocean have all been dammed. This is good for water supplies but bad for beaches. Just like our market-driven economy, the rules of supply and demand are followed in littoral drift. We've choked off the supply and now we have a deficit of sand. When beaches started shrinking, people built devices, like groins, to hold *their* sand in place. This stopped the conveyor belt and thus caused further erosion.

To help combat this erosion, communities truck in sand or dredge it from harbors and pipe it over to the beaches. These efforts have satisfied most towns that profit from beachside tourism. However, it is quite clear that methods of reestablishing the sand supply need to be found.

From a practical standpoint, beach visitors will find narrower beaches in the winter than during mid- and late summer visits. Some beaches lose all of their sand to winter storms, making castle building a summer-only proposition.

Speaking of castles, bring some putty knives, eating utensils, and a spray bottle on your next beach excursion. With these tools you'll be able to sculpt sand like the pros. To make a Central American pyramid, take a child's shovel or a putty knife, push the blade in about half an inch, then pull outward. Start at the top and work downwards. Practice and maybe you can join the pro sand sculptors at Imperial Beach for their annual October competition.

REGION 2

POINT LOMA TO PACIFIC BEACH

This diverse region begins with the rocky peninsula of Point Loma, which provides panoramic vistas of the San Diego skyline and vertigo-inducing views of the rugged shore beneath its tall cliffs. The cliffs give way to the wide sands of Ocean Beach, Mission Beach, and Pacific Beach's developed coastline. An astute observer will notice that these towns get progressively cleaner the farther north one goes. This also means the sights become more packaged and lack some of the individuality of the southern sprawl.

Point Loma offers a glimpse into California's past. The Old Point Loma Lighthouse and Cabrillo National Monument help prompt imaginations. Point Loma is the site of first landfall for Juan Rodriguez Cabrillo, the first European known to explore Southern California, during his 1542 expedition. The monument commemorates the event and gives a panoramic view of the bay. The old lighthouse brings to mind images of sailing ships seeking the bay's shelter while maneuvering along the rocky shores. This excellent place to watch for migrating gray whales offers coast access via steep stairs and pathways.

Ocean Beach—OB—to locals, is a surfer's beach. Sure, the sand is nice and volleyball is plentiful, but the beach is known for its surfing. This town has an unpolished quality that is refreshing in this era of prepackaged sterility.

Mission Bay is a boating enthusiast's dream with acres upon acres of smooth water to play on. This manmade water-oriented playground is swarming with recreational opportunities for the active crowd, plus it is home to Sea World.

Belmont Park's Giant Dipper, a classic wooden roller coaster, spills shrieks onto the sandy shores of Mission Beach, casting an amusement park atmosphere over the beach. The park offers a full midway and an historic swimming pool called the Plunge. Bonita Cove, a picnic and playground area, accents the southern end of this sandy shore.

Pacific Beach is a popular party spot for San Diegans. It has the reputation of being almost like La Jolla, meaning it is a bit cheaper and less pretentious than its northern neighbor, yet it's not as rough around the edges as OB. Pacific Beach feels a bit claustrophobic with its stacked houses sitting right along the sand accentuating the beach's partylike atmosphere. The main concern here is parking. There isn't much.

Access

I-5 and the Garnet/Balboa Ave. Exit mark the northern border of this region. The southern border is effectively the junction of I-5 and I-8.

POINT LOMA TO PACIFIC BEACH

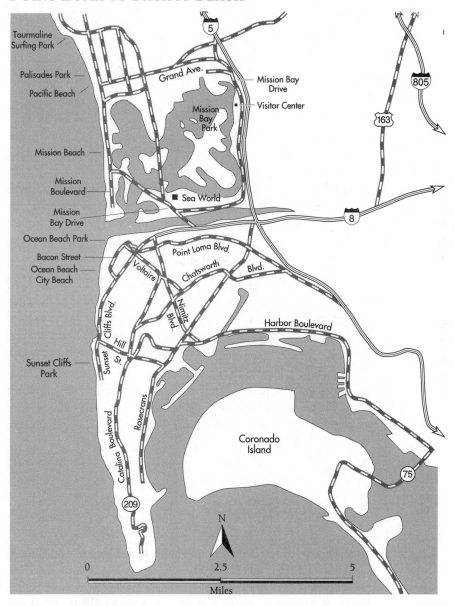

Tourmaline Surfing Park

Palisades Park

Pacific Beach

Grand Ave.

Mission Bay Drive

Visitor Center

Mission Bay Park

Mission Beach

Mission Boulevard

Sea World

Mission Bay Drive

Ocean Beach Park

Bacon Street

Ocean Beach City Beach

Point Loma Blvd.

Voltaire

Chatsworth

Blvd.

Nimitz Blvd.

Cliffs Blvd.

Harbor Boulevard

Sunset Hill St.

Sunset Cliffs Park

Catalina Boulevard

Rosecrans

Coronado Island

N

0   2.5   5

Miles

Beaches

Sunset Cliffs Park

Ocean Beach City Beach

Mission Bay Park

Mission Beach

Pacific Beach

Palisades Park

Tourmaline Surfing Park

Other points of interest

Sea World—619-226-3901, 1720 South Shores Rd., San Diego. Shamu and friends play in their 150-acre marine-life entertainment park on Mission Bay. $32.95 adults, $24.95 kids 3 to 11. Hours vary seasonally.

Belmont Park—619-491-2988, 3146 Mission Blvd. #F, San Diego. The Giant Dipper Roller Coaster is a classic, wooden thriller.

Cabrillo National Monument and Point Loma Lighthouse—619-557-5450, TDD 619-224-4140. This site commemorates Cabrillo's 1542 exploration of the California coast. The lighthouse, built in 1855, and the monument are reached by passing through Fort Rosecrans Military Reservation and its cemetery. Whale watching, a preserved coastal sage/scrub ecosystem, and the Point Loma Tide Pools are popular here. Open 9:00 A.M. to 5:15 P.M. $5.

Shelter and Harbor Islands—These two manmade islands jut into the north end of San Diego Bay. Shelter Island has a free, small boat launch and a public fishing pier among hotels, yacht clubs, and restaurants. Harbor Island is similar, minus the freebies.

SUNSET CLIFFS PARK

Sunset Cliffs Park's rocky, cliffside vantage point grants sweeping views of the Pacific from a path that skirts the edge of an eroding bluff. A stairway leads down to a rocky portion of coast located at the park's south end, where Ladera Street and Sunset Cliffs Boulevard meet. Despite the difficult access, surfing and diving are popular pastimes. Romantic couples park along the bluff and . . . uh . . . take in the view. The offshore kelp beds keep the water smooth while tickling surfers and swimmers.

ACCESS: Take I-5 to I-8. Follow I-8 westbound toward the Pacific. I-8 ends with a choice of Sea World Dr. or Sunset Cliffs Blvd. Turn left onto Sunset Cliffs Blvd.

A STAIRWAY DESCENDS THE SUNSET CLIFFS, PROVIDING SURFERS, SWIMMERS, AND DIVERS WITH OCEAN ACCESS.

and follow it to its southern terminus. After Point Loma Ave., the road meets the cliff and winds southward along it.

PARKING: Free parking is available along Sunset Cliffs Blvd. There is also a parking lot on Cornish Dr. at the park's southern end. Cornish Dr. leaves Sunset at the park's north end.

HOURS/FEES: Free.

AMENITIES: Restrooms, benches, stairway access.

ACTIVITIES: Surfing, diving, tide pools, romantic sitting.

OCEAN BEACH CITY BEACH

A nice mix of rocks and sand allow a wide range of fun here. While it doesn't feel secluded, the rocks make natural dividers to help with crowd control. The pier at the beach's north end is the longest on the West Coast (2,100 feet) and offers full service to anglers.

There's a special place for dog owners. The north section of beach, affectionately called Dog Beach, allows canines to play without restraint (i.e., no leash required). With this in mind, those heading for the ocean may want to cross the sand in the south end of the park. In-line skaters frequent the promenade while the well-kept grass offers space for a few picnickers.

In the not too distant past, OB seemed a rundown haven for beach bums. The town still boasts a large population of broke beachers sharing tiny, shacklike houses, but there has also been an influx of big money. Hopefully this won't ruin the charm of a coastal community of beach people doing what it takes to afford the life they enjoy—sun, sand, and surf.

ACCESS: From I-5, take I-8 toward the ocean. When I-8 ends, follow Sunset Cliffs Blvd. to the left.

To reach the beach's north end and the pier, turn right on Narragansett then turn right (north) on Bacon St. The beach officially begins at Niagara St. (the pier) and runs north to the river. Dog Beach starts at Voltaire St. and continues north to the river.

To reach the south end of the beach, continue on Sunset Cliffs Blvd. to Pescadero Ave. and turn right. The end of Pescadero marks the southern end of the beach. The ends of Narragansett, Santa Cruz, Orchard, and Bermuda Aves. all access the southern beach.

PARKING: Turn left off Bacon at Newport St. to park in the 110-space lot. There is a 300-car lot at the start of Voltaire St. About 70 more spaces are at the base of Santa Monica Ave. next to the lifeguard station. Del Monte Ave. also has beach parking. Turn left off Narragansett onto Bacon. Del Monte is the next street.

HOURS/FEES: The use of the pier and beach is free and always open.

AMENITIES: Pier, food concession, volleyball nets.

ACTIVITIES: Surfing, swimming, tide pools, fishing, volleyball, dogs.

FOR MORE INFORMATION:

Lifeguard Station—619-221-8899.

Surf/weather Report—619-221-8884.

Coastline parks—619-221-8901.

Water-quality Hotline—619-338-2073.

MISSION BAY PARK

Take a calm bay of clean water, add islands with names like Vacation Isle and Fiesta Island, toss in a city bent on playing in the sun, and the result is Mission Bay. There are 27 miles of sandy shore in this 4,600-acre park, providing San Diegans an aquatic playground with everything except wave-oriented activities. Sea World is an added draw to this former marshland turned water park conceived by city planners in 1960. The marsh was named False Bay by Juan Rodriguez Cabrillo when he "discovered" the area in 1542. Crown Point's nature reserve gives a glimpse of what wildlife remains and is a good birding location.

One note for weak swimmers or parents of small children: The calm waters here do have a hidden hazard. A drop-off exists and the water depth suddenly increases enough to submerge a child.

ACCESS: From the north—Take southbound I-5 and exit onto Mission Bay Dr. For Sail Bay, Riviera Shores, and Crown Point Shores, turn right on Balboa Ave. to Ingraham St., then turn left and continue to Riviera Dr. and follow the signs. For De Anza Cove, East Shore, and Fiesta Island stay on Mission Bay Dr. and follow the signs.

From the south—Take I-5 northbound, exit onto westbound I-8, then follow the signs to Sea World. Continue past Shamu's house (Sea World) on Ingraham St. to reach Vacation Isle and Ski Beach. If Dana Landing, Quivira Basin, Ventura Cove, Bonita Cove, El Carmel Point, or Santa Clara Point is your destination, exit onto West Mission Bay Dr. and follow the respective signs.

PARKING: Signs lead to parking in all areas except Sail Bay and Riviera Shores, which require on-street parking.

HOURS/FEES: There is neither a fee nor hours for the park proper. No parking is allowed between 2:00 A.M. and 4:00 A.M. to keep people from camping. Sea World costs about $25 for adults with some discounts available.

AMENITIES: This park offers everything but waves and shells. The main San Diego visitor center is in the park. All areas have sandy beaches except Sea World, Quivira Basin, and Dana Landing.

ACTIVITIES: Boating, waterskiing, Jet Skis, volleyball, swimming, sunning.

FOR MORE INFORMATION:

Lifeguard Service—619-221-8899.

Surf/weather Report—619-221-8884.

San Diego Convention and Visitors Bureau—619-236-3101, www.sandiego.org.

Coastline Parks—619-221-8901.

Water-quality Hotline—619-338-2073.

MISSION BEACH

This is a classic Southern California beach scene: in-line skaters, bikers, and strollers roll along the promenade, Ocean Front Walk, in differing stages of undress

Mission Bay Park in San Diego is an aquatic playground encompassing 4,600 acres.

while others relax on the sandy shore. As lifeguards watch over the ocean, surfers and swimmers are kept segregated by buoys. The beach features Belmont Park, home of the Giant Dipper Roller Coaster, the Plunge swimming pool, and the family playland of Pirates Cove. Crystal Pier marks the beach's north end and the basketball courts mark South Mission Beach.

ACCESS: From the north—Exit I-5 southbound onto Grand Ave., turn right, then turn right again onto Garnet Ave. Continue on Garnet just over 2 miles to Mission Blvd. and turn left. The beach officially starts at Santa Rita Place.

From the south—Exit I-5 northbound onto I-8, then exit onto Midway Dr. northbound (toward Sea World). Exit onto West Mission Bay Dr. and follow it to Mission Blvd. Turn left at Mission to reach South Mission Beach. That's Belmont Park up ahead on the left.

PARKING: There are a couple of free lots north and south of Belmont Park and one at the start of West Mission Bay Dr. Two more lots lie across the street from Bonita Cove. Metered street parking is also available. If it's summer and the sun's out, parking will be scarce.

HOURS/FEES: Mission Beach is open twenty-four hours a day, seven days a week, and there is no entrance fee. Entrance to Belmont Park is free and rides cost a few clams.

AMENITIES: Amusement park, picnicking, basketball courts, volleyball nets.

ACTIVITIES: Biking, strolling, basketball, volleyball, sunbathing, roller coaster, pool, swimming, surfing (designated areas).

FOR MORE INFORMATION:

Lifeguard Service—619-221-8899.

Surf/weather Report—619-221-8884.

Belmont Park—619-488-3110.

Coastline Parks—619-221-8901.

Water-quality Hotline—619-338-2073.

PACIFIC BEACH

Crystal Pier, a popular public fishing platform, marks the midsection of this wide, gently inclined section of sand. When heading to the water, look both ways before crossing the paths that parallel the shore. There's a path for walkers and one for wheeled travelers—meaning bikers and skaters—that has an 8 miles per hour speed limit. On the water side of the path lie the volleyball courts and the sunbathers and surf frolickers who flock to this beach. It's a scene right out of a Beach Boys song, with the scents of vanilla and coconut added.

ACCESS: From I-5 take the Grand/Garnet Avenue Exit toward the ocean. Stay on this road (it becomes Balboa Ave., then Grand Ave.) all the way to Mission Blvd., just a block from shore. Turn right on Mission Blvd. Pacific Beach Park actually starts 2 miles south of the pier, which is two blocks to the left. A turn to the right leads to parking.

PARKING: Streetside parking is all that is available. Keep your eyes peeled as you head up Mission Blvd. and jump at any open spot. When there aren't any (and there won't be) turn right on Law St. and right again on Bayard St. Bayard St. often has open spots, as does Felspar St. There is a small pay lot on Felspar St. between Mission Blvd. and Bayard St. If you still haven't found a spot, work inland. Good luck!

HOURS/FEES: Crystal Pier keeps hours of 7:00 A.M. until sunset and is free. The beach itself is free and usually has lifeguards posted from 9:00 A.M. until 6:00 P.M. Surfing is allowed before 11:00 A.M., at which time the surf cats have to hand the ocean over to swimmers.

AMENITIES: Restrooms, volleyball nets, bike path, pedestrian path, pier, picnic area.

ACTIVITIES: Surfing, swimming, volleyball, biking, walking, fishing.

FOR MORE INFORMATION:
Coastline Parks—619-221-8901.
Lifeguard Service—619-221-8899. ·
Surf/weather Report—619-221-8884.
Water-quality Hotline—619-338-2073.

PALISADES PARK

Palisades Park isn't the one they talk about in the song. That one's in New Jersey. This park humbly offers a nice place to picnic and a sandy beach. It's really part of the same sandy stretch as Pacific Beach and has the same swim and surf rule: Surf until 11:00 A.M., then swimming only. It also shares the parking ailments of its southern neighbor, offering only streetside parking.

ACCESS: From I-5 take the Grand/Garnet Ave. Exit toward the ocean. Stay on this road (it becomes Balboa Ave. and then Grand Ave.) all the way to Mission Blvd. just a block from shore. Turn right on Mission Blvd. Stay on Mission about 0.75 mile to Law St., which marks the park's southern boundary.

PARKING: Start searching for a spot at Law and turn around after passing Loring St. Start circling the blocks on both sides of Mission and a place will show up.

HOURS/FEES: Another free beach; the park has sunrise to sunset hours.

AMENITIES: Restrooms, picnic tables.

ACTIVITIES: Swimming, surfing, strolling.

FOR MORE INFORMATION:
Coastline Parks—619-221-8901.
Lifeguard Service—619-221-8899.
Surf/weather Report—619-221-8884.
Water-quality Hotline—619-338-2073.

TOURMALINE SURFING PARK

This rocky section of coast, just south of False Point, marks the start of La Jolla's jeweled shore. Tourmaline is off-limits to swimmers, making it popular with water-borne recreationists. Watching the surfers and kayakers head out among the rocks is breathtaking. Don't be surprised to see bipedal creatures with brightly colored tanks on their backs exiting the water here.

ACCESS: Exit I-5 via Grand/Garnet Ave. and head west toward the ocean. Turn right on Mission Blvd. Drive through Pacific Beach and turn left as the road joins La Jolla Blvd. Turn left on Tourmaline St., descend the steep hill, and park in the lot.

PARKING: Parking is easier to come by here than at the beaches to the south. If there's no space in the free 175-space lot, look along the residential streets and check the parking signs for regulations.

HOURS/FEES: Parking and park use are free, and Tourmaline is always open.

AMENITIES: Lifeguard, restrooms, showers, wheelchair accessibility, picnic area.

ACTIVITIES: Fishing, surfing, kayaking, diving, tide pools.

FOR MORE INFORMATION:

Coastline Parks—619-221-8901.

Lifeguard Service—619-221-8899.

Surf/weather Report—619-221-8884.

Water-quality Hotline—619-338-2073.

THE PULSE OF THE PACIFIC

The ocean experience is different for every individual. For some it holds deep spiritual or symbolic meaning. Others see it from a more scientific perspective. Each side sees the other as missing part of the ocean's mystery. Some can see both sides and are awed by each. I'll attempt to discuss waves from both perspectives. Hopefully, one method will convey my respect for it.

Take One: Birth of a Wave

Earth, basking in the warmth of the Ancient One's embrace, whispers to the Ocean, sending shivers along her skin. The more passionate the words, the stronger the shivers, which race down Ocean's arms to her fingers, which in turn caress the Earth. This pleases the Ancient One.

Take Two: Waterborne Energy Transfer

A wave's relationship to the water is difficult to visualize. A wave is not water rolling onto the beach. The water is simply the medium in which a wave flows. A wave is energy whose source is difficult to pinpoint. The easiest part of a wave's formation to describe is the moment the energy moves into the water.

When air flows across water's surface it encounters friction, which causes a bit of the water's surface to move. The water is actually receiving a chaotic bit of the air current's energy, and eventually small wind waves are formed. Wind waves are short period waves, which means the bits of energy are close together. When the wind blows in the same direction over the same area for a long time, called a fetch, the chaotic bits of energy bang into each other, join together, and become orderly. This orderly energy is called a swell. The swell rolls along in the ocean unhindered until it hits something less liquid, such as land. When a swell encounters water that is just a bit deeper than the swell's height (1.3 times the swell's height to be specific), the energy can no longer travel in its orderly form. Here, breakers develop as the energy is dissipated.

The difficult thing to understand is that the wave isn't the original surface water that was present during the energy transfer. The energy has been moving *through* the water. As the energy passes, the water moves in a circular motion, starting and finishing in the same place. Breakers form when there isn't enough room for the water to make that circle. The size of the circle is dependent on the size of the swell, which is dependent on the speed, direction, and duration of winds that created it.

You could simply say that waves are created by the wind on the water. However, the wind doesn't create the energy that it transfers. The air actually works like a fluid and has waves and currents. The sun heats the earth, which immediately sheds as much of the energy as it can to the air. The surface air, now heated, rises and starts to shed as much of the energy as it can. Toss in a spinning globe-shaped planet and you have swirling pools of air. Some of these swirls become storms, which may form over a body of water and transfer some of its energy to the water below. Of course, storms gain and dissipate energy much like the waterborne waves.

So, the sun starts the whole engine. Well, no. Something started the sun. One can follow this logic all the way to the friction of two hydrogen molecules running into each other, thus causing the big bang, which means surfers are actually riding upon the very energy that created the universe.

As with anything so complex, it is very simple. Perhaps this is why wave riders often have Taoist beliefs. While pondering the creation of a wave, one becomes aware of how simplicity and complexity are interconnected. One doesn't exist without the other. The more one looks at anything, the more one finds. The more one knows, the less one understands. The less one understands, the more one knows.

Those interested in swells on a daily basis have a number of tools to help them forecast wave activity. Surf reports available on a telephone hotline are usually recorded in the morning by a lifeguard or surfer. Professional forecasters and meteorologists predict where the waves will be on sites accessible via the Internet, including the following:

Wave-height graphs (locations and wave heights graphed)

San Diego County—cdip.ucsd.edu/models/sd_hs.gif

Orange County—cdip.ucsd.edu/models/orange_hs.gif

Los Angeles County—cdip.ucsd.edu/models/la_hs.gif

Ventura County—cdip.ucsd.edu/models/vent_hs.gif

Point Sal to Santa Barbara—cdip.ucsd.edu/models/barb_hs.gif

Point Sal to the Mexican Border—cdip.ucsd.edu/models/coast_hs.gif

Coastal wave-height models (colors on a coastal map represent predicted wave heights)

Point Conception to the Mexican border—cdip.ucsd.edu/models/socal_now.shtml

Point Conception to Ventura—cdip.ucsd.edu/models/sb_channel.gif

Long Beach to Huntington Beach—cdip.ucsd.edu/models/spc.gif

Point Conception to Half Moon Bay (Central CA)—cdip.ucsd.edu/models/conception.gif

California wave models

cdip.ucsd.edu/homepage.html

Channel Islands

cdip.ucsd.edu/models/islands.gif

San Pedro Bay (Newport Beach and Catalina)

cdip.ucsd.edu/models/spc.gif

Pacific wave heights (a map showing the entire Pacific with colors representing swell heights and arrows showing wave directions)

www.fnoc.navy.mil/wam/gifs/wam_wvht_000_pac.gif

Pacific satellite picture with wind and pressure shown

lumahai.soest.hawaii.edu/gifs/models/AVN/pac_AVNgoes.gif

Buoy data (raw data from National Weather Service buoys)

www.nws.fsu.edu/buoy/sw.html

Region 3

La Jolla to Torrey Pines

La Jolla (pronounced Lah HOY ya) is an exclusive community on an exquisite shore. The rocky, cliff-lined coast is set with small coves of sand massaged by aquamarine water creating a scene that stuns coastal connoisseurs.

The southern portion of coast is rich with tide pools, lying behind offshore rocks facing powerful waves. As the coast winds inland, it widens then makes a return to cliff-backed beaches as it turns northward. With Scripps Institution of Oceanography nearby, the water seems cleaner—and somehow it actually is.

Depending on who's talking, La Jolla either means jewel or is an old Mexican geographical term to describe wave-worn hollows. Either goes a long way in describing what many feel is the best place to live on the coast. It's definitely one of the most expensive regions to call home. The caves, the tide pools, and the wealth of the locals are all part of the charm. All it really lacks is the rough edges of the struggling beach bums. After a day here it's not hard to see why La Jolla is *the* San Diego destination of choice. Of course that makes space a hot commodity that, in turn, makes parking quite scarce. Be patient, flexible, and ready to walk a few blocks to the beach.

Access

The region is bound by I-5 on the east, Genesee Ave. on the north, and Grand Ave. on the south. The Ardath Rd. Exit, also marked Hwy 52, is a central access point from I-5.

Parking

Parking in La Jolla is usually an on-street affair. However, following are addresses for the parking garages that will allow up to three hours of free parking with merchant validation:

1298 Prospect

Cave and Prospect

7979 Ivanhoe Ave.

Herschel and Silverado

1010 Coast Blvd.

888 Prospect

Fay and Prospect

1111 Prospect

LA JOLLA TO TORREY PINES

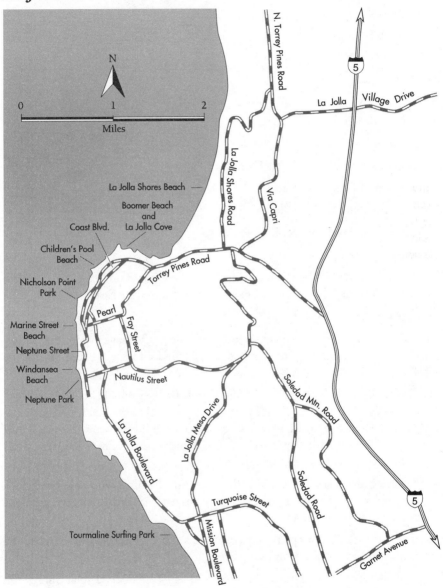

7825 Fay Ave.

7850 Fay Ave.

7777 Fay Ave.

7680 Girard Ave.

Beaches

Neptune Park

Windansea Beach

Marine Street Beach

Nicholson Point Park and Coast Boulevard Park

Children's Pool Beach

Boomer Beach and La Jolla Cove

La Jolla Shores Beach and Kellogg Park

Camping

Sorry, land here is gold, which means luxurious lodging (read "expensive") in hotels. Look south to Mission Bay or north to San Elijo State Beach.

Other places of interest

Cliff Walk—A rugged path along the north-facing bluffs that's not for the dexterously challenged. Look for the entrance next to the La Jolla Cave and Shell Shop at 1325 Coast Blvd.

La Jolla Cave and Shell Shop—619-459-0746 or 619-454-6080, 1325 Coast Blvd. Follow 144 wooden steps down through a damp tunnel to the inside of Sunny Jim Cave, which looks out to sea. $1.25 adults, 50 cents children 3 to 11. Open Monday through Saturday 10:00 A.M. to 5:00 P.M., Sunday 11:00 A.M. to 5:00 P.M. They stay open later during busy summer days.

Bird Rock—Surfers and divers share the area with the birds who've left their, uh, markings on the large rock. A stairway from the end of Bird Rock Ave. gets one down to the tide pools below.

Calumet Park—A pleasant picnic area overlooks a rocky, undeveloped beach at the end of Midway St. west of Calumet Ave.

Scripps Institution of Oceanography—619-534-3474, 8602 La Jolla Shores Dr. (just up the hill). These guys wrote the book on oceans. An impressive display of tide pools along with an aquarium are open from 9:00 A.M. to 5:00 P.M. daily on a donation basis.

Stephen Birch Aquarium and Museum—619-534-8665 or 619-534-7523 or aquarium.ucsd.edu. Just across the street from Scripps, this museum-aquarium combo runs educational programs and is often booked long in advance, so call early.

Scripps Shoreline Underwater Reserve and San Diego-La Jolla Underwater Park—These reserves represent the coast from Torrey Pines State Beach to Goldfish Point. Great tide pools for beachgoers—just don't touch! The underwater park is extremely popular with divers.

Prospect St./Fay Ave./Pearl St./Girard Ave./Herschel Ave—This ritzy shopping zone sees a lot of credit card abuse. Shoppers should take advantage of the parking garages and watch the plastic sizzle!

Mount Soledad—An excellent place to get an overview of this area. From the south side of town, take Nautilus St. east, uphill, and turn left on Scenic Dr. From the north side of town, follow Ardath away from the ocean and turn right on Hidden Valley Rd.

NEPTUNE PARK

Neptune Park is the southern jewel of the shore along Neptune Place. Windansea to the north is the other. The two are separated by a pair of one-way streets, Playa del Sur and Playa del Norte. This is a good surf and swim spot and has a pathway along the bluff for strolling. The beach can get washed away by winter storms, leaving just the rocks and tide pools.

ACCESS: From the north—Take I-5 south to the Grand/Garnet Exit and turn right onto Garnet Ave. Remain on the main road as it turns into Balboa and then Grand. When the road Ts into Mission Blvd., turn right and follow Mission through Pacific Beach to Turquoise St., turn left and follow Turquoise as it bears right, becoming La Jolla Blvd. Follow La Jolla Blvd. to Palomar Ave. and turn left. Turn right onto Neptune Pl. The park is on the wet side of Neptune Pl.

From the south—Take I-5 north to the Grand Ave. Exit and head toward the ocean. Turn right on Mission Blvd. Follow Mission through Pacific Beach to Turquoise St., turn left and follow Turquoise as it bears right, becoming La Jolla Blvd. Follow La Jolla Blvd. to Palomar Ave. and turn left. The park is on the wet side of Neptune Pl.

PARKING: Find a spot somewhere on Neptune Pl. or loop back to Vista del Mar Ave.

HOURS/FEES: It costs all of nothing and is open twenty-four hours a day, seven days a week.

AMENITIES: Walkway, steps to beach.

ACTIVITIES: Surfing, swimming, tide pool, fishing, strolling.

FOR MORE INFORMATION:

Lifeguard Service—619-221-8899.

Surf/weather Report—619-221-8884.

Coastline Parks—619-221-8901.

Water-quality Hotline—619-338-2073.

WINDANSEA BEACH

This is the northern part of the area known as Neptune Park. Windansea is home to the Windansea Surf Club, which means it's a great place to watch some excellent surfing. However, it's not the best place for nonlocals to surf. The surfing phenomenon called localism is fairly prevalent here. Basically that means that the locals get the good waves and *maybe* a nonlocal will get a wave. Nonetheless, this is a fine specimen of La Jolla coast. Be careful as the surf can be big with strong rip currents and no lifeguards.

ACCESS: From I-5 take the Grand/Garnet Exit and turn west onto Garnet Ave. Remain on the main road as it heads toward the ocean. When the road Ts into Mission Blvd., turn right and follow Mission through Pacific Beach. Turn left onto La Jolla Blvd., then turn left onto Palomar Ave. Finally, turn right onto Neptune Pl. The beach is accessed via stairs at the end of Vista de la Playa and Fern Glen.

PARKING: Park on Neptune Pl. or Vista de la Playa if one of the eighteen spots is available. Otherwise, fan out and start the search. It's worth it.

HOURS/FEES: Free and always open. However, heed all parking signs.

AMENITIES: Stairs.

ACTIVITIES: Surfing, swimming, tide pools, sunbathing.

FOR MORE INFORMATION:

Lifeguard Service—619-221-8899.

Surf/weather Report—619-221-8884.

Coastline Parks—619-221-8901.

Water-quality Hotline—619-338-2073.

MARINE STREET BEACH

Sand and rocks mixed with some fantastic surf make up this La Jolla offering. It receives a lot of the overflow from Windansea due to Horseshoe Reef, which stirs up the surf. The same reef sees diving action on flat days.

ACCESS: From I-5 take the Grand/Garnet Exit and turn west onto Garnet Ave. Remain on the main road as it heads toward the ocean. When the road Ts into Mission Blvd., turn right and follow Mission through Pacific Beach. Turn left onto La Jolla Blvd. Follow La Jolla Blvd. to Marine St. and turn left. The stairs at the end of Marine St. and Sea Lane access the beach, as does a path at Vista del Mar's terminus.

PARKING: Marine St. offers the closest parking. However, if none is available, look down Vista del Mar, Monte Vista Ave., or Olivetas Ave.

HOURS/FEES: Another free beach that's open twenty-four hours. Check the parking regulations at your spot to avoid any trouble.

AMENITIES: Stairs.

ACTIVITIES: Swimming, surfing, sunbathing, fishing, scuba diving.

FOR MORE INFORMATION:

Lifeguard Service—619-221-8899.

Surf/weather Report—619-221-8884.

Coastline Parks—619-221-8901.

Water-quality Hotline—619-338-2073.

NICHOLSON POINT PARK AND COAST BOULEVARD PARK

These beaches tend to be passed over by visitors. Finding the access path opens up a sandy chunk of coast worth a big bite of anyone's time. Coast Boulevard Park is easiest to find and offers a picnic area in addition to its rock and sand beach. Nicholson Point Park is tough to find but less crowded.

ACCESS: From the north—Take I-5 southbound, exit at La Jolla Village Dr., and keep right. In 0.7 mile, North La Jolla Scenic Dr. leaves to the left. Either turn on La Jolla Scenic Dr. or travel another 0.1 mile to Torrey Pines Rd. and turn left. The La Jolla Scenic Dr. route requires a right turn onto Ardath Rd. after 1.8 miles, which then joins Torrey Pines Rd. in another 0.5 mile. Continue on Torrey Pines Rd. into La Jolla, then turn right onto Prospect St., then take the next right onto Coast Blvd. Coast Boulevard Park comes into sight after Cuvier St. Continue to weave around on Coast Blvd. just over a mile to the street address, 202 Coast Blvd. The path to Nicholson Point Park lies between 100 and 202 Coast Blvd.

From the south—Take I-5 northbound, exit onto Ardath Rd., and follow it over I-5. North La Jolla Scenic Dr. joins Ardath about 1.5 miles after exiting. Follow the directions above from there.

From Pacific Beach—Follow Mission Blvd. northbound, with the ocean on the left, and turn left onto La Jolla Blvd. Remain on La Jolla Blvd. and cross over Prospect St. Turn left as the road Ts into Coast Blvd. and proceed to 202 Coast Blvd. to find Nicholson Point Park. Turn right to find Coast Boulevard Park.

PARKING: Yet another on-street-only parking situation. You may have to park in the lot for Children's Pool Beach.

HOURS/FEES: Open twenty-four hours, and it's free. Parking regulations may apply.

AMENITIES: Stairs.

ACTIVITIES: Fishing, body surfing, swimming, tide pools, diving.

FOR MORE INFORMATION:

Lifeguard Service—619-221-8899.

Surf/weather Report—619-221-8884.

Coastline Parks—619-221-8901.

Water-quality Hotline—619-338-2073.

CHILDREN'S POOL BEACH

If the name Children's Pool conjures up images of a carefree swimming area, you've been deceived. Lifeguards are on duty year-round to look over the sometimes-strong rip currents that can drag unsuspecting waders down into the rocks and possibly out to sea. The shore is protected by a brick seawall that was meant to keep things mellow. However, sand filled in behind the wall. It's possible to walk on the wall via a paved path. The shore's rocky, shallow incline is a haven for tide-pool life. Squeals of discovery are heard from children of all ages, 2 to 102. A reef just offshore makes this a good place to scuba and snorkel. The area is also part of San Diego-La Jolla Underwater Park. From a distance, observe the seals that may be resting on the beach.

ACCESS: From the north—Take I-5 to the La Jolla Village Dr. Exit and keep right (westbound). Turn left on Torrey Pines Rd. and follow it to Prospect St. Turn right. Watch for Coast Blvd. and bear right.

From the south—Take I-5 north to Ardath Rd. Continue on Ardath Rd. as it becomes Torrey Pines Rd. Follow Torrey Pines Rd. to Prospect St. and turn right. Bear right onto Coast Blvd.

PARKING: Available on the street along Coast Blvd. This time some spaces have actually been allotted. Four nearby parking garages offer free parking with merchant validation: 1010 Coast Blvd., 888 Prospect St., Fay and Prospect, and 7850 Fay Ave.

HOURS/FEES: Open twenty-four hours, and it's free.

AMENITIES: Stairs, lifeguard.

ACTIVITIES: Fishing, swimming, tide pools.

FOR MORE INFORMATION:

Lifeguard Service—619-221-8899.

Surf/weather Report—619-221-8884.

Coastline Parks—619-221-8901.

Water-quality Hotline—619-338-2073.

BOOMER BEACH AND LA JOLLA COVE

Bodysurfers have all heard of Boomer Beach since Boomer and Newport's Wedge are possibly the sport's most famous breaks in California. The grassy bluff top of Ellen Scripps Park provides tables, barbecue pits, and even shuffleboard among queen palms and torrey pines. La Jolla Cove lies just to the right while looking seaward around Point La Jolla. The cove, probably the most famous chunk of the La Jolla coast, is a short, wide, sandy shore that is often packed with bodies from the sea to the tall cliff that backs the beach. From both ends of the cove, stairs drop from the cliff's top to the sand below. At the southern end of the park—left while looking to sea—there's a small cave that leads to Shell Beach, a rugged and secluded section of coast. San Diego-La Jolla Underwater Park lies offshore, making scuba a popular pastime here. Board surfing is *not* allowed at the cove.

ACCESS: From the north—Exit I-5 southbound at La Jolla Village Dr. and keep right. In 0.7 mile North La Jolla Scenic Dr. leaves to the left. Either turn on North La Jolla Scenic Dr. or travel another 0.1 mile to Torrey Pines Rd. and turn left. The North La Jolla Scenic Dr. route requires a right turn onto Ardath Rd. after 1.8 miles, which then joins Torrey Pines Rd. in another 0.5 mile. Continue on Torrey Pines Rd. into La Jolla, turn right onto Prospect St., then take the next right onto Coast Blvd. The park is located at Coast Blvd. and Girard Ave.

From the south—Exit I-5 northbound at Ardath Rd. and follow it over the interstate. North La Jolla Scenic Dr. joins Ardath about 1.5 miles after the exit. Follow the directions above from there.

From Pacific Beach—Follow Mission Blvd. northbound, with the ocean on your left, and turn left onto La Jolla Blvd. Take La Jolla Blvd. about 3 miles, bear right onto Prospect St., and start looking for Girard St. to head off to the left and follow it left until it runs into Coast Blvd. The park lies straight ahead. The stairs to the cove are at 1100 Coast Blvd.

PARKING: On-street parking. The nearest parking garages are at 1010 Coast Blvd., 888 Prospect St., 1111 Prospect St., 1298 Prospect St., and 7979 Ivanhoe Ave. These garages offer up to three hours free with merchant validation.

HOURS/FEES: Open twenty-four hours, and it's free.

AMENITIES: At the park—restrooms, wheelchair-accessible path, stairs, picnic tables, barbecue , shuffleboard. At La Jolla Cove—lifeguard.

ACTIVITIES: Swimming, bodysurfing, tide pools, scuba, sunbathing, picnicking.

FOR MORE INFORMATION:

Lifeguard Service—619-221-8899.

Surf/weather Report—619-221-8884.

Coastline Parks—619-221-8901.

Water-quality Hotline—619-338-2073.

LA JOLLA SHORES BEACH AND KELLOGG PARK

Where's Gidget? La Jolla Shores Beach is an excellent first-stop beach! The beach is wide with plenty of room to watch everyone watching everyone else, and there's a consistent beach break that brings the surfers. Kellogg Park, the grassy picnic area, provides some parking to the early and the lucky. Scripps Beach, just past the research pier on the beach's north end, offers unspoiled tide pools. Look but don't touch in this protected area. The Scripps Institution of Oceanography lies farther up La Jolla Shores Drive and has an aquarium in addition to tide-pool displays. The shoreline here is part of San Diego-La Jolla Underwater Park, which means, again, look but don't touch.

ACCESS: From the north—Take I-5 southbound and exit at La Jolla Village Dr., keeping right. In 0.7 mile, North La Jolla Scenic Dr. leaves to the left. Either turn on North La Jolla Scenic Dr. or travel another 0.1 mile to Torrey Pines Rd. and turn left. The North La Jolla Scenic Dr. route requires a right turn onto Ardath Rd. after 1.8 miles, which then joins Torrey Pines Rd. in another 0.5 mile. Just after Torrey Pines Rd. and Ardath Rd. come together, turn right onto La Jolla Shores Dr., then turn left on Calle Frescota or Camino del Oro and start looking for a parking space. The parking lot is at 8200 Camino del Oro.

From the south—Take I-5 northbound and exit onto Ardath Rd., following it over the interstate. North La Jolla Scenic Dr. joins Ardath about 1.5 miles after exiting. Follow the directions above from there, turning almost immediately onto North La Jolla Shores Dr.

From Pacific Beach—Follow Mission Blvd. northbound, with the ocean on the left, and turn left onto La Jolla Blvd. Take La Jolla Blvd. about 3 miles and bear right onto Prospect St., following it to Torrey Pines Rd. Turn left on Torrey. In a mile the road forks. Keep left onto North La Jolla Shores Dr. and follow the directions above.

PARKING: A large parking lot is available to early birds or the patient. For the rest of us, on-street parking is plentiful. The walk from the car is all downhill—it's the return trip that has legs aching.

HOURS/FEES: Open twenty-four hours, and it's free.

AMENITIES: Restrooms, year-round lifeguard, showers, picnic tables, barbecue, handheld boat launch, promenade.

ACTIVITIES: Surfing, fishing, diving, swimming, sunbathing, kayaking, strolling.

FOR MORE INFORMATION:

Lifeguard Service—619-221-8899.

Surf/weather Report—619-221-8884.

Coastline Parks—619-221-8901.

Water-quality Hotline—619-338-2073.

LIQUID ISLANDS

As the tide recedes, life-giving liquid slowly flows down time-worn channels or spontaneous canals formed in the sand, leaving behind liquid islands among a barren, seaside landscape. These liquid islands are tide pools. In them some of the planet's most fascinating life-forms can be found surviving in a habitat where temperature changes, salinity changes, and the pounding of the ocean's waves keep other life-forms from establishing themselves.

Tides mark the rising and falling of the ocean's level and set the rhythm for these creatures' dance of life. While every celestial body with mass affects tide levels, the moon has the greatest effect. The nearer the moon, the higher and lower the tides or the greater the tide range, with the ocean acting as would water in a bowl: When the water level rises on one side, it drops proportionally on the other. The closer the moon, the more the bowl's contents tilt. The sun either pulls with the moon or against it, which results in the range between high and low tides being greater during full and new moons.

It takes the beaches in this book more than six hours to reach a new tide peak, averaging two high tides and two low tides every day. One of the high tides is

THE FASCINATING BUT FRAGILE LIFE-FORMS THAT INHABIT TIDE POOLS ARE BEST OBSERVED BUT NOT TOUCHED.

higher than the other and is labeled high-high tide versus low-high tide. The same difference occurs with low tides, creating a low-low tide and a high-low tide.

Extremely low tides are called minus tides for the fact that the ocean's actual level drops below the point labeled 0 feet in elevation, which is the average level of low tide. All tide heights are measured from that zero point. Thus a tide of -.5 feet is half a foot below the average level of the lowest tide.

This is all as clear as the water being turned up in the surf zone, right? Luckily, most fishing, surfing, and dive shops have a tide booklet that gives a prediction for each day's tides. Best of all, these booklets are usually free. A good rule of thumb is that extremely low tides are most common around the full moon when our celestial sister has the greatest effect on tides.

When looking at tide pools, keep in mind the fragility of these creatures. While some life-forms can handle brief removal from their environment, for others it would be like being placed on the moon without a spacesuit. Also, many areas have "Look but don't touch" regulations. Please check with the powers that be before handling the wildlife. Probably the best thing to do is use only your eyes at the pools and save the touching for one of the touch tanks run by educational groups.

REGION 4

TORREY PINES TO SAN ONOFRE

Thin strips of sand clinging to high, eroding bluffs characterize this region's beaches. Oceanside, a manmade harbor, has disrupted the flow of sand along the coast, and the beaches are fighting a battle to keep their sand. California has recognized the problem and is taking steps to repair some of the damage done by "progress." The coast seems to be responding by widening its beaches.

San Onofre State Beach, home to the world-famous surf break Trestles, sets the tone for the region with thin sandy beaches, rugged bluffs, and powerful surf. Camp Pendleton, a marine base, has placed an officer housing development here on what used to be some of the area's last virgin bluff tops. Following the coast southward toward San Diego, you see a gradual increase in civilization while the beaches continue to greet the ocean's many moods, oblivious to the surrounding population. Torrey Pines, the region's southern border, is the last stand of a tree that has suffered from man's need for elbow room. Towns along the way from north to south are Oceanside, Carlsbad, Encinitas, Solana Beach, and Del Mar.

The marine base, Camp Pendleton (619-725-5566), occupies a lengthy portion of coast between San Onofre and Oceanside. Access here is restricted.

Oceanside's beaches are wide and full of activity. Volleyball scenes like that from the movie *Top Gun*, which was filmed here, are common. The area is a popular fishing base, boasting one of the best small-craft harbors in the nation to go along with its long, wooden pier. Mission San Luis Rey, the largest of the California missions, is one way to observe the heavens locally. Another, the 200-inch Hale telescope, is at nearby Mount Palomar Observatory.

Carlsbad's sands are narrow and often hidden by high tide. Without much room to sun bake, people move inland. The city has attempted to create a European flavor noticeable in the architecture. Carlsbad Village has plenty to satisfy the shopping bug and a tree-shaded cafe to sit at and relax. The nearby Flower Fields of Carlsbad Ranch are a colorful morsel for the eyes to savor.

Ever-growing Encinitas is gobbling up the towns around it. The region is marketed as the "Flower Capital of the World" because of its numerous commercial flower farms. Its shores include San Elijo and Cardiff State Beaches.

Solana Beach is wedged between Del Mar and Encinitas. A good deal of its charm lies in the apparent struggle between becoming a tourist spot or staying quaint and quiet. The beaches here are mostly of the cove variety.

The healthy beaches of Del Mar are often crowded with the overflow from La Jolla. The town is one on the rise. Already known for its Del Mar Thoroughbred Club and Del Mar Fairgrounds, the town is trying to parlay its popularity to become a full-fledged resort town, as it was in the past. Bing Crosby, Betty Grable,

Torrey Pines to San Onofre

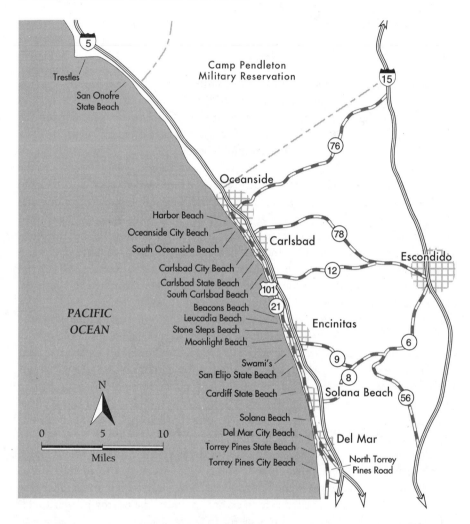

Desi Arnaz, and Jimmy Durante are among those who brought Hollywood glamour to Del Mar, the gateway to San Diego.

Access

I-5 feeds traffic into the region from the Orange County line. Basilone Rd., also known as the San Onofre Exit, marks the northern border for the region. The southern border, also marked on I-5, is represented by La Jolla Village Dr.

Beaches

Torrey Pines City Beach (Black's Beach)

Torrey Pines State Beach

Del Mar City Beach

Solana Beach

Cardiff State Beach

San Elijo State Beach

Swami's

Moonlight Beach

Beacons Beach and Stone Steps (Leucadia State Beach)

Carlsbad State and City Beaches

South Oceanside Beach

Oceanside City Beach

Harbor Beach

San Onofre State Beach South (Bluff Beach)

Trestles

Camping

San Mateo Campground—Reservations at 800-444-7275, information at 916-653-6995, cal-parks.ca.gov/travel/reserve/index.htm. 162 sites, 40 with hookups, dump station, hot showers, $17 to $24.

San Onofre State Beach—800-444-7275, cal-parks.ca.gov/travel/reserve/index.htm. 230 sites for tents or RVs, cold showers, $19 to $22.

Paradise by the Sea—760-439-1376, 1537 South Coast Hwy. From Oceanside, take Hwy 78/Vista Way west to South Coast Hwy and turn right. 100 sites with hookups, no tent sites, showers, cable TV hookup, hot showers, pool, Jacuzzi, telephone, grocery, clubhouse, $30.

Casitas Poquitos—760-722-4404, 1510 S. Coast Hwy, Oceanside. 140 sites with full hookups, showers, pool, Jacuzzi, park, $22 to $32.

South Carlsbad State Beach—800-444-7275, cal-parks.ca.gov/RESERVE/resindex.htm. 224 sites for tents or RVs, showers, water, toilets, dump station, $19 to $24.

San Elijo State Beach—800-444-7275, cal-parks.ca.gov/RESERVE/resindex.htm. 171 sites for tents or RVs, toilets, showers, water, dump station.

Oceanside Harbor—760-966-4580, 1540 Harbor Dr. North. Nearly one thousand small-craft are kept here. This full-service harbor is a floating city.

Other points of interest

Palomar Observatory—760-742-2119, astro.caltech.edu/observatoryies/palomar/public/visitor.info.html. Exit I-15 onto eastbound CA 76 and go to CR S6 which winds its way up the mountain to the observatory. This home to one of the largest telescopes in the world lies at the end of the Highway to the Stars. It sits a full mile above sea level. Open year-round 9:00 A.M. to 4:30 P.M., except Christmas Eve and Christmas Day. Daytime visits only as the telescope is a science-only proposition.

Torrey Pines City Park—619-221-8901. At the end of Torrey Pines Scenic Dr. lies this bluff-top park that draws hang-glider and model-airplane enthusiasts.

Torrey Pines Golf Course—760-452-3226. Golf fans, or should I say aficionados, have all heard of this world-class course.

Del Mar Fairgrounds and Racetrack—760-755-1161 and 760-755-1141, www.delmarfair.com and www.dmtc.com. Home to Del Mar Turf Club's thoroughbred racing from late July through mid-September. The fair runs from mid-June to early July. Polo season is May through October (760-481-9217).

Self-realization Fellowship Hermitage Grounds—619-753-2888. A unique place to stroll and think among gardens and Eastern architecture. Feel the stress of today's world melt away here! Professional photography is prohibited, as is beach attire.

Buena Vista Lagoon Ecological Reserve—760-439-2473, 2202 South Hill St., Oceanside. A simple way to view the wetlands. Exhibits and trails offer views of the plants and birds of the lagoon. Maxton Brown Park is another place to see the pond. Open 10:00 A.M. to 4:00 P.M., 1:00 to 4:00 P.M. on Sunday. Closed Monday.

Batiquitos Lagoon—619-943-7583 or 619-439-2473. These wetlands, between Leucadia and Carlsbad, are the result of a marine habitat trade-off. This environmental success is a result of the enlarging of the Port of Los Angeles. Batiquitos is now the largest freshwater habitat in San Diego County. An easy trail gives visitors a tour of the lagoon.

Agua Hedionda Lagoon—760-434-3080, 4215 Harrison St. Boating, waterskiing, and fishing are all popular here. Snug Harbor Marina has a ramp along with food, bait, equipment, and restrooms.

San Diego Wild Animal Park—760-747-8702 or 619-234-6541, 15500 San Paqual Valley Rd., Escondido. A drive-through zoo! It's a bit eerie to be the exhibit while driving within the bounds of a wild animal's home. Admission is $18.95 for adults, $11.95 for kids, and includes an hour-long guided monorail ride. Open 9:00 A.M. to 5:00 P.M daily, Thursday to Sunday until 10:00 P.M. mid-June through August.

Flower Fields at Carlsbad Ranch—760-930-9123, 5600 Avenida Encinas, #106, Carlsbad. Fields full of flowers for viewing and a place to buy them.

Quail Botanical Gardens—230 Quail Gardens Dr., Encinitas. Over 140 types of palm trees and the largest bamboo collection in the United States, all within a 30-acre exotic garden complete with waterfall and picnic area. Open daily 9:00 A.M. to 5:00 P.M. Adults $3, children 5 to 12 $1.50.

California Surf Museum—760-721-6876, 223 North Coast Hwy, Oceanside. A "no experience necessary" look into wave sliding's past, present, and future. Also doubles as an art gallery featuring surf-related art and/or artists.

Heritage Park Village and Museum—760-433-8297, 220 Peyri Rd., Oceanside. A look into Oceanside's past, including original buildings in a park setting.

Mission San Luis Rey—760-757-3651, 4050 Mission Ave., Oceanside. Known as the "king" of the Spanish mission system, the site includes a historic church, museum, and 56 acres of gardens.

TORREY PINES CITY BEACH (BLACK'S BEACH)

This news-making beach is famous for its fashion sense or, more accurately, its lack-of-fashion sense. It is currently illegal to be nude here, but the law is, apparently, unsupported as are the genitalia of some of this beach's visitors. The weather-worn cliffs behind the beach protect the eyes of those who can't bear flesh as well as those who can bare theirs. Black's is also famous for its steep, grinding waves that chew up and spit out surfers who err in the powerful break.

ACCESS: From I-5—Take the La Jolla Village Dr. Exit (right if southbound, left if northbound) and remain on La Jolla Village Dr. past Gilman Dr. The road bears right and becomes North Torrey Pines Rd. Take the next, obtuse left onto La Jolla Shores Dr. and then immediately turn right onto La Jolla Farms Rd. Weave on this road for about 2 miles to the point that Black Gold Rd. meets La Jolla Farms Rd. for the second time. The path here leads to the beach. Careful—it's a steep, rugged path requiring patience and attention.

By hiking—The beach can be reached by hiking north from La Jolla Shores Beach past Scripps Beach and Pier or by walking south from Torrey Pines State Beach. Black's Beach is marked by the presence of nudes. Keep an eye on the tide to ensure a dry walk back.

PARKING: Park along La Jolla Farms and Black Gold Rds. if using the path. If this is full or the strictly enforced, two-hour time limit is a concern, consider hiking from farther down the road at La Jolla Shores Beach or Torrey Pines State Beach.

HOURS/FEES: Black's, like many of life's best things, is free and always available.

Amenities: Only what nature has provided.

Activities: Fishing, surfing, swimming, nude sunbathing, strolling.

For more information:

Lifeguard Service—619-221-8899.

Surf/weather Report—619-221-8884.

Coastline Parks—619-221-8901.

Water-quality Hotline—619-338-2073.

Torrey Pines State Beach

Home of the last mainland concentration of Torrey Pine, *Pinus torreyana*, the beach lies within the Torrey Pines State Reserve. It is described by rangers as a "wilderness island in an urban sea," so please use no-trace practices while enjoying the scenery. The visitor center is a good place to gear up for the park's 8 miles of walking trails. Rangers guide nature walks at 11:30 A.M. and 1:30 P.M. weekends and holidays. The beach itself extends northward from Black's Beach.

Access: Exit I-5 at Carmel Valley Rd. and follow it west (right if southbound, left if northbound) or 1.5 miles to Coast Hwy 101 and turn left. The entrance will be on the right in about a mile. If you start to go up the Torrey Pines grade, you have passed it. The Beach Trail starts at the restrooms just south of the visitor center and is listed as the "least scenic" of the park's trails.

Parking: The lot is big enough here for most imaginable situations. Some additional parking is found on nearby streets characterized by the beat-up surfmobiles.

Hours/fees: Day use only, 8:00 A.M. to 11:00 P.M., with the parking lot closing at sundown. The visitor center opens at 9:00 A.M. $4.

Amenities: Parking, restrooms, lifeguard, handicapped accessible, picnic area, self-guided nature trails.

Park Rules:

No dogs, no horses.

No vehicles other than wheelchairs and strollers allowed on trails.

Smoking allowed only on beach or on the porch of the museum.

No picnicking in the reserve. Picnicking is allowed on the beach.

No food or drink on any trail except to get them to the beach.

No bicycles, motorcycles, or any other vehicle permitted on any trail, except baby strollers and wheelchairs.

ACTIVITIES: Surfing, swimming, hiking, nature viewing, beach picnics.

FOR MORE INFORMATION:

Torrey Pines State Reserve and Beach—619-755-2063, www.torreypine.org.

DEL MAR CITY BEACH

Del Mar, the self-titled "Gateway to San Diego," sees a lot of beach traffic that spills over from its huge neighbor to the south. This means parking trouble and crowds. The good news is this beach is wide enough to handle all who find a parking space. It's hard to imagine that the 1900 census was 228 with only 32 coastal dwellers. Powerhouse Park, at the beach's southern end, provides a place to picnic near the site of the old powerhouse that powered part of Del Mar's past and now makes a romantic, bluff-top viewpoint. Del Mar Bluffs City Park lies north of the San Dieguito River and supplies additional space to lounge on and a prime fishing spot.

ACCESS: From the south—Take the Del Mar Heights Rd. Exit west from I-5. Turn right onto Camino del Mar. Access the beach between 18th and 29th Sts.

From the north—Take the Via de la Valle Exit, turn right, continue to Court St., and turn left onto Camino del Mar. Access the beach between 29th and 18th Sts.

From La Jolla—Take North Torrey Pines Rd. (Hwy 21) and drive north to Del Mar by remaining on this road.

PARKING: There's a parking lot at the Amtrak station located on Zuni Dr., west of Coast St. Metered parking is also available on Coast St. Good luck!

HOURS/FEES: The beach is free, but parking isn't. The price varies with the Amtrak pay lot probably the best bet.

AMENITIES: Showers, year-round lifeguard.

ACTIVITIES: Surfing, swimming, sunbathing, fishing.

SOLANA BEACH

Del Mar Shores Terrace, Seascape Surf, Fletcher Cove Park, and Tide Beach Park all make up Solana Beach, another busy place for sun lovers from San Diego. Parking is a bit easier to find here than in Del Mar proper. Once you are on the wide sandy beaches, it won't matter what town you're in!

ACCESS: From I-5—Take the Lomas Santa Fe Dr. Exit toward the ocean and cross Hwy 21. In one block, Sierra Ave. intersects. Take a right to Tide Beach and Fletcher Cove. Turn left on Sierra for Seascape Surf and Del Mar Shores.

From La Jolla—Take North Torrey Pines Rd. (Hwy 21) and drive north through Del Mar and into Solana Beach.

To Tide Beach—Stairway to beach at Pacific Ave. and Solana Vista Dr.

To Fletcher Cove—Ramp to beach at 111 South Sierra Ave.

To Seascape Surf—Stairway to beach at 501 South Sierra Ave.

To Del Mar Shores Terrace—Stairway to beach at 108 Del Mar Shores Terr.

PARKING: There are parking lots at 111, 335, 550, 721, and 733 South Sierra Ave. All are open twenty-four hours; however, the lots maintain hours of 6:00 A.M. to 10:00 P.M. in the summer and 6:00 A.M. to 6:00 P.M. in the winter.

AMENITIES: Lifeguard, volleyball nets, basketball court, shuffleboard.

ACTIVITIES: Surfing, swimming, sunbathing, fishing, volleyball, diving.

FOR MORE INFORMATION:
Surf/weather Report—619-755-2971.

CARDIFF STATE BEACH

This sunbathing haven offers a wide, flat sandy beach bordered on the south by tide pools and on the north a boat launch. Surfing is best here on a west swell; otherwise it gets fairly mushy. The San Elijo Lagoon lies on the dry side of the highway. This saltwater marsh was freshwater prior to human "improvements" in the area. Nature continues to adapt, with the region still offering refuge to a variety of migrating birds and small mammals such as the southern pocket gopher. Cardiff is an excellent place to nature watch.

ACCESS: From I-5 take the Lomas Santa Fe Dr. Exit and head toward the ocean. Turn right on Old Hwy 101 and follow it about 1 mile to the beach's parking area.

PARKING: A fee parking lot is provided. Parking is also available at nearby Tide Beach Park.

HOURS/FEES: The day-use fee for the parking lot is $4 with hours of 7:00 A.M. to sunset. The beach is open from 6:00 A.M. to 11:00 P.M.

AMENITIES: Restrooms, lifeguards, wheelchair access, hand-launch/boat-launch zone.

ACTIVITIES: Swimming, surfing, boating, tide pools, wildlife watching.

FOR MORE INFORMATION:
Cardiff State Beach—760-753-5091.
San Diego Coast District Headquarters—619-642-4200.

SAN ELIJO STATE BEACH

San Elijo is one of the better beach campgrounds on the coast, which means a bluff top covered in RVs. The camp offers everything a roadside camper could need, including a laundry facility and a grocery store. Check out the native plant garden and tide-pool displays at the park headquarters to learn more about nature's ecosystem. The beach is pretty rocky and better suited to tide-pool exploration than reclining.

ACCESS: From I-5 take the Lomas Santa Fe Dr. Exit and head toward the ocean. Turn right on CR S21 and follow it about 1 mile to the beach's parking area.

PARKING: A fee parking lot is provided for day use. Some surfers park along CR S21 for free.

HOURS/FEES: The day-use fee for the parking lot is $4 and camping runs $18 to $25 with tent sites available. Beach use is free.

AMENITIES: Restrooms, lifeguards, wheelchair access, showers.

ACTIVITIES: Swimming, surfing, diving, tide pools, fishing.

FOR MORE INFORMATION:
San Elijo State Beach—760-753-5091.
California State Parks, San Diego District—619-642-4200.
Reservations—800-444-7275, cal-parks.ca.gov/RESERVE/resindex.htm.

SWAMI'S

Swami's is a small rock and sand beach hidden beneath a grassy, bluff-top picnic area complete with grills and restrooms. The area is a famous surfing spot named after the Self-realization Fellowship Hermitage grounds on the hill to the north. There's not really any room to spread out on the thin band of sand, which makes water activities the main draw here. The surf zone's outer point bears the name "The Boneyard," though its bark is said to be worse than its bite. Knowing that surfers tend to name breaks after an onshore landmark, it's likely the break is named after the secluded coast just north of Swami's, which happens to be a place for romantics and nudists. I'll let you figure out the rest.

ACCESS: Exit I-5 at Encinitas Blvd. and head toward the ocean. After ducking under the railroad bridge, turn left on 1st St. Continue to 1298 and the parking lot.

PARKING: Free parking lot at 1298 1st St.

HOURS/FEES: Swami's, a free beach, is practically always open. The 5:00 A.M. to 2:00 A.M. hours are designed to stop camping.

AMENITIES: Shower, wheelchair restrooms, tables, grills, lifeguard, stairs.

ACTIVITIES: Surfing, fishing, diving, picnicking, nude swimming.

FOR MORE INFORMATION:

Swami's—760-633-2880.

MOONLIGHT BEACH

Moonlight Beach, a wide, flat field of sand tucked away behind a cliff that juts into the ocean, has all the amenities of a resort without the cost. At the end of D Street, about 0.2 mile south, is a park with benches for romantics to bask in the lunar glow or stroll down the stairway to the tide pools and beach. Nighttime picnics were commonplace here in the early 1900s.

ACCESS: Exit I-5 at Encinitas Blvd. and head toward the ocean. After crossing the railroad tracks, make a jog to the right and continue heading toward the ocean on B St., which deadends at the beach.

PARKING: Free parking is at the end of C St., along C St., and along 4th St.

HOURS/FEES: 5:00 A.M. to 2:00 A.M. In other words, *No Camping.* The beach is free.

AMENITIES: Shower, wheelchair restrooms, tables, grills, lifeguard, volleyball, tennis, beach rentals, snack shack.

ACTIVITIES: Surfing, fishing, diving, picnicking, swimming.

FOR MORE INFORMATION:

Moonlight Beach—760-633-2880.

Community Services—760-633-2740

California State Parks, San Diego District—619-642-4200.

WHAT A RIP!

The Sun reflects off the glassy ocean like multifaceted sparkles in a field of diamonds. The waves are small, spilling gently onto the beach. A child plays near a rocky jetty, happily frolicking in the foam. He stumbles backward as the sand slopes sharply. He laughs as his bottom hits the water. Here the water is moving quickly toward the sea. The child, a good swimmer, finds the water is now deep and the ground is beyond his extended toes. Instinctively, the child tries to swim to shore. The current is too strong and the child soon tires and continues to be pushed out to sea.

Rip currents, also called a rip tide, the undertow, or simply a rip, are strong currents that form along beaches. A combination of forces sends water up and onto a beach. This water, like all liquids, seeks a level state. Thus, the water recedes to the ocean. Liquids also "stick" together, and this ocean water forms a river of sorts that seeks the easiest route back to sea. One portion of shore can have a number of these extremely powerful rip-current rivers. Rip currents can form on any shore and often are found alongside breakwaters or other big objects in the water. Rips can even form where large groups of bathers create a breakwater.

The best way to avoid rip currents is to check with a lifeguard, who will tell you where and where not to swim. Even when swimming in an approved area, be alert to changing conditions and swim parallel to shore.

If you find yourself caught in one of these "rivers," don't panic. Panic is not a survival tool! After not panicking, get your bearings while waving for help. The rip is rushing to sea and you want to be on the land. However, a human is not stronger than the ocean. If you've stayed calm and waved for help, by now you know which way the current is flowing, so swim perpendicular to it. In almost every case, this will mean swimming parallel to the shore, meaning up or down the beach and not toward it.

While you are still in the grip of the rip, you will continue to be swept toward the open ocean. Continue swimming perpendicular to the ocean. You will eventually exit the current and your seaward motion will cease and desist. Get your bearings again, wave for help again, don't panic again, and make sure you're really out of the rip current before swimming back to shore.

Don't fight the ocean. You will lose. Work with it to get back. The wave energy can help you to shore. Don't exhaust yourself. Tread water and rest as necessary. Swim at a pace that won't use up all your energy. And keep remembering not to panic.

Of the rescues made by beach lifeguards, 80 percent are necessitated by rip currents. The currents themselves are perfectly natural. They simply command respect. Be aware and swim with care.

A good website with rip current information is at http://www.ci.imperial-beach.ca.us/riptide.htm.

BEACONS BEACH AND STONE STEPS BEACH (LEUCADIA STATE BEACH)

Leucadia, meaning "sheltered place" in Greek, was the former name for this cliffside play place. Surfers used to call it "The Beacon." However, with time surfers will make any name plural—hence, Beacons Beach. Fishing and diving are good here. Encinitas Beach lies to the south and is only accessible from this or Stone Steps Beach. Stone Steps is accessed via, you guessed it, stone steps from the end of South El Portal, just down Neptune Avenue from Beacons, and is a good surfing spot. The cliff at the base of the ninety-seven steps (some are wooden) is undercut by the high tide, making this a low-tide-only trip.

ACCESS: Exit I-5 at Leucadia Blvd. and head to the water. Cross Old Hwy 101 (CR S21) and bear right as the road finds Neptune Ave. The parking lot is dead ahead. Follow the path to the beach. Access to Stone Steps lies left down Neptune Ave. Turn right onto South El Portal.

PARKING: Free parking in the lot at the end of Leucadia Blvd. There is also on-street parking for Stone Steps on Neptune Ave.

HOURS/FEES: 5:00 A.M. to 2:00 A.M., in other words, no camping.

AMENITIES: Beacons, parking lot, stone steps.

ACTIVITIES: Surfing, fishing, diving, swimming, tide pools, stroll on beach.

FOR MORE INFORMATION:

Encinitas Automated Information Line—760-633-2880.

Community Services—760-633-2740.

California State Parks, San Diego District—619-642-4200.

CARLSBAD STATE AND CITY BEACHES

The black stuff seen at these beaches is naturally occurring tar. What isn't natural is how the sand is disappearing. It used to be replenished annually from the north. However, Oceanside Harbor has changed how things work. Construction at Oceanside Harbor has disrupted the natural transport of sand along the coast so the beach can no longer replenish itself. Nonetheless, this beach is still pleasant and steps to help nature move and keep sand here are in place. The state beach is an excellent place to picnic with its grassy, ocean vistas. The paved path here is wheel-free, making romantic strolls carefree. Surfers are restricted to the morning hours at the city beach, and both beaches limit lifeguard service to summer. Following in the footsteps of places like Tourmaline Surfing Park, Tamarack Surfing Park at the intersection of Carlsbad Boulevard and Tamarack Avenue allows surfing at any time.

ACCESS: From the south—Take I-5 northbound, exit via Tamarack Ave., turn left, travel 0.5 mile to Carlsbad Blvd., and turn right. Stairs are off Sycamore, Maple, Cherry, Hemlock, and Tamarack Aves.

From the north—Take I-5 southbound, exit via Elm Ave., turn right, and travel 0.5 mile to Ocean St. Stairs to the beach lie ahead and a block in either direction, with a parking lot to the left where Ocean St. and Carlsbad Blvd. meet.

PARKING: On-street parking along Carlsbad and Ocean. There's a parking lot where Carlsbad Blvd. and Ocean St. meet and another at Carlsbad and Tamarack.

HOURS/FEES: A free beach with free parking.

AMENITIES: Wheelchair-accessible restrooms, lifeguard.

ACTIVITIES: Surfing, swimming, fishing, diving.

FOR MORE INFORMATION:

California State Parks, San Diego District—619-642-4200.

Carlsbad and South Carlsbad State Beach—760-438-3143.

Carlsbad Chamber of Commerce—800-227-5722 or www.carlsbadca.org.

SOUTH OCEANSIDE BEACH AND BUCCANEER PARK

The sand is showing signs of returning here after its harbor-induced disappearance. Because it requires a bit more effort to reach than Oceanside's northern beaches, the shore is less crowded. Buccaneer Park is a full-service park nestled against the still waters of Loma Alta Marsh and the railroad tracks.

ACCESS: From I-5, exit on Cassidy St. and head toward the ocean. Cross Hill St. and continue to Pacific St. Stairs to the beach lie dead ahead and to the right at 1639 and 1587 Pacific St. Buccaneer Park lies farther down Pacific St. at Morse St.

PARKING: Along Pacific St. and at Buccaneer Park. A complete list of Oceanside's numerous parking lots is available at the visitor center.

HOURS/FEES: Twenty-four hours. Free.

AMENITIES: Snack shack, volleyball courts, basketball courts, athletic fields, shower, covered picnic area, playground, wheelchair-accessible restrooms, walking path.

ACTIVITIES: Surfing, swimming, fishing, volleyball, basketball, bird-watching, strolling, tide pools.

FOR MORE INFORMATION:

Beach Community Center—760-966-4549.

Oceanside Visitor Center—800-350-7873 or 760-721-1101.

Chamber of Commerce—www.oceansidechamber.com.

OCEANSIDE CITY BEACH AND PIER

The West Coast's longest pier bisects this widening strip of sand popular for sunning, surfing, and strolling. Beach rescue efforts have the sands widening after suffering from the construction of Oceanside Harbor's breakwater. The beach is flanked by the Strand, which in turn is paralleled by Tyson Park, which provides a green backdrop to the light, adjacent sands. The park's palm-lined walkway strolls south along the Strand, then leads up some stairs to Linear Park and its benches. The pier, 1,954 feet long, offers free fishing and has wheelchair-accessible trolley service to its terminus.

SUNBATHERS, SURFERS, AND STROLLERS ALIKE FLOCK TO THE BEACH AT OCEANSIDE.

ACCESS: Exit I-5 on Hill St. Turn left onto Pier View Way to reach Pacific St. Access to the beach and parking lies ahead and in both directions.

PARKING: Lots at the end of Breakwater Way, Forster St., Hayes St., Pier View Way, Windward Way, and Wisconsin St. A complete list of Oceanside's numerous parking lots is available at the visitor center.

HOURS/FEES: Free beach use. The fees for parking vary from free to 50 cents an hour.

AMENITIES: Beach—shower, covered picnic area, grill, restrooms, lifeguard, walkway, volleyball. Pier—bait shop, restaurant, trolley, gym.

ACTIVITIES: Surfing, swimming, fishing, volleyball, strolling, sunbathing.

FOR MORE INFORMATION:

Oceanside Lifeguard—760-966-4535.

Beach Community Center—760-966-4549.

Oceanside Visitor Center—800-350-7873 or 760-721-1101.

Chamber of Commerce—www.oceansidechamber.com.

HARBOR BEACH

This is where the resurgence of Oceanside's beaches begins. Sand dredged from the harbor is deposited here rather than being lost to offshore canyons. What this means to beachgoers is a wide expanse of clean sand protected by a series of breakwaters that make for excellent swimming, surfing, and fishing. The harbor offers restaurants, shops, and whale-watching trips in addition to standard boating activities.

ACCESS: Exit I-5 on Harbor Dr. and turn left to weave around the southern end of the harbor.

PARKING: The end of Harbor Dr. South has a lot. A complete list of Oceanside's numerous parking lots is available at the visitor center.

HOURS/FEES: Open twenty-four hours. $5 per car.

AMENITIES: Barbecue grills, wheelchair-accessible picnic area, lifeguard, playground, RV campsites.

ACTIVITIES: Surfing, swimming, fishing, camping, picnicking, sunning.

FOR MORE INFORMATION:

Beach Community Center—760-966-4549.

Oceanside Visitor Center—800-350-7873 or 760-721-1101.

Oceanside Harbor—760-966-4580.

Chamber of Commerce—www.oceansidechamber.com.

San Onofre State Beach South (Bluff Beach)

Once the exclusive playground of the San Onofre Surf Club, Bluff Beach is readily accessible to all who wish to recreate within a stone's throw of a nuclear power plant. The beach is of the wide, sandy variety at the base of tall, eroding bluffs. Among the scrub-line trees and shrubs atop the bluffs sits a popular campground, which provides trails along the cliff sides that offer dizzying vistas of the ocean half a football field below. Signs tell you where to tune in the event of a nuclear warning siren. However, you may just want to sit and watch from the bluff's edge.

Access: The exit from I-5 is marked for San Onofre. Take the exit and follow the signs either to the campground or past the power plant to the beach access.

Parking: The day-use lot is huge and more than capable of handling the largest of crowds. A shuttle bus even services this lot.

Hours/Fees: Day use is $4 and camping ranges from $18 to $25. Campers will need to make a reservation via Destinet to have any shot at a site.

Amenities: Lifeguard, wheelchair-accessible restrooms, campground, picnic area, barbecue grills, showers, trails.

Activities: Surfing, nature viewing, biking, hiking, protesting.

For more information:

San Onofre State Beach—714-492-4872 or 714-492-0802.

Reservations—800-444-7275, cal-parks.ca.gov/RESERVE/resindex.htm.

Trestles

This is one of the primo surf spots on California's shores and is named for the old bridge trestle that surfers use to gauge where to sit in the water. A long trail provides access to this section of shore used almost entirely by surfers and their spectators. The parking lot can be used as an indicator of surf conditions: A full lot equals good surf.

Access: From I-5, take the Christianitos Rd. Exit and head away from the ocean. After 1.5 miles, turn right into San Mateo Campground. The 1.5-mile asphalt trail to the beach leaves from the lot.

Parking: Park in the campground's day-use lot.

HOURS/FEES: Day use is $4 and camping ranges from $15 to $25. The area keeps hours of sunrise to 10:00 P.M.

AMENITIES: Long, clean, point-peeling waves and a paved path to access them.

ACTIVITIES: Surfing, surf photography, surf dreaming, hiking with a surfboard, biking.

FOR MORE INFORMATION:

San Mateo Campground Reservations—800-444-7275, cal-parks.ca.gov/RESER-VE/resindex.htm.

ON A MISSION

Like the sweet smell of air after a rainstorm sweeps through, the missions of California have a profound effect on the senses. Wooden railings worn smooth by decades of human hands, roofs covered with green mold after years of shelter, gardens full of life next to cemeteries centuries old. This is history, not words in a book, actual history. Here, the breeze carries sounds to the imagination, creating a vision of the past. Odors and sights do the same. Being at one of California's twenty-one missions immerses you in history.

In 1769 Gaspar de Portolá sailed into San Diego with a holy fellow, Father Junípero Serro. The plan was to extend Spain's territory northward from Baja California, using missions and presidios. The indigenous people were to be converted to Christianity in the process of securing the area for Spain. The intentions of the monks were holy enough: Save the native people by teaching them Christianity. They even had laws that allowed the native Californians to control the land—after they learned to behave in a Spanish way.

Many indigenous people went along with the idea, and for the most part things went well. Unfortunately, the indigenous folk had never been exposed to the germs that accompanied the Europeans and thereby lost much of their population to disease. Another fallout was the disruption of trade. With the mainland tribes being converted to new ways of life, the island cultures lost valuable trading partners. Thus when food was scarce during severe El Niño conditions, they could choose starvation or move to the mainland and the missions. Many chose starvation, but eventually the tribes moved. Tribal identities were blurred through marriages to individuals of other tribes or persons of European descent.

When Mexico won its independence from Spain, the Spaniards sold off the missions. During this time, many of the buildings were destroyed or damaged as ranches absorbed them. Not soon after this, gold was discovered and California quickly became one of the United States. This meant native Californians had to deal with the U.S. government to keep their lands. In classic late-nineteenth-century fashion,

SAN BUENAVENTURA MISSION, FOUNDED IN 1782, STILL HOLDS MASS IN ITS VENERABLE CHURCH.

the tribes were given treaties that weren't honored and most found themselves without land. This was also a time of indentured servitude and flat-out murdering of the indigenous population, a fact that has been glossed over by most history books.

Zipping to the present, the missions are now very peaceful and calm. While plans called for more, twenty-one missions were built and all are within a day's horse ride from the next along the Camino Real, which is basically Pacific Coast Highway. Museums and gift shops help satisfy tourist curiosity and the mission churches are still available for worship.

Part of the beauty of history is that it isn't judgmental. It simply is. The original walls of these buildings saw everything that went on around them. They watched people behave as people do. Maybe someday we'll learn from history. Maybe today?

REGION 5

SAN CLEMENTE TO DANA POINT

The swallows of San Juan Capistrano return every spring to this region's mission of the same name. Not a bad place to come home to. The region delivers coastal good times and still has a village feel despite its rapid growth.

San Clemente's coastline is composed of eroding cliffs that cascade into the sand below, giving the beaches a secluded feel despite the closeness of the thriving beach community. From atop the steep hills overlooking the ocean, the town made headlines in the 1970s as Nixon's West Coast White House. In addition to its beaches, the community has fourteen parks spread throughout. The nucleus of tourist activities is the San Clemente Pier Bowl at the end of Avenida del Mar.

Capistrano Beach is a popular seashore playground. Volleyball nets, playground equipment, and a bike path provide onshore recreation while wide, sandy coast provides the rest. The town of Capistrano Beach sits along a cliff overlooking its beach of the same name. Unfortunately for the town's businesses, Highway 1 runs beneath the cliff, passing the town by.

Doheny State Beach made waves in the Beach Boys tune "Surfin' USA." Unfortunately for surfers, the harbor at Dana Point killed the famous waves. Still, the region has plenty of sand, sun, and surf to quench a hearty beach appetite. Doheny State Beach offers shoreside campers a home by the sea along with a marine education in its five aquariums and indoor tide pool. The beach itself is a continuation of Capistrano's sand and offers similar amenities. The two blend together. Dana Point's claim to fame lies in its harbor, pleasant parks, and ocean-view lookout points providing places to watch the annual whale migration.

San Juan Capistrano, home to the world-famous mission of the same name, lies inland. Despite being landlocked, tourism thrives here with mission memorabilia available in all shapes and forms. The buildings, new and old, all look to be from the same mission mold. The swallows arrive here, and up and down the coast, on March 15.

Access

Pacific Coast Hwy (Hwy 1) runs through the entire region and acts as the main access route. It can be reached via I-5. Exit the interstate on El Camino Real to reach the southern points. Use the Hwy 1 Exit to access Doheny and points north.

Beaches

San Clemente State Beach

Calafia Beach

SAN CLEMENTE TO DANA POINT

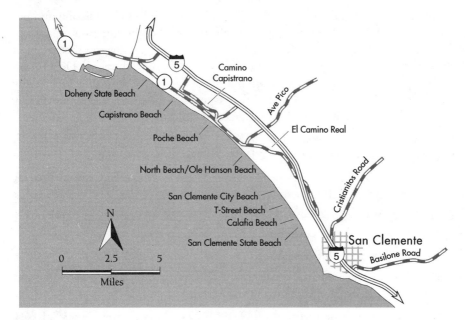

San Clemente City Beach and T-Street Beach

Ole Hanson Beach (North Beach)

Capistrano Beach and Poche Beach

Doheny State Beach

Camping

San Mateo Campground—949-361-2531. Reservations, 800-444-7275; information, 916-653-6995, cal-parks.ca.gov/travel/reserve/index.htm. 162 sites, 40 with hookups, dump station, hot showers, $17 to $24.

San Onofre State Beach—949-492-4872, 800-444-7275, cal-parks.ca.gov/travel/reserve/index.htm. 230 sites for tents or RVs, cold showers, $19 to $22.

San Clemente State Beach—949-492-0802 or 949-492-3156. Reservations, 800-444-7275, cal-parks.ca.gove/travel/reserve/index.htm. 157 sites, 72 with full hookups, hot showers, flush toilets, laundry tubs, dump station.

Doheny State Beach—949-496-6172. Reservations, 800-444-7275, cal-parks.ca.gove/travel/reserve/index.htm. 121 developed sites, picnic tables, fire rings, water, dump station.

Other points of interest

Mission San Juan Capistrano—949-493-1111 or 949-248-2048. Mission number seven in the chain of twenty-one that reach from San Diego northward past San Francisco. A celebration is held every spring to welcome spring and the return of the swallows. To see the mission, exit on Hwy 74 and follow the signs. Del Obispo St. (Hwy 74) continues to Hwy 1 from the city of San Juan Capistrano. Open daily from 8:30 A.M. to 5:00 P.M. Closed Thanksgiving, Christmas, and Good Friday afternoon. $5 for adults and $4 for seniors and children.

O'Neill Museum—949-493-8444, 31831 Los Rios St., San Juan Capistrano. A Victorian-era house, once called the Pryor House, turned museum.

The Heritage of San Clemente—949-369-1299, 415 North El Camino Real. A museum featuring the local history along with a visitor center.

Doheny Aquariums—949-496-6172. The park offers five aquariums and an indoor tide pool for paying customers.

Dana Point Harbor—949-496-1555.

Orange County Harbor Patrol—949-248-2222. Sportfishing, whale watching, and sailing are common activities based in the harbor.

Orange County Marine Institute—949-496-2274. Tours, "living history" classes, theater presentations, and the tall ship *Pilgrim* await.

San Clemente Bowl—949-492-1131. The area surrounding the municipal pier is a hub of tourist activity. Wining and dining is a common activity here.

SAN CLEMENTE STATE BEACH

A pair of steep paths wind down the eroding bluff to a cliff-lined beach. The nominal day-use fee and short but steep walk to the sand keep the crowds away. The beach's narrow nature lends itself to strolls rather than sunbathing. The cliff adds to the illusion of seclusion. Keep walking south to gain a view of the "West Coast White House" where Presidents Nixon and FDR both spent time. The surf spot off the shore here, Cottons, is named after the house's original owner, Hamilton H. Cotton.

ACCESS: From the north—Exit I-5 southbound at the Avenida Calafia Exit. Continue straight through the intersection, remaining on Avenida Calafia. The park entrance is on the left 0.4 mile from the highway.

From the south—From I-5 northbound, take the Cristianitos Rd. Exit. Turn right on Cristianitos Rd., then make an immediate left onto El Camino Real. Just over a mile from the exit, turn left onto Avenida San Luis Rey, cross over I-5, and turn right on Avenida del Presidente. Travel about another 0.5 mile and turn left onto Avenida Calafia. The park entrance is on the left, halfway down the hill.

Pay appropriate fees at the gatehouse and pick up a map. Two trails lead to the beach from the day-use parking area.

PARKING: Campers will be assigned a space. Day-use parking is reached by following the access road past the two camp area entrances to a 200-space parking lot.

HOURS/FEES: 6:00 A.M. to 10:00 P.M. $5 day use.

AMENITIES: Restrooms, picnic tables, barbecue grills, fire pits on beach, trails, campfire programs, ranger-led hikes.

ACTIVITIES: Swimming, surfing, fishing, scuba diving, hiking.

FOR MORE INFORMATION:

San Clemente State Beach—949-492-0802 or 949-492-3156.

Orange County Beaches—www.oc.ca.gov/pfrd/hbp.

Coastal Weather—949-496-2210.

Surf/weather Report—949-492-1011.

San Clemente Chamber of Commerce—949-492-1131.

Beach Closure Hotline—949-667-3752.

CALAFIA BEACH

Calafia, much wider than San Clemente State Beach, its neighbor to the south, is more popular with the sunbathing and volleyball crowd. A surfside eatery adds condiments to this sandy recipe for summer fun.

ACCESS: From the north—Exit I-5 southbound at the Avenida Calafia Exit. Continue straight through the intersection, remaining on Avenida Calafia. The road dives toward the coast and ends in a parking lot.

From the south—From I-5 northbound, take the Cristianitos Rd. Exit. Turn right on Cristianitos Rd., then make an immediate left onto El Camino Real. Just over a mile from the exit, turn left onto Avenida San Luis Rey, cross over I-5, and turn right on Avenida del Presidente. Travel about another 0.5 mile and turn left onto Avenida Calafia. The road dives toward the coast and ends in a parking lot.

PARKING: A metered parking lot greets beachgoers. Some cars park along Avenida Calafia. If doing so, look around for the sign posting that particular area's regulations.

HOURS/FEES: Dawn to midnight. Parking is metered.

AMENITIES: Snack shack, restrooms, showers, volleyball nets.

ACTIVITIES: Volleyball, swimming, sunbathing, body surfing.

FOR MORE INFORMATION:

Orange County Beaches—www.oc.ca.gov/pfrd/hbp.

Coastal Weather—949-496-2210.

Surf/weather Report—949-492-1011.

San Clemente Chamber of Commerce—949-492-1131.

Beach Closure Hotline—949-667-3752.

SAN CLEMENTE CITY BEACH AND T-STREET BEACH

The movers and shakers of the surfing world rub elbows on T-Street Beach, vying for publicity from locally based surf magazines. The beach is a soft strand of sand backed by bluffs vegetated with houses. Railroad tracks, with their rocky embankment, divide the beach from the bluff. The municipal pier extends into the ocean from Avenida del Mar, providing tidy ocean viewing and dining. Volleyball and picnicking lie in the pier's shadow.

ACCESS: From the north—Exit I-5 southbound at Avenida Palizada and keep right on Avenida Palizada. Turn left onto El Camino Real (Hwy 1), travel about 0.6 mile and turn right onto Avenida del Mar. Stay on this road as it winds down to the ocean. The beach is accessed via a walkway adjacent to the pier.

From the south—Exit I-5 northbound onto El Camino Real (Hwy 1), turn left, and remain on El Camino Real as it passes beneath I-5. Turn left onto Avenida del Mar and follow it down to the parking area. T-Street Beach lies a short walk southward from the pier.

PARKING: There's a metered lot at the junction of Avenida del Mar and Victoria. Free roadside parking is available to a select few along Victoria. Parking is available along most roads. Be sure and check the signs as regulations vary widely.

HOURS/FEES: An hour before sunrise to midnight for this free beach.

AMENITIES: Pier, volleyball nets, coin-operated binoculars, parking lot, picnic tables (some covered), playground, lifeguards, shopping, dining.

ACTIVITIES: Surfing, swimming, sunbathing, picnicking, volleyball.

FOR MORE INFORMATION:

Coastal Weather—949-496-2210.

Surf/weather Report—949-492-1011.

Orange County Beaches—www.oc.ca.gov/pfrd/hbp.

San Clemente Chamber of Commerce—949-492-1131.

Beach Closure Hotline—949-667-3752.

San Clemente Pier—949-492-8335.

OLE HANSON BEACH (NORTH BEACH)

A small playground and restroom across the railroad tracks from a commuter's parking lot mark Ole Hanson Beach. The recreation center of the same name overlooks the beach from a parklike perch just inland and has a popular swimming pool. Be careful when crossing the railroad tracks to this swath of sand.

ACCESS: From either direction on I-5, take the Avenida Pico Exit and head toward the ocean. That's a right if southbound, a left if northbound. Continue down the road to El Camino Real (Hwy 1). Ole Hanson Beach lies across this intersection and has some parking. However, turn right on El Camino Real, then take an immediate left into the large parking area. The beach is reached via a pedestrian railroad crossing.

PARKING: The commuter train's parking lot is available for beach use after 8:00 A.M. Pay by the hour at a ticket-dispensing pay station.

HOURS/FEES: 8:00 A.M. to midnight.

AMENITIES: Grassy bluff park, restrooms, showers, playground equipment, train station.

ACTIVITIES: Swimming, sunbathing, volleyball.

FOR MORE INFORMATION:

Coastal Weather—949-496-2210.

Surf/weather Report—949-492-1011.

Orange County Beaches—www.oc.ca.gov/pfrd/hbp.

San Clemente Chamber of Commerce—949-492-1131.

Beach Closure Hotline—949-667-3752.

CAPISTRANO BEACH AND POCHE BEACH

Capistrano Beach follows a common Southern California template: a central area for playgrounds, volleyball pits, picnic tables, restrooms, and a parking lot, with beach extending in both directions. Poche Beach is basically the southern extension of Capistrano without all the parking.

ACCESS: From I-5 take the Avenida Pico Exit and head toward the ocean. That's a right if southbound or a left if northbound. Continue down the road to El Camino Real (Hwy 1), turn right. Travel almost 3 miles and turn left into the parking lot.

PARKING: The lot offers metered parking spaces. Free parking is available from Capistrano Beach northward on Hwy 1. Pedestrian walkways are used to cross the railroad tracks from these spots.

HOURS/FEES: 6:00 A.M. to 10:00 P.M. Beach use is free.

AMENITIES: Restrooms, showers, volleyball nets, picnic tables, and lifeguard.

ACTIVITIES: Swimming, surfing, in-line skating, and biking.

FOR MORE INFORMATION:

County of Orange (Harbors, Beaches and Parks)—949-834-5536.

Orange County Beaches—www.oc.ca.gov/pfrd/hbp.

Coastal Weather—949-496-2210.

Surf/weather Report—949-492-1011.

Beach Closure Hotline—949-667-3752.

DOHENY STATE BEACH (HOLE IN THE FENCE)

Doheny State Beach is actually the southern portion of Doheny State Beach Park. The park proper provides camping and an educational aquarium, and the beachfront lies south of these attractions. Day fees charged by the park are avoided by finding parking along Pacific Coast Highway and using one of the pedestrian bridges to access the beach. Thus Doheny's alias: Hole in the Fence. The facilities are standard state beach fare with a few restrooms complete with beach showers. A long and narrow parking lot parallels the beach.

ACCESS: From I-5 take the spaghetti-like exit onto Hwy 1 just south of San Juan Capistrano. To enter the park, turn right on Hwy 1. Turn left to access the beach without entering the park.

PARKING: Day-use parking is available in a lot that parallels the entire length of the beach. Free parking is found along Hwy 1, with access via pedestrian bridges that span the highway and railroad tracks.

HOURS/FEES: Sunrise to 10:00 P.M. $5 for day use.

AMENITIES: Restrooms, showers, lifeguard, camping, picnic area with barbecue grill, bike path, underwater diving park, horse trail, snack shack.

ACTIVITIES: Surfing, swimming, diving, volleyball, horseback riding (inland), tide pools (in the park proper).

FOR MORE INFORMATION:

Doheny State Beach—949-496-6171 or 949-496-6162.

Reservations—800-444-7275, cal-parks.ca.gove/travel/reserve/index.htm.

Orange County Beaches—www.oc.ca.gov/pfrd/hbp.

Coastal Weather—949-496-2210.

Surf/weather Report—949-492-1011.

Beach Closure Hotline—949-667-3752.

BIRDING

The silence grows louder as the birder melds into the surrounding shrubs. Raising the binoculars and gently nudging the focus knob makes the great blue heron's magnified image as crisp as the morning air. Excitement sends a wave of warmth to tingling toes combating the cold induced by a thirty-minute wait in the dewy dawn.

Bird-watching, or birding, was once a stodgy European pastime. Now, young and old enjoy this activity on a variety of different levels. Quite simply, it is humanity and wildlife sharing each other's presence. One of the beauties of birding is that it can be practiced anywhere and by anyone. Red-tailed hawks, kestrels, barn owls, and white-tailed kites are seen fluttering along coastal bluffs. Seabirds like the California brown pelican, surf scoters, and cormorants are seen foraging at sea, and godwits, oystercatchers, and plovers are just a few of the shorebirds that hang out on Southern California's beaches.

Many coastal birds, like the western gull, are colonial, meaning they exhibit distinctly social behaviors. Shorebirds, like the sandpiper, dart in and out of the waves. These little birds are virtually unidentifiable to all but the extremely patient.

HAWKS, PELICANS, PLOVERS, AND GULLS ARE AMONG THE BIRDS AN OBSERVANT VISITOR MAY SPOT ON OR NEAR SOUTHERN CALIFORNIA BEACHES.

Yet a good generalization will satisfy most bird watchers' curiosity. The ones with short bills are picking up food on the surface while those with long bills are digging for worms and crabs.

The sport doesn't require anything but eyes—and/or ears—and a desire to experience nature. Of course, certain tools of the trade help a birder see more good birds. (The phrase "good birds" refers to birds seen less commonly.) While watching any bird is rewarding, the serious birder actively seeks the ornithological find that is less commonplace.

With patience (waiting fifteen to thirty minutes) and silence, birds will often approach the viewer. While some find it tempting to manipulate the bird into flight, watching its ground behavior is much more rewarding. If the birds don't get close enough for your naked eye, binoculars will bring them to you. Good binoculars cost from $100 to $200, with extremely serious birders possessing binos costing more than $1,000. The reason for the price difference isn't solely magnification. The range of clarity and durability is vast. The better the glass, the better the binos, and the more money out of ye ole wallet. Often a higher power is less desirable. With a range of 7x (7 times normal vision) to 10x being common, an 8x binocular usually offers higher light-gathering power and closer focusing and is easier to hold steady than the more powerful 10x variety. To decipher what the eyes see, a field guide comes in mighty handy.

Remember that you don't *need* to know what you're looking at to appreciate its beauty.

GOOD PLACES TO BIRD:

Tijuana River National Estuarine Research Reserve—619-575-3613 or 619-435-5184, 301 Caspian Way, Imperial Beach. This is a great bird-watching spot with limited beach access, they even have free silhouette guides to help identify what you see. 10:00 A.M. to 6:00 P.M. Wednesday to Sunday.

Sweetwater Marsh National Wildlife Reserve—619-575-1290, 1000 Gunpowder Point Dr., Chula Vista. Located at the end of E St., this is the largest salt marsh in the bay area. A favorite for numerous birds, some endangered, and the site of the Chula Vista Nature Interpretive Center. A shuttle ride is required. Call for current information.

Buena Vista Lagoon Ecological Reserve—760-439-2473, 2202 South Hill St., Oceanside. A simple way to view the wetlands. Exhibits and trails offer views of the plant and birds of the lagoon. Maxton Brown Park is another place to see the pond. 10:00 A.M. to 4:00 P.M., 1:00 to 4:00 P.M. on Sunday, closed Monday.

Upper Newport Bay Ecological Reserve—949-640-6746. A 752-acre wetland full of birds and other estuary wildlife. Tours are offered every first and third Saturday at 9:00 A.M. Kayak tours are also available.

Crystal Cove State Park—949-496-3539. 2,791 acres of birds, fishing, coastal and canyon areas, nature walks, tours. 6:00 A.M. to sunset.

Bolsa Chica Ecological Reserve—714-840-1575. Protect a wetland by the sea and birds will come to stay.

Palos Verdes Estate Shoreline Preserve—The peninsula's rocky coastline offers lots of tide-pool fun and diving opportunities. Park on Paseo del Mar.

Point Mugu Lagoon—West of Hwy 1 on the Pacific Missile Test Center. Access is available for groups of fifteen to twenty-five only. Reservations are required a month in advance for these weekend-only tours. Pacific Missile Test Center Public Affairs Office: 805-989-8094.

Channel Islands National Park—805-658-5700. A safe haven for wildlife, birds are plentiful here. California brown pelicans, making a comeback from their DDT-caused near-extinction, have a rookery on Anacapa Island. Western gulls, Cassin's auklets, and the rare storm-petrel are just a few of the island chain's inhabitants.

McGrath State Beach—805-654-4744 or 805-899-1400. A river-mouth estuary and a small lake make this dune-filled beach a good birding locale. A nature trail with secluded benches makes for comfortable viewing. Watch out for poison oak.

Seaside Wilderness Park—805-652-4550. The trails in Hobo Park lead to the Ventura River and the wetlands that line it.

Andree Clark Bird Refuge—805-564-5421. Gardens and a saltwater marsh that connects to the Santa Barbara Zoo via a bike path make this a good place for hiking, biking, and birding.

Ash Avenue Wetland, Carpinteria Parks and Recreation—805-684-5405. A saltwater marsh home frequented by egrets, ospreys, and herons. Bat rays can be seen swimming in the channels. Kayaking and snorkeling are popular at the offshore reef. Kayak rentals are available.

Coal Oil Point Reserve—805-893-4127. The University of California uses this area to conduct scientific studies. They've provided a nature trail so visitors can enjoy the wildlife and coastal flora.

Oso Flaco Lakes—805-473-7230. The migratory birds of spring and fall pack the lakes' waters. A boardwalk extends out into the action.

Sweet Springs—This sanctuary between Montaña de Oro and Morro Bay State Park offers up-close views of the Morro Bay estuary along with a freshwater pond.

Morro Bay State Park—805-772-2560. A blue heron rookery (nesting site) is situated between the bay and the golf course. Informative signs and a nearby museum shed light on the area's avian species.

San Simeon State Beach—805-927-2068. The wide waterway here is protected from the Pacific by the sands of San Simeon. The result is a good birding location.

REGION 6

SOUTH LAGUNA BEACH TO NEWPORT BEACH

Sandy coves between rocky points create a coastline as eclectic as the towns that border it: South Laguna Beach, Laguna Beach, Corona del Mar, and Newport Beach. The water is usually very clear, creating a striking contrast of deep blue and light golden-tan.

The region also has Crystal Cove State Park, a large undeveloped area with 3.5 miles of coastline and an underwater park. Crystal Cove gives a welcome break from the shop-lined coast along Pacific Coast Highway.

South Laguna Beach has two excellent parks: Aliso Beach County Park and Salt Creek Beach Park. Both are well developed and often crowded. The offshore waters here are protected as a marine life refuge.

Laguna Beach's tourist brochure lists thirty beaches and coves on its 7-mile coastline. Doing the math tells one that the average beach here is 0.23 mile long. While the beaches aren't expansive, they aren't that small either. They're just separated by rocky, tide-pool areas and bluffs packed with homes. If you wander along the shore, be sure to stay below the mean high-tide line and explore to your heart's content. Glenn E. Vedder Ecological Reserve, just offshore, gives divers a living aquarium to explore. Laguna is hailed as a Mediterranean-style artist colony, and art events occur year-round.

Newport Beach and its suburbs, Corona del Mar and Balboa, are situated along 6 miles of wide, sandy coastline. Balboa Beach is home to the legendary Wedge, a wave that often reaches monstrous proportions due to refraction off the jetty. The entire coastal area is dedicated to ocean- and tourist-related activities. The Old Glory Boat Parade, annual sand castle contest, and gondola rides are some of the attractions here.

Access

From I-5 or I-405—Hwy 1, Pacific Coast Hwy (PCH), runs through the region. Take Hwy 133 westbound to join PCH in Laguna Beach. The beaches south of Laguna Main Beach lie to the south (left) of the junction of Hwy 133 and Hwy 1, while the rest are to the north (right).

To reach Newport Beach—Take Hwy 55 from I-5 or I-405 and head west into Newport Beach.

Beaches

Salt Creek Beach Park

1,000 Steps Beach

SOUTH LAGUNA BEACH TO NEWPORT BEACH

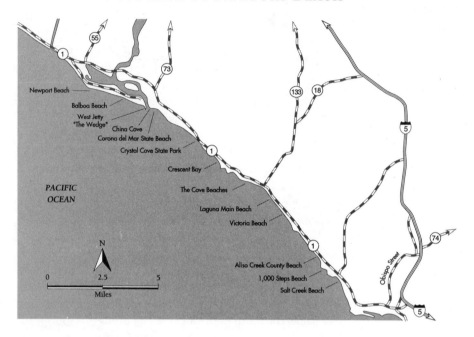

Aliso Creek County Beach

Victoria Beach

Laguna Main Beach

The Cove Beaches—(Diver's, Fisherman's, and Shaw's Cove)

Crescent Bay

Crystal Cove State Park

Corona del Mar State Beach

Newport Beach and Balboa Beach

Camping

Newport Dunes Resort—949-729-DUNE, 800-288-0770, 1131 Back Bay Dr. 403 sites with full hookups, boat launch, equipment rental, playground, restrooms, showers.

El Morro Canyon—949-494-3539, 471 Coast Hwy, Laguna Beach. Reservations, 800-444-7275, three campsites, pit toilet, picnic bench, no water (bring some), no fires, hiking, biking, horseback riding, birding. "Environmental camping" in El Morro Canyon, 2,200-acres of backcountry trails. There's a hike of 1.5 to 2.0 miles to reach the campground.

Other points of interest

Newport Harbor—949-723-4511. The area around the harbor is stocked with tourist-oriented shops and restaurants.

Upper Newport Bay Ecological Reserve—949-640-6746 or 949-640-1751.

Friends of Newport Bay—949-646-8009. 752 acres of wetlands full of birds and other estuary wildlife. Tours every first and third Saturday of the month at 9:00 A.M. Kayak tours and campfire programs are also available. 7:00 A.M. to sunset year-round.

Balboa Pavilion—949-675-9444, 400 Main St. In 1905 this was a Victorian bathhouse. Now, it's a gallery of historical photos. At night the structure is lit with 1,400 lights.

The Catalina Flyer—949-673-5245. This catamaran takes visitors 26 miles out to sea to Santa Catalina Island. Visitor center, 310-510-1520. Departs from the Balboa Pavilion.

Crystal Cove State Park—949-496-3539. 2,791 acres of coastal and canyon areas, nature walks, birding, fishing, tours. 6:00 A.M. to sunset.

Newport Nautical Museum—949-673-7863, 151 East Pacific Coast Hwy.

Pelican Hill Golf Club—Information, 949-759-5190; tee times, 949-760-0707, 22651 Pelican Hill Rd. South. Eighteen-holes of golf in Newport. Tom Fazio's design uses the canyons and ocean views for this golfing experience. Tee-time reservations up to seven days in advance.

Newport Beach Yacht Clubs:

Balboa Yacht Club—949-673-3515.

Balboa Island Yacht Club and Ferry—949-673-1070.

Lido Isle Yacht Club—949-673-6170.

Newport Harbor Yacht Club—949-673-7730.

Shark Island Yacht Club—949-760-0221.

South Shore Yacht Club—949-646-3102.

Gondola tours in Newport Harbor:

Gondola Company of Newport Beach—949-675-1212 or 949-675-4730.

Adventures at Sea—949-650-2412.

Still more points of interest:

Balboa Fun Zone—949-673-0408, Balboa Peninsula. Dating back to 1936, the Fun Zone has a Ferris wheel, merry-go-round, and bumper cars, along with a video arcade and shops full of souvenirs. Open 10:00 A.M. to 10:00 P.M.

The Environmental Nature Center—949-645-8489, 1601 16th St. (between Irvine Ave. and Dover Dr.), Newport Beach, home.earthling.net/~encnb. Designed especially for kids five and up, these trails weave through 2.5 acres of wildlife habitat. Open every day from 8:00 A.M. to 5:00 P.M.

Parks and Recreation Department—949-644-3151, 3300 Newport Blvd. Newport Beach parks have basketball and volleyball courts and equipment for beach use, and some include racquetball courts, athletic fields, baseball diamonds, barbecue grills, picnic tables, play equipment, restrooms, and parking lots.

Salt Creek Beach Park

Salt Creek Beach Park is tucked between the Pacific Coast Highway and the ocean on the only large, nondeveloped area in South Laguna. The long ribbon of sand that is the beach proper is formed from the sediment brought to the ocean from Salt Creek. Littoral (along the shore) currents put the sand where the waves can push it onto shore. The point to the south helps the current dump its load. Picnickers enjoy the park up on the hill

ACCESS: Follow Hwy 1 south from its intersection with Hwy 133, passing through Laguna Beach and into South Laguna Beach. Turn right onto Ritz Carlton Dr. and park in the lot.

PARKING: A lot full of meters is on Ritz Carlton Dr.

HOURS/FEES: 6:00 A.M. to 10:00 P.M. Parking meters are $1 an hour. County parking permits honored.

AMENITIES: Bike path, volleyball, restrooms, showers.

ACTIVITIES: Surfing, biking, volleyball, swimming, sunbathing.

FOR MORE INFORMATION:

Orange County South Coastal Operations—949-661-7013, www.oc.ca.gov/pfrd/hbp. Laguna Beach Visitor's Bureau—800-877-1115 or 848-497-9229, www.lagunabeachinfo.org.

1,000 Steps Beach

This thin beach in Three Arch Bay is accessed by a long staircase, which gives 1,000 Steps Beach its dubious moniker. The number is less than 1,000, but I won't spoil the fun of counting them. For a unique Southern California tour, you could check out this beach along with 1,000 Steps Beach in Santa Barbara, Stone Steps, and the steps in Shell Beach Ragged Point, topping it off with East Anacapa Island. The beach below is a prime surf spot and narrow beach.

ACCESS: From the north—At the junction of Hwys 1 and 133, head south on Hwy 1 to South Laguna. The steps are on the ocean side of the road across from 9th St.

From the south—Exit I-5 at Hwy 1 and follow it past Dana Point and into South Laguna. Look for 10th St. Next is 9th St.

PARKING: Park along Hwy 1. Be sure and check the parking signs. There is no parking for a few blocks.

HOURS/FEES: 6:00 A.M. to 10:00 P.M. Parking meters are $1 an hour.

AMENITIES: Stairs.

ACTIVITIES: Surfing, hiking the steps.

FOR MORE INFORMATION:

Orange County South Coastal Operations—949-661-7013, www.oc.ca.gov/pfrd/hbp. Laguna Beach Visitor's Bureau—800-877-1115 or 949-497-9229, www. lagunabeachinfo.org.

ALISO CREEK COUNTY BEACH

A fishing pier, picnic area, and snack bar make Aliso Creek County Beach the most developed beach in Laguna Beach. It even has an allotment of metered parking. This park spans both sides of Pacific Coast Highway (PCH) and reaches da' beaches via a pedestrian tunnel. Blessed by a point of land called Aliso Point, the beach was deposited in a protected cove. Laguna's rugged bluffs surround these sands.

ACCESS: From the junction of Hwys 1 and 133, head south on Hwy 1 to South Laguna Beach. Turn left onto Aliso Park Circle and hope for a space. Otherwise, well, hope for a space.

PARKING: The metered lot is the biggest in Laguna Beach.

HOURS/FEES: 6:00 A.M. to 10:00 P.M. Parking meters are $1 an hour. County parking permits honored.

AMENITIES: Pier, snack shack, picnic area, barbecue grills, restrooms, showers, lifeguards.

ACTIVITIES: Surfing, sunbathing, fishing.

FOR MORE INFORMATION:

Orange County South Coastal Operations—949-661-7013, www.oc.ca.gov/pfrd/hbp. Laguna Beach Visitor's Bureau—800-877-1115 or 949-497-9229, www. lagunabeachinfo.org.

VICTORIA BEACH

Victoria Beach is pitched by the tourism groups as a skim-boarding beach. A skim board is a piece of round or oval plywood that has been sealed to keep it from splintering. It's placed where the last bit of a wave retreats to the ocean. When the water starts to float the board, the rider runs and jumps on it, hydroplaning (skimming) to the shore break where he or she performs maneuvers of great daring and dexterity. Apparently this is the place in Laguna to skim board. Its flat sands and close-breaking waves are the reason.

ACCESS: Take Hwy 1 south from its intersection with Hwy 133. Turn right on Victoria Dr., then right on Sunset Terr.

PARKING: Very limited on-street parking.

HOURS/FEES: 6:00 A.M. to 10:00 P.M. Parking meters are $1 an hour.

AMENITIES: Volleyball nets, lifeguard.

ACTIVITIES: Bodysurfing, skim boarding, volleyball, sunbathing.

FOR MORE INFORMATION:

Orange County South Coastal Operations—949-661-7013, www.oc.ca.gov/pfrd/hbp. Laguna Beach Visitor's Bureau—800-877-1115 or 949-497-9229, www.lagunabeachinfo.org.

LAGUNA MAIN BEACH

Main Beach sits in Laguna's downtown where the continual row of businesses breaks, allowing a glimpse of the ocean. The playground and basketball courts mark the most visible portion of the park, with volleyball nets lining the bordering sand. The lifeguard tower was once part of a 1930s gas station in Laguna. Heisler Park, to the north of Main Beach, provides access to Picnic Beach, Rock Pile Beach, and Main Beach. The park itself has picnic tables and a place to play shuffleboard or even do some lawn bowling. Picnic Beach is reached by walking from Myrtle

Street down to the narrow band of sand below. Sleepy Hollow Beach is the name for the area to the south. These beaches all have different names partly because of the rocky points that separate the coves in Laguna and partly to allow the local chamber of commerce to boast of its 30 beaches.

ACCESS: The beach lies at the junction of Hwy 1 and Hwy 133. Legion St. is the access point. It lies about 0.25 mile south of the intersection, but continue to Cleo St., turn right, then right again on Sleepy Hollow. Heisler Park is reached by turning right onto Hwy 1 and heading north to Jasmine St., then turning left. The road runs into Cliff Dr., which traverses the park's length.

PARKING: Metered parking is available along Heisler Park at Cliff Dr. and its side streets. Otherwise, search the area around Cleo St.

HOURS/FEES: 6:00 A.M. to 10:00 P.M. Parking meters are $1 an hour.

AMENITIES: Basketball court, volleyball, restrooms, lifeguard, showers, picnic tables, boardwalk.

ACTIVITIES: Volleyball, basketball, surfing, swimming, picnicking.

FOR MORE INFORMATION:

Orange County South Coastal Operations—949-661-7013, www.oc.ca.gov/pfrd/hbp.

Laguna Beach Visitor's Bureau—800-877-1115 or 949-497-9229, www.lagunabeachinfo.org.

THE COVE BEACHES (DIVER'S, FISHERMAN'S, AND SHAW'S COVE)

These coves, popular spots to snorkel and scuba dive, are protected by protruding points, which help keep the visiblilty good for underwater activities. These areas, along with Crescent Bay, are within the Glenn E. Vedder Ecological Reserve. This means you can't take anything from the ocean, beach, or tide pools. Nothing. Not even shells or plants. So don't.

ACCESS: Follow Hwy 1 north from its intersection with Hwy 133. Turn left on Cliff Dr. or Fairview Dr. Cliff Dr. has paths to both Fisherman's and Diver's Coves. Fairview Drive leads to Shaw's Cove.

PARKING: There are some parking spaces for Heisler Park along Cliff Dr. and its side streets, but it's a crap shoot. Look inland and walk to the beach.

HOURS/FEES: 6:00 A.M. to 10:00 P.M. (unless you're over eighteen). Parking meters are $1 an hour.

AMENITIES: Nearest amenities are at Heisler Park.

ACTIVITIES: Snorkeling, scuba diving, tide-pool watching.

FOR MORE INFORMATION:

Laguna Beach Visitor's Bureau—800-877-1115 or 949-497-9229, www.lagunabeachinfo.org.

CRESCENT BAY

Known for good body surfing, Crescent Bay's beach has tubing waves that break close to the sandy shore. In winter, these same waves strip the sand away, leaving just Two Rocks Point. This is a natural process, and the sands return with summer's gentler surf. The region known as Pocket Beaches lies to the south and is accessed via stairways marked by "Coastal Access" signs. The park is a prime perch from which to watch the wildlife that frequents the cove.

ACCESS: Head north on Hwy 1 from Hwy 133 to Crescent Bay Dr. and turn left. The beach can be reached via stairs at Circle Way or a path at Barranca St.

PARKING: Limited on-street parking.

HOURS/FEES: 6:00 A.M. to 10:00 P.M. Parking meters are $1 an hour.

AMENITIES: Volleyball nets.

ACTIVITIES: Surfing, diving, tide pools.

FOR MORE INFORMATION:

Laguna Beach Visitor's Bureau—800-877-1115 or 949-497-9229, www.lagunabeachinfo.org.

CRYSTAL COVE STATE PARK

Crystal Cove State Park has 3.5 miles of beach and 2,000 acres of undeveloped woodland, which is popular for hiking and horseback riding. The offshore waters are designated as an underwater park and are frequented by scuba divers. The sandy beach at Reef Point is popular with swimmers and surfers. Surrounded by ocean and 100-foot cliffs, it qualifies as secluded. The beach all but disappears at the park's north end, allowing tide-pool viewing. Picnickers and fishermen use Pelican Point. The park is within the Irvine Coast Marine Life Refuge and special regulations are enforced. The expansive upland area provides a unique opportunity to be in the backcountry yet next door to Los Angeles. Many of the plants along the 17 miles of trails are rare or endangered native species.

ACCESS: The park is located off Pacific Coast Hwy between Corona del Mar and Laguna Beach. Beach-access trails begin at the parking lots.

PARKING: The park's 3.2 miles of beach are served by three large parking areas: Reef Point, Pelican Point, and Los Trancos.

HOURS/FEES: 6:00 A.M. to sunset. $5.

AMENITIES: Lifeguard, restrooms, bike trails, hiking trails, horse trails.

ACTIVITIES: Swimming, surfing, sunbathing, scuba and skin diving, fishing, mountain biking, tide pools, hiking.

FOR MORE INFORMATION:

Crystal Cove State Park—949-494-3539.

CORONA DEL MAR STATE BEACH

Though they are named separately and are worlds apart, Corona del Mar Beach and Little Corona del Mar Beach are actually one beach. The big version is a massive field of sand covered with volleyball nets and beach blankets. The little beach is a cove hidden around the southern point of the main sands and is a wet dream for scuba divers, snorkelers, and tide-pool enthusiasts. Kinda like the main beach is for, uh, people watchers.

Another pair of beaches hide upcoast, over the breakwater. China Cove and Bayside Drive County Beach face Newport Bay and have calm waters and wide sands. Bayside Drive is another big volleyball beach.

ACCESS: From the north—From I-405, take Hwy 73 (Corona del Mar Freeway) to Hwy 1 and turn left to follow the directions below.

From the south—From I-405, take MacArthur Blvd. westbound to Hwy 73, continue to Hwy 1, and turn left.

From the junction of Hwys 1 and 73 in Corona del Mar—Head south for eight blocks on Hwy 1 and turn right onto Marguerite Ave. Turn right on Ocean Blvd. and follow the signs to the parking entrance. To reach Little Corona del Mar Beach turn left on Ocean Blvd., continue to Poppy Ave., make a right, and follow the road to the beach.

PARKING: The bluff has a large metered parking lot. Bayside requires on-street parking.

HOURS/FEES: 6:00 A.M. to 10:00 P.M. Parking fees vary.

AMENITIES: Volleyball courts, picnic tables, showers, restrooms, snack shack, lifeguard, walking path, fire rings.

ACTIVITIES: Volleyball, volleyball, volleyball, surfing, picnicking, sunbathing.

FOR MORE INFORMATION:

Corona del Mar State Beach—949-644-3044.

Beach, Park, and Recreation Information (surf and water report)—949-673-3371.

Newport Beach Visitor Information—800-94-COAST, www.newportbeach.ca.us.

Newport Lifeguard Emergencies—949-673-3360.

Newport Lifeguard Business—949-644-3047.

Newport Beach Parks, Beaches and Recreation Department—949-644-3151.

NEWPORT BEACH AND BALBOA BEACH

Newport Municipal Beach starts at the Santa Ana River and stretches southward to Balboa Beach, which includes West Jetty and the Wedge. The Wedge is world-famous for its body surfing. The energy of the ocean's swell hits the jetty and actually increases in strength from the refraction. The result is a large wave that crashes into about a foot of water. These daredevils aren't beginners! A wrong move can put the rider headfirst in the sand from 10 feet or higher in the air. "That's not much of a good thing," I overhead someone say. West Jetty Park gives a good vantage point to watch this show. The rest of the beach is pretty standard. The golden sands are narrow near the Santa Ana River, become wider to the south, and include a couple of piers and areas for barbecuing and picnicking. To borrow volleyball equipment, call Parks and Recreation at 949-644-3151 (3300 Newport Boulevard). Park at either pier and bring along your patience as traffic can get pretty heavy. Surfers tend to cluster offshore by the jetties and near the ends of 56th, 24th, and 18th Streets.

ACCESS: From Hwy 1—Turn toward the ocean on Newport Blvd. Turn right on 22nd or continue as the road becomes Balboa Blvd. Look for the parking signs.

From Pacific Coast Highway—Take the Newport Blvd. turnoff and proceed west, watching for signs directing traffic to the pier. The pier sits at the foot of McFadden Pl.

PARKING: There's metered parking on the streets surrounding McFadden Sq. next to Newport Pier. For the southern end, park in lots A and B near Balboa Pier. There are some metered spots at West Jetty Park. Call 949-644-3344 for meter information or 949-644-3121 for permit info.

HOURS: 6:00 A.M. to 10:00 P.M.

AMENITIES: Two piers, playground, bike path, snack shack, volleyball, lifeguard, showers, restrooms.

ACTIVITIES: Surfing, body surfing, sunbathing, fishing, volleyball, kite flying.

FOR MORE INFORMATION:

Beach, Park, and Recreation Information (surf and water report)—949-673-3371.

Newport Lifeguard Emergencies—949-673-3360.

Newport Lifeguard Business—949-644-3047.

Beach Police—949-644-3717.

Newport Beach Parks, Beaches and Recreation Department—949-644-3151.

Newport Beach Visitor Information—800-94-COAST, www.newportbeach.ca.us.

Balboa Pier—949-499-3312.

SAILING

One's vision focuses upon the taut fabric of a full sail as a lone soul harnesses the wind and heads seaward on a beam reach. Imagination takes flight and the observer's vision heads toward the horizon, squinting to see farther, to see more. Sailing is like life—you can't direct it but you *can* adjust the sails. Attitude and response are things we *can* control.

All the harbors and marinas in Southern California offer opportunities to learn sailing through local yacht clubs and city park and recreation programs. They also host a number of concessionaires who have vessels available for charter.

Mission Bay and Oceanside are popular sailing locations within this guide's southern reaches. Both offer a number of amenities that help make sailors feel at home.

The Santa Barbara Channel, protected from the brunt of most Pacific storms by the Channel Islands, is a world-class sailing location. The islands help keep swells at a size most skippers can handle and provide a spectacular destination for a sailing excursion. Marina del Rey, Channel Islands Harbor, Ventura Harbor, and Santa Barbara Harbor allow easy access to these waters.

Port San Luis has a friendly and reasonably priced boatyard for those who do their own repairs.

Morro Bay's harbor entrance is narrow and often has dangerous waves and currents. However, it is another friendly port for those sailors en route to San Francisco or exploring Point Sal or Point Conception. Point Conception is known to be a rough place to sail and has claimed a fair number of ships. It also requires contacting Vandenberg Air Force Base to be certain the ship won't be hit by any missile tests.

REGION 7

HUNTINGTON BEACH TO SEAL BEACH

The sandy coast slopes up to the edge of car-lined Pacific Coast Highway (Hwy 1), where thong-clad humans feed parking meters. The beach seems very planned, which feels unnatural. In the 1960s the ocean tried to wash away the Surfside-Sunset Beach area. Four million cubic yards of sand were brought in to save the dwellings. The ocean still pushes into coastal homes here as if to remind humanity who's really the boss. Part of the region's plan includes a 7-mile bike path that runs from Huntington State Beach to Bolsa Chica State Beach.

Huntington has long been recognized as a surf capital. While the waves may not always be the best, the overall scene is "Surf City" all the way. A busy beach in summer, this playground of the Inland Empire is empty during the winter months as Californians hide from the hideously cold 60-degree temperatures. As the summer heats up, so do the crowds, which is part of Huntington's charm. Seal Beach, just up the coast, offers more of the same on a smaller scale.

Both Seal and Huntington Beaches have piers providing prime perches for fishing and viewing while surfers slide down the waves below.

The international museum of surfing is a must-see in this author's eyes. While not quite as awesome as a mackin', head-high set, the museum sheds light on this often misunderstood pastime. Scope out the scene, Dude.

The Waterfront, the area's glitzy mall, opens its doors for shopaholics who need a shoreside fix. Huntington Harbor and Sunset Marina give boaters access to the watery depths, as well as places to stroll, picnic, and play.

Access

From the north—Choose a route to the junction of I-405 and I-605 and continue southbound on I-405. The region's northern portion is reached via Seal Beach Blvd. and the southern portion via Hwy 39.

From the south—Take I-405 northbound to enter the region.

From Hwy 1—Hwy 1 parallels the region's shoreline and can be reached from the north off I-405 in Long Beach. From the south, pick up Hwy 1 in Newport Beach.

Beaches

Huntington State Beach

Huntington City Beach

Bolsa Chica State Beach

Sunset Beach (Surfside Beach)

Seal Beach

HUNTINGTON BEACH TO SEAL BEACH

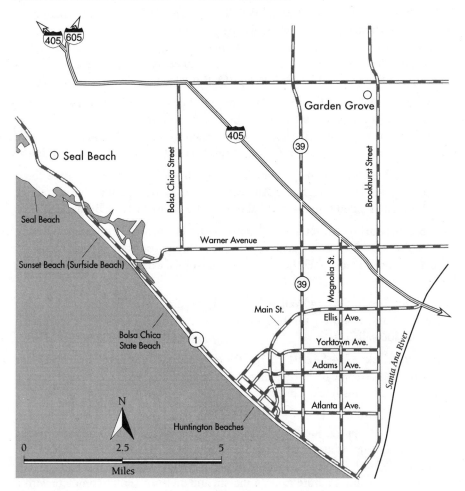

Camping

Huntington by the Sea RV Resort—800-439-3486, 0.5 mile south of the junction of Hwys 39 and 1 on Newland St. 141 sites with full hookups, pool, laundry, showers.

Huntington City Beach RV Facility—714-969-5621 or 714-536-5280, between Main St. and Beach Blvd. on Pacific Coast Hwy. Overnight parking for RVs from June to September (first come, first served), waste disposal, fire rings, outdoor showers. $15. Check in between 6:00 P.M. and 11:00 P.M. and be out by 8:00 A.M. the next morning.

Bolsa Chica State Beach—714-846-3460 or 714-848-1566. RV camping with some full hookups available, showers extra. $14. Reservations, 800-0444-7275, calparks.ca.gove/travel/reserve/index.htm.

Other points of interest

Seal Beach (Anaheim Bay) National Wildlife Refuge—562-598-1024. This winter home for the Pacific golden plover is also part of a naval weapons station. A tour on the last Saturday of the month can be arranged through the refuge manager. The request must be made at least three weeks in advance. Refuge Manager, U.S. Fish and Wildlife Service, Seal Beach NWR, P.O. Box 815, Seal Beach, CA 90740.

Bolsa Chica Ecological Reserve—714-846-1114 or 714-897-7003. Two parking lots along Pacific Coast Hwy (one at the beach's entrance, the other at Warner Ave.) allow viewing and trail access of this wetland reserve. Signs and benches are provided for self-guided viewing. Tours available the first Saturday of the month.

Huntington Beach Wetlands (Talbert Marsh)—714-963-2123. 25 acres of restored saltwater marsh next to the Santa Ana River. There's a bike path with informative signs for a self-guided tour. Located along Pacific Coast Hwy at Brookhurst St.

International Surfing Museum—714-960-3483, 411 Olive St., Huntington Beach. A gathering of stuff significant to surfing. Soothing strains of surfing songs accompany gnarly videos to set the tone for the historical exibits. Wednesday through Sunday, 12:00 P.M. to 5:00 P.M. $1.

Huntington Beach Surfing Walk of Fame—Extending from the corners of Pacific Coast Hwy and Main St. Granite stones representing surfing's VIPs are placed along the sidewalk.

Skate Zone Rink—714-842-9143, 16091 Gothard St., Huntington Beach. A place to cool off and do some in-line skating of the original kind—on ice. Also the home ice of the Sun Devils hockey team.

Huntington Central Park—714-960-8847. This park has picnic tables, barbecues, restrooms, several playgrounds, a golf course, and 6 miles of trails. The park's picnic area and small amphitheater are available for groups (714-536-5281). Shipley Nature Center (714-960-8867) is a nature preserve in the middle of Huntington Central Park that includes nature trails, a marsh, and a visitor center complete with a nature museum. There's even an equestrian center (714-848-6565) in this park!

Sunset Marina Park—714-846-3460 or 714-848-1566, enter at the west end of Edinger Ave. A public, multilaned boat launch ramp, a 276-slip marina, boat and trailer parking, and a boat repair yard accompany the park's picnic areas.

Imperial Woods Trail (Santa Ana River Bike Trail). Mostly flat riding for 30 miles along the Santa Ana River from Huntington Beach to the Riverside County Line.

San Gabriel River (Coyote Creek Trail)—A biking and hiking trail along the San Gabriel riverbed from I-605 at Katella Ave. to Ocean Ave. in Seal Beach to its Seal Beach Pier completion.

Huntington Beach Mall—714-897-2533. A million square feet of shopping at Beach Blvd. and Edinger Ave. in Huntington Beach.

Grass Roots—562-799-9550, www.g-roots.com/ hemp_c.

Old World Village Shopping Center—714-898-3033, 7561 Center Ave., Huntington Beach. Bavarian-style shops with a variety of imported goods including cuisine. Some of the store owners live in their stores, just like in the Old World.

On the Break (billiards at the beach!)—714-374-0546, 300 Pacific Coast Hwy, Huntington Beach.

Rockets and Pockets (more billiards at the beach!)—714-965-2240, 19092 Beach Blvd., Huntington Beach.

Pacific Electric Red Car Museum—Only open on the second and fourth Saturday of each month from 1:00 P.M. to 4:00 P.M., this museum offers a glimpse into the history of public transportation in Southern California. The Red Car was even mentioned in the movie *Who Framed Roger Rabbit*.

Electric Avenue—142-C Main St., Seal Beach. Clothes, hemp shoes, organic cotton, natural body care, hemp housewares.

HUNTINGTON STATE BEACH

For 2 miles along Huntington's beach belt, Huntington State Beach delivers the goods with expansive sands, good surf, throngs of revelers, and the facilities to support them. From the ocean's perspective, this is simply a continuation of Huntington City Beach and it's mostly a carbon copy, save the lack of the pier. This stretch of sand can get a bit crowded: About 4 million people visit here every year, with most of the hoards visiting in the summer. Your mouth may salivate to the aroma here. Locals often call this "cookout beach" in reference to the numerous fire pits.

Across the road lies Huntington Beach Wetlands, a 114-acre chunk of land watched over by the California Department of Fish and Game. The California least tern and the snowy plover take sanctuary here in their plight to avoid extinction.

ACCESS: From I-405, exit onto Hwy 39 and continue south for 5.7 miles, through the city of Huntington Beach to Pacific Coast Hwy (Hwy 1/PCH) and turn left. Travel 1.2 miles to reach the beach, which is across from Magnolia Ave. on PCH.

PARKING: A lot is provided off PCH across from Magnolia Ave. Metered parking is also available along PCH and in the city. To contest a parking ticket in Huntington, call 800-553-4412 or visit www.hbpd.org/traffic_citehear.htm.

HOURS/FEES: Sunup to sundown. $5 to park in the lot.

Amenities: Bike path, fire rings, restrooms, snack shack, showers, volleyball nets.

Activities: Biking, blading, strolling, picnicking, bonfires, surfing, fishing, volleyball—everything under the sun and in the water.

For more information:

714-536-1454 or 714-848-1566.

Bike Trails—www.biketrails.com/orange.html.

Surf and Weather Report—714-536-9303.

Huntington City Beach

This is Surf City's beach and the beach blanket bingo for the new millennium plays here daily. Huntington Beach, also known as Surf City, boasts 8.5 miles of sandy shoreline. The smallest in the continuous string of beaches, Huntington City Beach, is also the most popular. Starting from the pier, where the beach's modern, orange-roofed, green-windowed building provides a bizarre contrast to the natural beauty of the ocean's blue-green hues, the wide sands bend southeast to Beach Boulevard where they miraculously become Huntington State Beach. While lifeguards are on daylight duty every day of the year, it's the perennial summer crowd that creates the charm of HB.

The pier is a popular fishing spot and provides an offshore perspective of the scene. Surfers have been known to "shoot the pier," meaning they've caught the wave on one side then ridden it to the other.

The city does a good job of bringing a variety of attractions to the beach. Professional roller hockey, along with skateboarders and aerial acrobats leaping in and out of a half-pipe ramp on bicycles, are just some of the events that happen here.

Access: From I-405, exit onto Hwy 39 and continue south for 5.7 miles through the city of Huntington Beach where the road becomes Beach Blvd. Continue to Pacific Coast Hwy (Hwy 1/PCH). The beach lies dead ahead and runs northward (to the right).

Parking: From Beach Blvd. to the pier are big parking lots. Metered off-street lots are on the wet (ocean) side at Golden West, a metered lot by the Warner Fire Station boat ramp. There are meters from Beach Blvd. northward to Bolsa Chica State Beach. The lot between the pier and Beach Blvd. charges $6 per day and has entrances at Beach Blvd., First St., and Huntington St. There is an 830-space parking and retail structure on the east side of Main St. between Walnut and Olive Sts. The parking fee is $2 for the first hour and an additional $1 per hour with a $5 maximum. The first 60 minutes are free Monday through Friday until 6:00 P.M. To contest a parking ticket in Huntington, call 800-553-4412 or visit www.hbpd.org/traffic_citehear.htm.

HOURS/FEES: Curfew is 10:00 P.M. to 5:00 A.M. and is strictly enforced. The beach is free. Budget $5 or $6 for parking.

AMENITIES: Food and rental concessions (open during prime season), restrooms, showers, fire rings, lifeguard, bike path, volleyball nets.

ACTIVITIES: Sunbathing, volleyball, swimming, surfing, biking, blading, watching.

FOR MORE INFORMATION:

Beach Headquarters—714-536-5281 or 714-536-5280, 103 Pacific Coast Hwy. Office hours, seven days a week, 8:00 A.M. to 5:00 P.M., emergencies, 714-536-2581.

Surf/weather report—714-536-9303.

Huntington Pier—714-536-5281.

Huntington Beach Visitors Bureau—800-SAY-OCEAN.

Events listing—www.hbonline.com.

BOLSA CHICA STATE BEACH

Bolsa Chica, meaning "little pocket" in Spanish, is appropriate for this refuge of nature in the southern sprawl of civilization. It was called "Tin Can Beach" before the state kicked out the homeless. The 6-mile shoreline arcs ever so slightly on a southeast path toward Huntington City Beach. The sand is scarce along the southern reaches of the area and is all but gone during high tide. However, the beach widens as it arcs northward to the main parking lots. Bolsa Chica's neighboring ecological reserve has top-notch facilities, and camping is available to RVs. A paved bikeway connects all the way to the Newport Pier, 10 miles to the south.

The big, cement fire rings make this a popular bonfire location. Get here early if fire making is in your plans. If you're a dog owner, a "dog beach" has been set up for leashed use at Golden West Street and Pacific Coast Highway.

ACCESS: From I-405, exit onto Hwy 39 and continue south for miles through the city of Huntington Beach, where the road becomes Beach Blvd. Continue to Pacific Coast Hwy (Hwy 1/PCH) and turn right. The access road is between Golden West St. and Warner Ave.

PARKING: The state has graciously provided 2,500 spaces of parking in lots along the beach.

HOURS/FEES: 6:00 A.M. to 10:00 P.M., with the gates closing at 9:00 P.M. RV camping costs $14 per night.

AMENITIES: Camping, bike path, restrooms, lifeguards, showers, fire rings, snack shack, volleyball.

ACTIVITIES: Biking, birding, fishing, swimming, surfing, roller blading, volleyball.

FOR MORE INFORMATION:

Bolsa Chica State Beach—714-846-3460 or 714-848-1566.

Huntington Beach Visitors Bureau—800-SAY-OCEAN.

Amigos de Bolsa Chica—714-897-7003.

SUNSET BEACH (SURFSIDE BEACH)

Nope, this isn't the Sunset Beach that's famous. That one's in Hawaii. This Sunset Beach is a strip of coast between the private community of Surfside and Bolsa Chica State Beach. Volleyball nets and lifeguards are provided for this wide, ruler-straight beach with views of the Long Beach skyline. A park in the center median of Pacific Avenue provides restrooms and free parking. The area north of Anderson Street is Surfside Beach, which is shoreward of the private, gated community. To access it, walk northward along the shore.

ACCESS: From I-405 take Seal Beach Blvd. southbound to Pacific Coast Hwy (Hwy 1) and turn left. Continue for 1.6 miles to Anderson St. or 2.9 miles to Warner Ave. Turn right (seaward) on any street between Anderson St. and Warner Ave. to reach the linear park on Pacific Ave.

PARKING: 627 spaces along a linear park with public restrooms and a playground.

HOURS/FEES: 6:00 A.M. to 10:00 P.M. No fee, yet. There is talk of putting up meters.

AMENITIES: Parking, restrooms, playground, bike path, lifeguard, volleyball nets. A public boat launch is located on Warner Ave, east of PCH.

ACTIVITIES: Swimming, surfing, sunning, volleyball.

FOR MORE INFORMATION:

Surfside Beach—562-430-2613.

Sunset Beach and Harbor—714-723-4511.

Sunset Aquatic Marina—561-592-2833.

SEAL BEACH

A wide, flat expanse of light sand, Seal Beach stretches from the San Gabriel River to Anaheim Bay. During the summer, water activities are regulated. In English, that means you can't surf the whole beach. Of course, you really couldn't as the beach's waters are crowded when Los Angeles heats up. L.A. television stations show live shots of Seal Beach during the weather report, which ensures the media-loving Inland Empire will be on the beach the next day. Eisenhower Park, located at the base of the pier, provides a good starting point for exploring Seal Beach. The southern jetty and the pier are good places to stroll without having to dodge children or step over towels.

ACCESS: From I-405 take Seal Beach Blvd. southbound to Pacific Coast Hwy (Hwy 1) and turn right. Continue for eight blocks, turn left on Main St., follow it westward to Ocean Ave., and turn right. Parking at 8th St. is one block ahead.

PARKING: 8th St. and 1st St. both have parking lots that are accessible from Ocean Ave.

HOURS/FEES: 6:00 A.M. to 10:00 P.M. $4 to park.

AMENITIES: Restrooms, lifeguard, bike path, pier, playground.

ACTIVITIES: Surfing, sunning, swimming, biking, fishing.

FOR MORE INFORMATION:

Seal Beach—562-431-2527.

Seal Beach Pier—562-598-8677.

Seal Beach Chamber of Commerce—562-799-0179.

THAR SHE BLOWS!

Multihued reflections ripple off the harbor's looking-glass waters while morning fog clings to mast tops like a dreamer clings to sleep. I step aboard *Vanguard*'s deck. A guttural rumble comes from the stern as the captain fires up the engines. We move into the harbor, our hull slicing the glassy water. A patch of blue sky opens up over us as we pass by the breakwater's protection and are birthed into the Pacific Ocean. The whale-watching trip has begun.

Twice a year gray whales, *Eschrichtius robustus,* make a near-shore commute between Baja California and Alaska. This whale species is the most common one seen off the Southern California coast. Well, that's not quite true. Dolphins, also in the cetacean (whale) order, are frequently seen here. However, it's the bigger mammals that are the quarry of the whale-watching boats.

The recipe for fun on a whale-watching trip is simple: Dress warmly and keep your eyes open. Morning and afternoon trips are commonly offered, and the advice holds true for both. The morning chill is usually replaced with sun, making layered clothing a must. Afternoon sun tends to give way to wind, making a windbreaker useful. Whether you pack a snack or visit the boat's galley, you'll want to keep energy levels high and vision keen. Polarized sunglasses will help you see the whales that often swim a few feet beneath the surface.

The area between East Anacapa Island and Port Hueneme is the narrowest point of the Santa Barbara Channel, making the area one of the best whale-watching locales in the world.

The gray whales travel 5,000 miles from Baja California to the Bering and Chukchi Seas off Alaska's shores. They leave the cold waters of the north in fall to return to the Baja to calve, then return north. March to May is the zenith of the gray's northward migration off the SoCal coast. The return trip happens between October and December.

The gray was almost hunted into oblivion with as few as 1,500 in 1946. Today, gray whales are valued as an earthly neighbor rather than a commodity.

It's possible to view the spouting whales from land-based lookout points. Simply scan the horizon from right to left for telltale white plumes. (Our eyes tend to pick up movement better when scanning from right to left.) If something pops up closer to you, your eyes will pick it up.

In addition to spouting behavior, whales can be seen breaching, sounding, and spy hopping. Breaching is where the whale leaps out of the water. Sounding describes a whale that is putting its fluke (tail) out of the water. A spy-hopping whale is one whose head is bobbing out of the water, affording it a topside view.

Seasickness can drastically reduce a trip's fun quotient. If you think you're a candidate for it, motion-sickness medicine is available over the counter at local drugstores. Another trick to combating this equilibrium-attacking sickness is to focus on the horizon. Most people find that they can handle the sea without any ill effects, but if you succumb to it, stay outside and near the stern. This makes things easier for all concerned.

Sharing a morning or afternoon with these gentle giants eases stress and makes one wonder who is more intelligent: a mammal that runs itself ragged in a race to gather up possessions or one whose patient, nomadic lifestyle keeps it vigorous and free.

Here's a quick listing of some cetaceans you could see off these shores: gray whale, blue whale, fin whale, humpback whale, sperm whale, minke whale, pygmy sperm whale, dwarf sperm whale, Cuvier's beaked whale, Baird's beaked whale, Hubb's beaked whale, Stejneger's beaked whale, Hector's beaked whale, Blainville's beaked whale, harbor porpoise, killer whale, false killer whale, short-finned pilot whale, Risso's dolphin, Pacific white-sided dolphin, bottlenose dolphin, common dolphin, and striped dolphin.

REGION 8

SANTA CATALINA ISLAND

Twenty-two miles westward of the immense Inland Empire that is the Los Angeles Basin lies a place that boasts of clean air, clear waters, vast valleys, quaint coves, and 2,000-foot peaks. Here lies a 76-square-mile mix of ecological awareness and capitalistic reality named Santa Catalina Island, simply called Catalina by those in the know.

The Santa Catalina Island Conservancy owns 88 percent of the island and runs it as a nonprofit business, which has kept things quite pristine and makes camping, scuba diving, snorkeling, and boating especially popular here. A pair of harbors, named Avalon and Two Harbors, make up the remaining 12 percent vying for tourist dollars. The drawback to this setup is that things in town are a wee bit pricey, though most visitors think this is a fair trade to experience island life so close to Los Angeles.

Boat passage or a helicopter flight is required to reach the island. Cars are not an option. However, rental bikes are easily obtained near the ferry landings, as are bus tours and taxis. There are even rental "golf" carts available.

Once a playground for the Hollywood elite, Catalina's recreations are exhaustive. Horseback riding, Jet Skiing, scuba diving, snorkeling, golf, glass-bottom boat rides, jeep tours, open-air buses, kayak trips, parasailing, and raft trips are some of the most common pleasures provided by a wide range of tour operators.

Access

The only way to reach the island is through the air or sea. The following companies are among those that offer passage.

Air

Island Express—310-510-2525. A 15-minute helicopter ride. A cab ride from the Pebbly Beach landing pad is needed to reach Avalon. $66 one-way, 25-pound baggage limit. Helicopters tours priced from $50 per person.

Catalina Airlines/Island Hopper—610-279-4595. Based in San Diego with service to Catalina's Airport in the Sky.

Sea

Catalina Cruises—800-228-2546. About two hours on a large boat with a chance to see seabirds, dolphins, and maybe even whales. $12.50 one-way, 100 pounds of baggage per person. $3 for bikes and surfboards. Covered parking available for $7.50. ·

Catalina Express—799-464-4228. Depending on the boat, it's an hour or a ninety-minute ride. Hostess service as well as private party rooms are available. $18 one-way, 70 pounds of baggage allowed in four bags. $3 for bikes and surfboards. Open-air parking costs $7 a day.

Santa Catalina Island

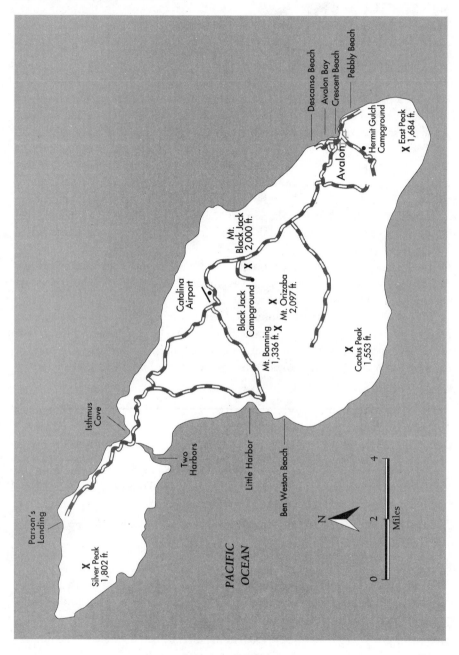

Catalina Flyer Terminal, Newport—714-673-5245. At 9:00 A.M. every day, this three-decked catamaran makes its trip from Newport Beach to Avalon in seventy-five minutes. It returns from Avalon at 4:30 P.M. $36 round-trip (reservations required), two bags of handheld luggage allowed, $7 round-trip for bikes. Parking available for $7 a day.

Transportation on the Island

Permits are required for hiking (free) and biking (see below). The Santa Catalina Island Conservancy issues the permits in Avalon (310-510-1421); at the Catalina Interpretive Center (310-510-2514); at the Airport in the Sky (310-510-0143); and at the Cove and Camp Agency in Two Harbors (310-510-0303).

Biking outside of Avalon is allowed on the main road from Avalon to Emerald Bay. The regulations require mountain bikes, helmets, and a permit. The permit may be obtained at the locations listed above and costs $50 for an individual or $75 for a family. Biking the trails is not allowed. (See below for rental info.) Permission to bike the trails is not granted with the permit.

Brown's Bikes Bicycle Rentals—310-510-0986, 107 Pebbly Beach Rd. in Avalon. (They have wheelchairs and strollers, too.)

Catalina Auto and Bike Rentals—310-510-0111, corner of Metropole and Crescent in Avalon.

Island Rentals—310-510-1456, 125 Pebbly Beach Rd. in Avalon.

Cartopia Golf Cart Rentals—310-510-2493, 615 Crescent Ave. in Avalon.

Morning Van to the Airport—310-510-0143. A van takes hikers ($5) and bikers ($7) to the Airport in the Sky at 7:30 A.M. If you already have permits, the van will drop you anywhere on the route. Otherwise, the airport has the permits needed for hiking and biking along with a restaurant that serves breakfast.

Catalina Safari Bus—800-785-8425. This bus links Avalon and Two Harbors with departures twice daily. It also serves the airport and Little Harbor. $29 round-trip or $14.50 one-way with a fare reduction for stops at places in between.

Catalina Cab Company—310-510-0025. $50 an hour. A cab, which can hold six people, will cost $75 from Avalon to Little Harbor.

Beaches

Descanso Beach

Crescent Beach

Pebbly Beach

Ben Weston Beach

Little Harbor

Parson's Landing

Two Harbors

Isthmus Cove

Camping

Hiking and biking on the island both require a permit (see above). Two Harbors Visitor Services can make reservations to the campgrounds listed below (800-785-8425 or www.catalina.com/twoharbors/index.html#Reservations).

Hermit's Gulch Campground—310-510-8368. Closest to Avalon. 60 sites for tents, no pets, hot showers, toilets, tables with barbecue grill, fire ring. $7.50 per person/per night.

Little Harbor Campground—310-510-2800 or 310-510-0303. Space for 150 campers, no pets. Showers, chemical toilets, tables with barbecue, phone. Shuttle avoids 7-mile hike. $7.50 per person/per night.

Black Jack Campground—310-510-2800 or 310-510-0303, located 9.5 miles northwest of Avalon off of Old Stage Rd. Space for 75 campers, no pets. Water, chemical toilets, barbecue grill, phone, showers. $7.50 per person/per night.

Isthmus Cove Campground—310-510-2800 or 310-510-0303. 54 sites, no pets. Water, chemical toilets, tables with barbecue, cold showers, sunshades. $7.50 per person/per night.

Parson's Landing Campground—310-510-2800 or 310-510-0303, located between Lands End and Arrow Point. 6 sites for tents, no pets. Fire rings, pit toilet, some water available. $15, plus $5 per additional person up to $50 for eight.

Catalina Island Visitors Bureau—310-510-1520. This organization can provide information on hotel availability.

Camping on your boat or on primitive beaches is also allowed. Call Catalina Island Camping at 310-510-7265 for more information.

Other points of interest

The Casino and Catalina Island Museum—310-510-2414. In Avalon's often-photographed casino, this museum keeps the island's history, going back 7,000 years! $1.50. Open 10:30 A.M. to 4:00 P.M.

Wrigley Botanical Gardens and Wrigley Memorial—1400 Avalon Canyon Rd. This 37-acre garden focuses on plants endemic to this and other California islands. The Wrigley Memorial honors the chewing-gum king William Wrigley Jr., who happened to be a key figure in the island's past. It's about a mile walk from Avalon or $7 for a cab. $1 admission, open 8:00 A.M. to 5:00 P.M.

The Santa Catalina Island Interpretive Center—Situated in a canyon above Avalon, this interpretive center is is a natural history museum covering the island's human and geological history along with information on the plants and animals below and above the sea. Hiking trails start here and are free with a permit available at the center.

Catalina Mountain Bikers—310-510-1355. A club for resident riders offering guided trips of the island's interior.

Tour Providers and Rental Companies

Scuba diving, kayaking, snorkeling, glass-bottom boats, jeep rides, and more are all available through a variety of tour companies. The equipment for many of these same activities is available to rent for the do-it-yourselfer. Following are some of the businesses that can help you plan your island adventures. Keep in mind that some rental groups offer tours and some tour groups offer rentals.

Discovery Tours—310-510-2500, 800-428-2566, www.Catalina.com/discovery_land_tours.html. In business since 1894. If you can imagine it, odds are they offer the tour.

Catalina Adventure Tours—310-510-2888, www.catalina.com/adventure. Wide range of land and/or sea tours.

Catalina Ocean Rafting—310-510-0211 or 800-990-RAFT (California only).

Argo Diving Services—310-510-2208.

Catalina Divers Supply—800-353-0330.

Catalina Island Expeditions—310-510-1226. Rents kayaks specially designed for scuba use. Guided kayak tours.

Catalina Scuba Luv—800-262-DIVE. Full-service dive shop.

Catalina West End Dive Center—800-785-8425. Full-service dive shop.

Catalina Snorkeling Adventures—800-877-SNORKEL. On-site at Lover's Cover.

Descanso Beach Ocean Sports—310-510-1226. Rents snorkels, masks and fins, and kayaks and "view" rafts.

Snorkeling Catalina—310-510-0455. Guided tour, gear included.

Wet Spot Rentals—310-510-2229. Rents snorkel gear, kayaks, beach equipment, tours available.

West End Dive Center—800-785-8425, in Two Harbors. Rents scuba gear, kayaks, and Aqua View paddleboards.

King Neptune—800-262-DIVE. Dive tours.

Scuba Outpost—At Emerald Bay. A west-end base for scuba diving, kayaking, and hiking.

High Tide Traders—310-510-1612. Fishing tackle and licenses.

The Two Harbors General Store—310-510-7625. Fishing, camping, general supplies.

Live Bait Barge—Near Avalon at Abalone Point.

Rosie's Fish Market—Avalon's green pier. Live fishing bait.

Avalon Boat Stand/Joe's Rent-a-Boat—Avalon's green pier. Boat rental. Fishing gear sold and rented.

Island Kayak Adventures—310-510-2229. Kayaking and snorkeling tours.

Blue Cavern Sailing Charters—Full and half-day trips (including kayaks).

FOR MORE INFORMATION:
Catalina Island Visitors Bureau and Chamber of Commerce—310-510-1520.
Catalina's online presence—www.catalina.com.
Two Harbors Visitors Information Center—310-510-0303.
Catalina Island Harbor Department—310-510-COVE.
Avalon Harbormaster—310-510-0535.
Two Harbors Harbormaster—310-510-2683.
Avalon Marine Dock—310-510-0046.
Santa Catalina Island Conservancy—310-510-2595 or 310-510-2202.

FISHIN' IN THE DEEP

There are two ways to fish the deep: your own boat or someone else's. A party boat, also called a CPFV (Commercial Passenger Fishing Vessel), is a great way to try sportfishing. These boats are found at party-boat landings, which also rent and sell the proper tackle for whatever you're heading out to catch, as well as one-day licenses

A COMMERCIAL PASSENGER FISHING VESSEL, OR "PARTY BOAT," IS A GREAT WAY TO SAMPLE DEEP-SEA SPORTFISHING.

EARLY MORNINGS AT SEA CAN BE CHILLY, SO DRESSING IN LAYERS IS A GOOD IDEA.

to those just starting out. A one-day, fin-fish-only license is $6.55. For $18.65 you're legal for a year of ocean fishing. It's a perfect way to learn ocean fishing from the pros.

The boats usually leave around 6:00 A.M. and 9:00 A.M., weather and bookings permitting. Some landings also offer 1:00 A.M. departures. The ocean and early morning mean cold. Dress in layers. The boats usually have full-service galleys to keep anglers warm and energetic. The deckhands will clean your catch for a small fee and some will even cook some up for you. Pack a cooler in your car for the catch.

When on the boat ask and *listen* to the deckhands' advice. These guys fish every day and love what they're doing. Don't be shy about asking them for help. Do be grateful for the help and tip appropriately after the trip.

If you aren't familiar with the reels, be sure to get a quick lesson from a deckhand. A birdnest (a backlash tangle) when the fishing is hot is very frustrating. It *will* happen at one time or another. Ask for help to get back in the game quickly.

The following areas have numerous sportfishing concessions: San Diego, Oceanside, Dana Harbor, Long Beach, Marina del Rey, Catalina Island, Channel Islands Harbor, Ventura Harbor, Port San Luis, and Morro Bay.

REGION 9

LONG BEACH TO PALOS VERDES

Long Beach, while not a very creative name, is certainly descriptive of this region's coastline. Stretching for 5.5 miles, the wide, sandy beach provides towel space for a good many sun sirens. Long Beach, the city, is a massive sprawl of humanity that ranks as California's fifth largest.

This population pressure has created a city on the sea with civilization almost pushing back the water. Having run out of room, the people have taken to the ocean. The *Queen Mary* is a popular attraction/hotel here with its lit silhouette reflecting off the bay at night creating a postcard atmosphere for anyone in Shoreline Village.

The $650 million Queensway Bay project was designed to revitalize the area's tourist appeal. Rainbow Harbor, complete with the tall ship *Californian* and the Aquarium of the Pacific is surrounded by a palm-lined esplanade, shops, restaurants, and entertainment venues.

The Long Beach Aquarium of the Pacific, with 12,000 specimens of more than 550 species, boasts one million gallons of informative marine exhibits that tell the story of the world's largest ocean. The shark tank should keep peoples' jaws gaping.

Belmont Shores and Naples Island capture the essence of this city on the beach with a 15-block eclectic collection of restaurants and gondoliers in Italian costumes pushing their boats along canals backed by high-dollar homes.

At the tip of the San Pedro Peninsula, the Point Vicente Lighthouse and its accompanying park offer views into the Pacific as well as lessons in local history. The peninsula is host to Los Angeles Harbor, along with its share of sandy shore and a shoreline preserve. Also on the peninsula is the Cabrillo Marine Aquarium, a free museum that includes a hands-on exhibit allowing people to touch the animals.

At the farthest southwest corner of the peninsula, near Frank A. Venderlip Sr. Park, lies the southwesternmost tip on the North American continent. It's marked by a tower at Long Point on the old Marineland of the Pacific site.

Access

I-405 parallels the outskirts of the region and connects to Los Angeles International Airport, Long Beach Airport, and John Wayne Airport. I-110 and I-710 both feed traffic into the region from I-405 and regions farther north. I-710 terminates at Ocean Blvd., which is the main waterfront road in Long Beach. I-110 crosses the Pacific Coast Hwy (Hwy 1) to end in L.A. Harbor and the west end of Ocean Blvd. and the Vincent Thomas Bridge or Faffey St., which leads to San Pedro and the lighthouse. Hwy 1 is the access road for reaching Palos Verdes.

LONG BEACH TO PALOS VERDES

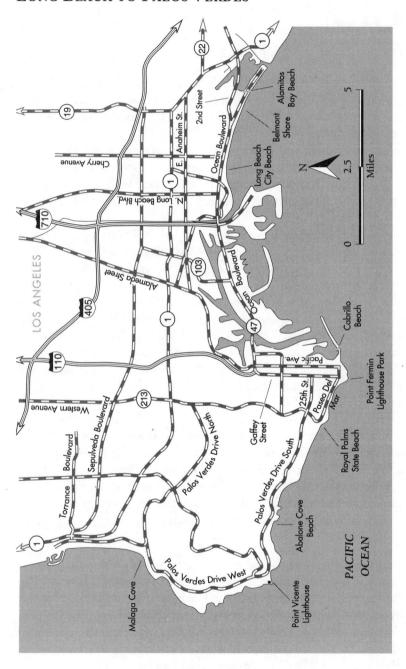

Beaches

Alamitos Bay Beach

Belmont Shore

Long Beach City Beach

Cabrillo Beach

Royal Palms State Beach

Abalone Cove Beach

Point Vicente Fishing Access

Malaga Cove

Camping

Golden Shore RV Park—562-435-4646. 80 sites with full hookups. Swimming pool, rec room, showers, laundry, general store.

Dockweiler State Beach to the north and Bolsa Chica State Beach to the south offer coastal camping; Anaheim, near Disneyland and Knott's Berry Farm, offers RV spaces.

Other points of interest

Alamitos Bay—This is where the castaways of the SS *Minnow* set sail on their three-hour tour to Gilligan's Island. (See Alamitos Bay Beach.)

Shoreline Marina and Village—562-437-0375. A place to ride bikes, walk, and to park your boat. There's also plenty of shopping here.

Shoreline Park—Off Ocean Blvd. on Shoreline Drive. Biking, picnicking, and strolling by the lagoon and Queensway Bay.

Queen Mary—562-435-3511, www.queenmary.com. Explore the historic ship/hotel from wheelhouse to engine room. The ship also doubles as a hotel.

The Aquarium of the Pacific—562-590-3100, 100 Aquarium Way, just off Shoreline Dr. in Long Beach, www.aquariumofpacific.org/visitor/visitorinfo.html. One million gallons of marine-life displays plus snacks and souvenirs.

Murals—310-983-3820. Long Beach has an expansive art gallery kept outside on walls throughout the city. The Mural and Cultural Arts Program of the Public Corporation for the Arts is responsible. A free brochure-guide can be found in the visitor center.

Los Angeles Harbor ("Worldport LA")—310-831-0287, Berth 84. Ports O'Call Village (Berth 77) and Whalers Wharf offer shopping and dining with a historic New England feel. The harbor also provides access to Catalina Island. Nearby John S. Gibson, Jr. Park (310-548-7756) and the Maritime Museum (310-548-7618) tell the harbor's story in pictures and memorabilia in a park setting. The knot exhibit is gripping!

S.S. *Lane* Victory Memorial Museum—310-519-9545, Berth 94, Los Angeles Harbor. This ship saw service in three wars.

The Fort MacArthur Museum—310-548-2631 or 310-548-7705. The history of Fort MacArthur, the U.S. Army's guard of Los Angeles Harbor from 1914 to 1974, is preserved here. Open noon to 5:00 P.M., Tuesday, Thursday, weekends and holidays.

Point Fermin Lighthouse Park—At the end of Gaffey St. and Paseo del Mar lies a bluff-top park for picnics with a path to tide pools below. Unfortunately the old lighthouse is off-limits.

Point Vicente Lighthouse—310-377-5370. Teetering on a cliffside in Point Vicente Park, this tower of history doubles as a good whale-watching site. A natural history museum in the park sheds light on the peninsula's plants, animals, and geology. 10:00 A.M. to 5:00 P.M. every day, later in summer.

Palos Verdes Estate Shoreline Preserve—The peninsula's rocky coastline offers lots of tide-pool fun and diving opportunities. Park on Paseo del Mar.

South Coast Botanic Garden—213-377-0468, 26300 Crenshaw Blvd. A true Cinderella story! More than 2,000 species of plants on 87 acres of a former waste dump. Open daily 9:00 A.M. to 5:00 P.M., except Christmas.

Cabrillo Beach Pier—This 1,200-foot-long concrete pier has all the trappings for anglers. Unfortunately, the fish don't seem to cooperate. A good place to see the harbor's activity.

Belmont Pier—Another long, concrete pier (1,265 feet) with more cooperative fish. The lights stay on until 10:00 P.M.

The Long Beach Bike Trail—This 17-foot-wide paved path reserves 12 feet for two bike lanes and gives the remaining 5 feet to pedestrians. It's 3.1 miles long and can be connected to the San Gabriel River Bike Trail (38 miles long) and the Los Angeles River Bikeway (28 miles long).

California Department of Fish and Game—310-590-5132. If you ever want to make a personal visit, this agency's southern office is in Long Beach. It serves Southern California from Santa Barbara to the Mexican Border.

Marine Mammal Care Center—310-548-5677. A rehabilitation location for seals and sea lions that often has up to fifty animals under care. Viewing is allowed and on-site exhibits deliver info on the mammals. Open every day 8:00 A.M. to 4:00 P.M. Free.

Long Beach Area Convention and Visitors Bureau—310-436-3645 or 800-4LB-STAY, 1 World Trade Center, Suite 300, Long Beach. Visitor information Monday to Saturday, 9:00 A.M. to 5:00 P.M.

ALAMITOS BAY BEACH

Alamitos Bay is where the SS *Minnow* set sail on its three-hour tour back in 1964 only to be tossed onto the airways and into the hearts of America as it ran aground on Gilligan's Island. The beach offers calm waters off a sandy shore well-suited to sunbathers.

Please sing the following description to the tune of the *Gilligan's Island* theme:
Just sit right back and you'll hear a tale.
A tale of a sandy beach.
That sits along Alamitos Bay
near the Long Beach coast.
The water here is mighty calm,
the facilities few but sure.
Sunbathers set down towels each day
upon these sandy shores.
Upon these sandy shores.
The weather is usually great,
tiny ships all in the moat.
If feeling the courage of the fearless few
rent a little boat.
Rent a little boat.
The bay surrounds the shores of this
charted Naples isle . . .
with its canals,
the yacht club too,
millionaires
and their wives,
movie stars,
and the rest
all on Naples Isle.

ACCESS: From I-110 or I-710, exit onto Hwy 1 South. Follow Hwy 1 through the Alamitos circle by keeping right and staying on Hwy 1. Turn right onto 2nd St. and travel past the marina and over the island of Naples. Turn left on Bayshore Ave. immediately after the road crosses the bay for the second time. The beach runs between 54th Pl. and 2nd St.

PARKING: Free parking is available along Bayshore Ave.

HOURS/FEES: 5:00 A.M. to 10:00 P.M. Free.

AMENITIES: Restrooms, lifeguard, kayak rentals.

ACTIVITIES: Swimming, kayaking, sunning, gawking.

THE SANDY STRAND AT LONG BEACH STRETCHES AN IMPRESSIVE 5.5 MILES LONG.

FOR MORE INFORMATION:

Long Beach Marine Services—310-594-0951.

Long Beach Lifeguards—562-570-3400.

Long Beach Lifeguard Division—562-570-1287.

Long Beach Lifeguards Headquarters—562-570-1360.

City of Long Beach Parks and Recreation—562-570-1707.

Long Beach Area Convention and Visitors Bureau—310-436-3645 or 800-4LB-STAY.

BELMONT SHORE

This is the southern end of Long Beach City Beach, stretching from Belmont Pier to the Alamitos Peninsula. It's a wide expanse of white sand used extensively for volleyball and sunning, There's not much water play beyond swimming, but recreation abounds with a long bike path and a competitive basketball court.

ACCESS: From the south, take Westminister Ave. from I-405 toward the coast. At Hwy 1 the road changes to 2nd St. Remain on 2nd St. over Naples. After crossing Alamitos Bay for the second time, the road enters Belmont Shore. Every other road to the left is a one-way leading to East Ocean Blvd. and the beach that lies along it.

PARKING: Metered parking along East Ocean Blvd. and side streets. The Belmont Plaza Olympic Pool also has a pay parking lot. Termino Ave.'s metered parking is convenient for pier users. A fee lot at East Ocean Blvd. and 72nd Pl. works well for visiting the Alamitos Peninsula.

HOURS/FEES: Beach—5:00 A.M. to 10 P.M., free. Pier—one hour before sunrise to one hour after sunset, free.

AMENITIES: Beach—bike path, restrooms, lifeguard, playground, basketball court, volleyball nets, small boat launch. Pier—bait, snack shack, restrooms, boat trips.

ACTIVITES: Volleyball, biking, boating, swimming, basketball, fishing, gawking.

FOR MORE INFORMATION:

Long Beach Lifeguards—562-570-3400.

Long Beach Lifeguard Division—562-570-1287.

Long Beach Lifeguards Headquarters—562-570-1360.

City of Long Beach Parks and Recreation—562-570-1707.

Long Beach Visitors Bureau—562-435-3645 or 800-4LB-STAY.

Long Beach Chamber of Commerce—562-436-1251.

Long Beach Marine Services—310-594-0951.

LONG BEACH CITY BEACH

With a length of 5.5 miles, the city's namesake is aptly named. The southern portion of this beach, known as Belmont Shore, described above, runs from the north side of Belmont Pier up to the Downtown Long Beach Marina. The beach offers a unique view into Long Beach Outer Harbor and its "oil hotels." The four visible islands are oil rigs with false fronts to make the postcards look better. Perhaps it's this "style over substance" attitude that has Long Beach scrambling for more attractions like an insecure teen seeking to impress a lover. Bixby Park and Bluff Park, both along East Ocean Boulevard., are nice picnic areas overlooking the beach as well as a welcome splash of greenery in this concrete jungle.

ACCESS: Take I-710 westbound from I-405 or Hwy 1. I-710 deposits you onto Ocean Blvd. Follow the signs for East Ocean Blvd. and exit I-710. Remain on East Ocean Blvd. and the beach will reveal itself after you pass Shoreline Park.

PARKING: On-street, metered parking. Start looking from Alamitos Ave. and a spot should rear its head before the pier on 39th Pl. Bixby and Bluff Parks should have parking available as well.

HOURS/FEES: 5:00 A.M. to 10:00 P.M. Free.

AMENITIES: Lifeguards, restrooms, showers, bike path, snack shack.

ACTIVITIES: Swimming, sunning, biking.

FOR MORE INFORMATION:

Long Beach Lifeguards—562-570-3400.

Long Beach Lifeguard Division—562-570-1287.

Long Beach Lifeguards Headquarters—562-570-1360.

City of Long Beach Parks and Recreation—562-570-1707.

Long Beach Marine Services—310-594-0951.

Long Beach Visitors Bureau—562-435-3645 or 800-4LB-STAY.

Long Beach Chamber of Commerce—562-436-1251.

CABRILLO BEACH

The San Pedro Breakwater has split the personality of Cabrillo Beach. On one side lies the calm waters of San Pedro Bay while on the other side great combers break with the raw power of the untamed Pacific. The inside beach offers a four-lane boat launch and a large, sandy play area with gentle waters lapping at the shore. The outside beach sees the sea roll in unfiltered to crash upon the sand, creating a good place for beginning surfers to practice their craft.

The Cabrillo Fishing Pier allows anglers to tempt the ichthyoid palates with bait or lures, and the Cabrillo Marine Aquarium lets visitors touch some of the marine creatures that reside in its thirty-two aquariums.

ACCESS: From I-405 or Hwy 1—Take I-110 (Harbor Freeway) westbound to its terminus at North Gaffey St. Turn left onto Gaffey (Hwy 110) and continue toward the ocean. In about 2.5 miles turn left onto West 22nd St., travel two long blocks to South Pacific Ave., and turn right. Travel about 1.6 miles and turn left on Stephen W. White Dr., then keep left at the fork to reach the beach. The right-hand fork leads to Point Fermin Park's lower reaches.

From Long Beach City Beach—Drive north on East Ocean Blvd., which becomes West Ocean Blvd. then crosses Desmond Bridge and Vincent Thomas Bridge (50-cent toll) as is becomes Seaside Ave. Remain on this road across the bridges, then exit to Harbor Blvd./North Front St. Turn left after this horseshoe exit onto North

Front St. and follow it through the underpass and around to its junction with South Pacific Ave. Turn left onto Pacific and travel just over 5 miles to Stephen W. White Dr. and turn left.

PARKING: A parking lot is provided costing $5.50.

HOURS/FEES: Sunrise to 10:30 P.M. $5.50 to park.

MUSEUM: Tuesday through Friday, noon to 5:00 P.M.; weekends, 10:00 A.M. to 5:00 P.M. Free.

AMENITIES: Showers, lifeguards, tables, barbecue grill, boat lauch, restrooms, pier, aquarium, volleyball.

ACTIVITIES: Surfing, swimming, boating, tide pools, fishing, volleyball, diving.

FOR MORE INFORMATION:

Beach—310-831-8109.

Pier—310-832-1179.

Aquarium—310-548-7562.

Los Angeles County Southern Section Lifeguard Headquarters—310-372-2166.

San Pedro Peninsula Chamber of Commerce—310-832-7272, www.san-pedrochamber.com.

Pacific Region Recreation and Parks Headquarters—310-548-7671.

ROYAL PALMS STATE BEACH

Named for the Royal Palms Hotel that lost a battle with the sea in 1920, this rocky shore also includes White Point Beach. Tide pools and surfing are the main fare that lies beneath these rugged bluffs. The steep dirt trails that access the shore tend to keep the crowds small.

ACCESS: From I-405 or Hwy 1— Take I-110 southward toward the harbor. Remain on I-110 as it becomes Gaffey St. and keep heading south. Turn right on Paseo del Mar as Gaffey St. ends. The parking lot lies ahead on the left where Paseo del Mar turns north to become Western Ave.

From Cabrillo Beach—Take Pacific Ave. south to its junction with Shepard St. and turn right. Pass Point Fermin Park and follow the road as it becomes South Paseo del Mar and continue to the lot at Western Ave.

PARKING: Some free parking along Paseo del Mar. A pay lot at the beach.

HOURS/FEES: Sunrise to sunset. Free.

AMENITIES: Restrooms, lifeguard.

ACTIVITIES: Surfing, tide pool, swimming, diving.

FOR MORE INFORMATION:

Los Angeles County Southern Section Lifeguard Headquarters—310-372-2166.

San Pedro Peninsula Chamber of Commerce—310-832-7272, www.san-pedrochamber.com.

Pacific Region Recreation and Parks Headquarters—310-548-7671.

ABALONE COVE BEACH

The southernmost access point for the Palos Verdes region, Abalone Cove offers tide-pool exploration in an ecological reserve and bluff-top picnics. It's also common to see surfers skirting the shore on their journeys southward. Past the two points, Portuguese and Inspiration, lies Portuguese Bend, which boasts year-round surf and an occasional nude bather.

The Wayfarer's Chapel is tucked away just south of the parking area. The architechtural artwork, designed to blend into the natural surroundings, is worth a look regardless of your religious beliefs.

ACCESS: From I-405 or Hwy 1—Take Hwy 213 (Western Ave.) southbound to West 25th St. Turn right and wind about 10 miles up West 25th, which becomes Palos Verdes Dr. South en route. Abalone Cove Shoreline Park lies on the left with the beach accessed via dirt path.

From Torrance Beach, Redondo Beach, or Manhattan Beach—Take Hwy 1 south, exit on Palos Verdes Blvd., then keep right on Palos Verdes Dr. West. Follow the road around the peninsula. Abalone Cove lies 3 miles from Point Vicente.

PARKING: Pay lot on the wet side of Palos Verdes Dr. South. $5.

HOURS/FEES: Sunrise to sunset.

AMENITIES: Lifeguard, restrooms, tables.

ACTIVITIES: Surfing, diving, swimming, tide pool, picnicking.

FOR MORE INFORMATION:

Abalone Shoreline Park—310-377-1222.

Los Angeles County Southern Section Lifeguard Headquarters—310-372-2166.

Los Angeles County Lifeguard—310-832-1179.

San Pedro Peninsula Chamber of Commerce—310-832-7272, www.san-pedrochamber.com.

Pacific Region Recreation and Parks Headquarters—310-548-7671.

POINT VICENTE FISHING ACCESS

While lacking sand, Point Vicente Fishing Access does access the cobblestone shoreline and gives me a chance to not describe something as wide and sandy. Tide pools beckon nonanglers down a 0.5-mile trail that descends an eroding bluff. The lighthouse perched high above the shore isn't open to the public, but the park allows a good look and photo op. There's also a natural history museum in the park, shedding light on the peninsula's plants, animals, and geology. It's open 10:00 A.M. to 5:00 P.M. every day with extended hours during the summer.

ACCESS: From I-405 or Hwy 1—Take Hwy 213 (Western Ave.) southbound to West 25th St. Turn right and wind up West 25th about 10 miles. It becomes Palos Verdes Dr. South en route. Point Vicente is 3 miles past Abalone Cove

From Torrance Beach, Redondo Beach, or Manhattan Beach—Take Hwy 1 South, exit on Palos Verdes Blvd., and keep right on Palos Verdes Dr. West. Follow the road around the peninsula.

PARKING: Pull-over parking area along Palos Verdes Dr. West.

HOURS/FEES: 5:00 A.M. to 9:00 P.M. Free.

AMENITIES: Restrooms, trail, museum.

FOR MORE INFORMATION:

Rancho Palos Verdes Parks and Recreation Department—310-377-5370.

San Pedro Peninsula Chamber of Commerce—310-832-7272, www.san-pedrochamber.com.

Pacific Region Recreation and Parks Headquarters—310-548-7671.

MALAGA COVE

With sandy shores complete with volleyball nets, Malaga is Palos Verdes' only sandy strand. The beach blends into Torrance Beach to the north and fades into the rocky tide pools of Flat Rock Point to the southwest. If someone yells "RAT!" don't be alarmed. It's short for "Right after Torrance" and is this beach's alias.

This is also a surf spot called Haggerty's. It really macks with a big north and a medium tide. Totally epic, Dude. Translation: If you happen to be surfing here when a north swell of 5 to15 feet hits, and the tide isn't too high or low, the experience will be one to remember, as the waves will be well-shaped and powerful.

ACCESS: From Hwy 1 in Redondo Beach—Turn south onto Palos Verdes Blvd. Stay right on Palos Verdes Dr. West and continue to Paseo del Mar and turn right. Weave around the bluff to the parking lot.

The picturesque Point Vicente Lighthouse on Palos Verdes Peninsula was one of the last built on the West Coast, in 1925.

From I-405—Take Hwy 107 south to Hwy 1 and turn right, northbound, and follow the directions above.

PARKING: The lot seems adequate for the beach's use. If full, park at Torrance County Beach.

HOURS/FEES: Sunrise to sunset. Free.

AMENITIES: Restrooms, showers, lifeguards, volleyball nets, gazebo.

ACTIVITIES: Volleyball, surfing, tide pools, fishing.

FOR MORE INFORMATION:

Weather and Surf Conditions—310-379-8471

Los Angeles County Southern Section Lifeguard Headquarters—310-372-2166.

Pacific Region Recreation and Parks Headquarters—310-548-7671.

ODE TO A LIGHTHOUSE

Beacons in the darkest of nights. A guiding light for souls at sea. These sentinels perch on points and cling to craggy cliff tops, warning of shallow shore with lens and horn.

UNFORTUNATELY, THE QUAINT LIGHTHOUSE ON POINT FERMIN, AT LONG BEACH, IS NOT OPEN TO THE PUBLIC, BUT IT STANDS ON THE GROUNDS OF A CITY PARK.

It's hard to pinpoint the intrigue and interest lighthouses generate. Perhaps they are beacons to a time when humankind was still closely connected with the sea, when one person would spend time looking out for others. The varying styles of old lighthouses shine light on fertile imaginations. Some look like lone towers that conjure up images of Merlin standing atop with arms raised, commanding the wind, hail, and lightning. Others look like cottages that put a light on the roof just out of kindness to the sailors. Each brings different images of a simple time when someone could point out the hazards in our journeys, allowing us to steer clear and sail on.

Perhaps the new "robot lights" that sit atop sterile steel stands symbolize our society's current state: No one on watch, no one at the helm. Have we become observers who lack responsibility for our own actions, looking for others to blame? Or maybe lighthouses just look cool.

REGION 10

TORRANCE TO PLAYA DEL REY

Ask third-graders to draw a sandy shore and they'll give a good rendering of this coastline. It's basically one wide and sandy beach from Torrance through Playa del Rey. Bronzed men and women with chiseled bodies swarm on the South Bay Bicycle Trail that parallels the shore and holds the region together by creating a common thread between the towns.

The biggest difference among beaches here lies in the towns perched above them: Torrance, El Segundo, Redondo Beach, Hermosa Beach, and Manhattan Beach. Torrance and El Segundo are mostly inland cities with their fingers scratching the shore. The entire region is one wide band of sand that disappears into the rocky cliffs of Palos Verdes.

Torrance County Beach is considered by many as belonging to Redondo. Neither is as crowded as Hermosa or Manhattan Beach. That's a bit strange, seeing as there is plenty of parking there and the town is very tourist oriented, two qualities ignored by the other two cities. Goes to show that people like things to be difficult.

Hermosa Beach has a stereotypical California attitude. Things here are relaxed and the populace is very athletic. This is apparent when traveling on the bike path or sunbathing on the 2-mile-long beach.

Manhattan Beach is basically a continuation of Hermosa. The homes are so close together that you can borrow your neighbor's milk by reaching out the window. The whole town is built on a steep hill with buildings stacked shoulder to shoulder like spectators in a sold-out stadium. Like such an event, parking is elusive and costly.

El Segundo and Playa del Rey offer vast expanses of beach without the crowds. Unfortunately, manmade monstrosities, oil refineries, a sewage treatment plant, and a power plant back the beaches. Keep looking out toward the ocean and you'd never know how close to the L.A. infrastructure you really are.

Access

Hwy 1, Pacific Coast Hwy, and I-405 are the main north-south corridors for this region. However, it is often wise to avoid Hwy 1 near the airport.

To reach the northern beaches—Take I-405 to Hwy 90 West (Marina Freeway). After 3 miles, turn left onto Culver Blvd., which leads to the crossing over Hwy 1. Within 0.5 mile of the ocean, Culver Blvd. bears left and becomes Vista del Mar, which is the main access road for the northern section of the region.

To Manhattan Beach South—This beach is probably best accessed by taking I-405 to Hwy 91 West (Artesia Blvd.) and following it to Hwy 1.

Torrance to Playa del Rey

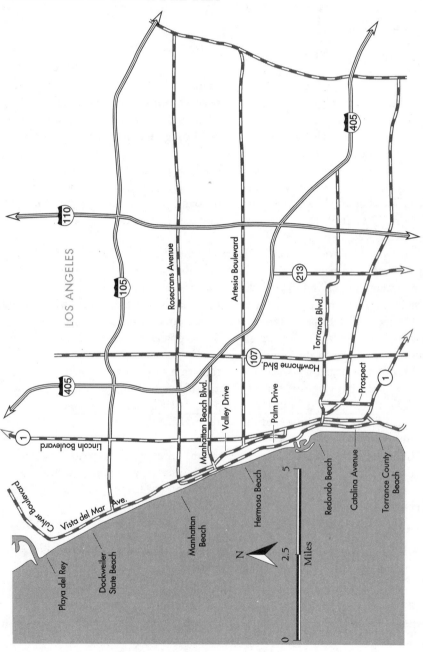

To Manhattan Beach and points north—Turn right on Hwy 1 (Sepulveda Blvd.) then left after 2 miles onto Manhattan Beach Blvd.

To points south—Turn left on Hwy 1.

Beaches

Torrance County Beach

Redondo Beach

Hermosa Beach

Manhattan Beach

Dockweiler State Beach

Playa del Rey

Camping

Dockweiler State Beach RV Park—800-950-7275 or 310-322-4951. 120 sites, most with hookups.

Hopkins Wilderness Park—310-318-0668. Tent camping in 11.5 acres of wilderness in a Redondo Beach residential area.

Other points of interest

Madrona Marsh Preserve—310-782-3989 or 310-32MARSH, 3291 Plaza del Amo. A natural history museum is the starting point for tours and nature activities through Torrance Parks and Recreation and the Friends of Madrona Marsh.

Miramar Park—310-618-2930 or 310-371-9332, 201 Paseo de la Playa, Torrance. A park with a seascape setting.

Horseshoe Pier and Monstad Pier—Almost a town on stilts, this pier complex offers fishing, dining, and strolling. The 300-foot public pier is one of the most popular fishin' spots on the coast and it's lighted and always open. No license required! The wooden structure is being changed to concrete so construction clutters things a bit, but access is maintained.

Redondo Sportfishing Pier—310-372-3566. This 250-foot wooden pier is behind the long, protective arm of King Harbor. Charters, whale-watching vessels, and party boats in search of yellowtail jack all call this home. The nearby electric plant attracts fish by warming the surrounding waters. Open 4:30 A.M. to 11:00 P.M. The "Fish Count Hotline" can be reached at 310-376-1622.

Redondo Fun Factory—310-374-9982. Classic boardwalk-style games and rides on the Redondo Beach Pier.

Hopkins Wilderness Park—310-318-0668. A small wildlife reserve in the midst of a residential Redondo Beach. Camping is permitted.

Dominguez Park—310-378-8555, 190th St. and Flagler Ln. This is Redondo's dog racing park and also home to Heritage Court and the Redondo Beach Historical Museum.

Redondo Beach Historical Museum—310-318-0610, ext. 3252, Dominguez Park Heritage Court. A restored Victorian home with pics, memorabilia, and other stuff documenting the area's past. Open weekends from 1:00 P.M. to 4:00 P.M. Free.

George Freeth Memorial—A memorial bust on the Redondo Beach Pier. George, one of the fathers of modern surfing, was showin' the locals how to ride waves in 1907! He was California's first lifeguard and invented that red torpedo thing that today's lifeguards use.

Seaside Lagoon—310-318-0682, corner of Harbor Dr. and Portofino Way in Redondo Beach. A heated saltwater swimming pool, sand volleyball courts, and a rentable rec room.

Alta Vista Park—310-318-0670, 715 Julia Ave. Lighted tennis and indoor racquetball courts. Reservations and variable fee required.

Hermosa Beach Municipal Pier—Concrete pilings stretch 1,100 feet to sea. On top sits the bait shop and restrooms. It is yet another popular fishing platform. Open sunrise to sunset.

Hermosa Skate Track—710 Pier Ave. An outdoor skate park, which gives boarders and bladers a place to play without getting arrested. Skating is not a crime!

The Roundhouse—310-379-8117, end of Manhattan Beach Pier. An educational aquarium offering public viewing. The touch tank allows one to get close and personal with the local sea life. Open Monday to Friday 3:00 P.M. to sunset, weekends 10:00 A.M. to sunset. Free (donations welcome).

Manhattan Beach Historical Society and Museum—310-374-7575, 1601 Manhattan Beach Blvd. A beach cottage (circa 1905) museum. Open weekends noon to 3:00 P.M. and by appointment.

South Bay Bicycle Trail—Stretching 22 miles from Torrance Beach northward to Will Rogers State Beach, this path guide the hardbodies of the Los Angeles Basin on their route to physical fitness. A mileage chart can be found online at members.aol.com/eathermosa/bicycle.html.

TORRANCE COUNTY BEACH

While perched above Torrance County Beach, it's easy to feel like a bird on the wing as the dots of color move about like ants on their hill. The serpentine route of the South Bay Bicycle Trail starts (or ends) here and creates a coastal bike highway to Will Rogers State Beach. The main visual difference between this wide beach and Redondo Beach, which connects to the north, is there's a different sponsor on the trash cans. Giant Mountain Dew cans were in use at Torrance, paying tribute to Andy Warhol's pop art. (Redondo Beach had Chock Full o' Nuts cans). The cliffs at Palos Verdes and Malaga Cove (also known as RAT Beach) are reachable by walking south.

ACCESS: From Hwy 1—Turn west onto Palos Verdes Blvd. In 0.6 mile turn right onto Via Riviera, then left onto Paseo de la Playa and park.

From the north—Exit I-405 southbound onto Hwy 107 southbound (Hawthorne Blvd.). Turn right onto Torrance Blvd., continue to Hwy 1, and turn left.

From the south—Exit I-405 northbound onto Hwy 91 westbound (Artesia Blvd.), turn left onto Hwy 107 southbound (Hawthorne Blvd.), continue on Hwy 1, and turn left.

PARKING: There are large pay lots at the beach and additional parking along Vista del Mar.

HOURS/FEES: 6:00 A.M. to 10:00 P.M.

AMENITIES: Volleyball, bike path, restrooms, snack shack, picnic area, grills, lifeguards.

ACTIVITIES: Surfing, biking, volleyball, sunbathing.

FOR MORE INFORMATION:

Los Angeles County Southern Section Lifeguard Headquarters—310-372-2166.

Torrance Chamber of Commerce—310-515-2558 or 310-540-5858, www.torrancechamber.com.

Torrance Parks and Recreation—310-618-2930 or 310-371-9332, www.tprd.torrnet.com.

Torrance Visitors Bureau—310-792-2341.

REDONDO BEACH

A long track of golden sand runs southward from a horseshoe-shaped pier to form Redondo Beach. Volleyball and sunbathing are pursued with equal vigor here. Avenue. I marks the spot for late teens and early twenty-something people to hang out. There seems to be a pecking order as the junior-high-aged locals are more prevalent at RAT Beach.

Parking here is easier than up in Hermosa or Manhattan but can still be a challenge. Get to the beach before 11:00 A.M. or after 3:00 P.M. (peak tanning hours) and spaces should be available. The surfers here deal with shifting peaks, meaning the sandy bottom's characteristics change, causing the waves to break in different places. The South Bay Bicycle Trail detours around the marina here and then wanders through the pier's parking building, necessitating a dismount.

ACCESS: From the north—Take Hwy 1 southbound, turn westward onto Torrance Blvd., then left onto South Catalina Ave. Travel one block, then bear right onto Esplanade St., which parallels the entire beach.

From the south—Take Hwy 1 northbound, turn left on Ave. I. Follow the road to Esplanade St.

From I-405 southbound—Exit onto Hwy 107 southbound (Hawthorne Blvd.). Turn right onto Torrance Blvd. and continue to South Catalina Ave.

From I-405 northbound—Exit onto Hwy 91 westbound (Artesia Blvd.), turn left onto Hwy 107 southbound (Hawthorne Blvd.), and continue to South Catalina Ave.

PARKING: There are pay lots by the piers and streetside parking along Esplanade.

HOURS: 6:00 A.M. to 10:00 P.M.

AMENITIES: Volleyball, bike path, restrooms, snack shack, picnic area, grills, lifeguards.

ACTIVITIES: Biking, surfing, volleyball, sunbathing, jogging, rollerblading.

FOR MORE INFORMATION:

Los Angeles County Southern Section Lifeguard Headquarters—310-372-2166.

Redondo Chamber of Commerce—310-376-6911.

Redondo Beach Recreation Department—310-318-0610.

Weather—www.smalltown.com/wx/weathertext.html.

Redondo Beach Visitor's Bureau—310-374-2171 or 800-282-0333, www.visit-redondo.com.

HERMOSA BEACH

Hermosa Beach plays host to hordes of people enjoying California's trifecta: sun, sand, and surf. The South Bay Bicycle Trail often feels like a log jam, with athletic men and women flexing and flirting as they walk, ride, or roll past the wide sands. The path is narrow as it skirts a pair of cement walls that divide the sand from the houses that line the beachfront. Volleyball is always happening during the summer, with other pairs watching and waiting for their rotation onto a court. Any game that has an object that can migrate onto the towel of a cute member of the opposite sex is played here. It's a wonder that all these people found a place to park! Surfers hang out by the pier and south toward the Redondo breakwater.

Access: From Hwy 1—Turn westward onto Pier Ave. in the town of Hermosa Beach. Follow Pier Ave. to Hermosa Ave. and turn right. The beach is accessed via walkways along Hermosa Ave.

From I-405—Exit on Hwy 91 (Artesia Blvd.) and head west. Turn left onto Hwy 1, right on Pier Ave., and left on Hermosa Ave.

Parking: Hermosa Ave. has meters along the median. There's a public lot at Hermosa Ave. and 11th, 13th, and 14th Sts.

Hours/fees: 6:00 A.M. to 10:00 P.M. 50 cents per hour.

Amenities: Bike path, volleyball, pier, snack shack, restrooms, showers, lifeguard.

Activities: Biking, fishing, surfing, volleyball, sunbathing, swimming.

For more information:

Los Angeles County Southern Section Lifeguard Headquarters—310-372-2166.

Hermosa Beach Parks and Recreation—310-318-0280, www.hermosabch.org/parks.

Hermosa Beach Chamber of Commerce—310-376-0951.

Strand Cam online video camera—www.eatgoodstuff.com/strandcam/index.html.

Another Hermosa Beach online video camera: www.hermosawave.net/wave/livecam.asp.

Volleyball/boardwalk online video cam: www-net.com/goodstuff/awn-hbs-nc.html.

Manhattan Beach and El Porto Beach

Manhattan Beach is where trendsetters go to play. No, let me correct that. This is where trend followers come to be seen following trends. It's a wide slab o' sand packed along an auditorium of houses that seem to lean toward the ocean. The average home here sells for $550,000, which is $100,000 more than Hermosa Beach property and almost double the beachfront price in Redondo Beach. However, as is apparent when looking for parking, a majority of the visitors just *want* to live here. Hardbodies stroll the shore between bouts of volleyball, and bronzed-beauties emerge from the ocean and walk to their towels, apparently oblivious to the open-mouthed stares of today's television-fed youths. Manhattan Beach has the sparkle and flash befitting the Hollywood execs who live here.

As the coast continues northward, the sands become El Porto Beach and the crowd thins. The beach is actually still Manhattan Beach, but the different moniker keeps the name-brand-oriented crowds to the south.

ACCESS: From I-405—Exit onto westbound Manhattan Beach Blvd. and continue straight to the coast.

From Hwy 1—Turn onto Manhattan Beach Blvd. and head west. Once in town, turn right on Highland Ave. to head through town or left on Hermosa Ave. to hit Hermosa Beach.

PARKING: There are parking structures along Highland at Rosecrans and at 12th St., five-hour parking meters at Highland and 14th St., and a five-hour lot at 12th and Highland. El Porto Beach has some metered parking at the end of 44th St. Otherwise, head to Hermosa and walk to Manhattan.

HOURS/FEES: 6:00 A.M. to 10:00 P.M. It's a free world, but parking here costs at least $1 an hour and the meters are limited to five hours. The Manhattan Beach Municipal Pier is open from 6:00 A.M. to midnight.

AMENITIES: Volleyball, bike path, restrooms, snack shack, picnic area, grills, lifeguards, pier, aquarium.

ACTIVITIES: Lots of volleyball, biking, surfing, sunbathing, being seen, swimming.

FOR MORE INFORMATION:

Los Angeles County Southern Section Lifeguard Headquarters—310-372-2166.

Manhattan Beach Pier—310-379-8117.

Manhattan Beach Chamber of Commerce—310-545-5313.

DOCKWEILER STATE BEACH AND EL SEGUNDO BEACH

Below a tall, steep bank lies Dockweiler State Beach, a wide, flat band of sand set directly beneath the flight path of Los Angeles International Airport. It's fun to look up at the jumbo jets and wonder if they're on their way to good or bad times—and aren't they envious as they look down on happy, relaxed beachgoers. It does get noisy, but the sand is nice and the crowd is well spread out. The south end of the strand is El Segundo Beach. Same beach, same management, same facilities—just farther south.

ACCESS: From Hwy 1 (Lincoln Blvd.) southbound—Turn right onto Culver Blvd. The road becomes Vista del Mar Ave. as it bends to the left. Dockweiler State Beach begins on the right in less than a mile.

From I-405—Exit on I-105 and continue west as it becomes Imperial Hwy, which runs straight to the beach.

PARKING: Vista del Mar offers streetside parking. The state-provided lots are usually sufficient for the crowds. The trend is less crowded the farther north you go.

HOURS/FEES: 6:00 A.M. to 10:00 P.M. $5 to park in the lots run by the state. Free parking along Vista del Mar.

AMENITIES: Bike path, snack shack, volleyball, playground, picnic area, grills, restrooms, showers, lifeguard, camping.

ACTIVITIES: Surfing, swimming, biking, sunbathing, volleyball.

FOR MORE INFORMATION:

State Parks Los Angeles Headquarters—818-880-0350.

Los Angeles County Southern Section Lifeguard Headquarters—310-372-2166.

El Segundo Chamber of Commerce—310-322-1220.

El Segundo Parks and Recreation—310-322-3842 or 310-322-1677.

PLAYA DEL REY

Playa del Rey can be a quiet place to recline on the wide, flat sands and watch the boats of Marina del Rey. It can also be a noisy dance jam that rocks the nearby weathered houses. The beach reaches from the entrance of Marina del Rey to El Segundo State Beach. The nearby del Rey Lagoon Park has playing fields and basketball courts. Sometimes the activities spill over to these sands. This is one of the few places where the pigeon is a seabird.

ACCESS: From Hwy 1 (Lincoln Blvd.) southbound—Turn right onto Culver Blvd. Stay right as the main road bends left to become Vista del Mar Ave. Turn left on Pacific Ave. and park. The beach is accessed at the end of Culver Blvd.

From I-405—Exit on I-105 and continue west as it becomes Imperial Hwy, turn right on Vista del Mar Ave. when the road hits Dockweiler State Beach. Turn left on Pacific Ave. just before Vista del Mar Ave. turns right to become Culver Blvd.

PARKING: Parking is available along Pacific Ave. at Del Rey Lagoon Park.

HOURS/FEES: 6:00 A.M. to 10:00 P.M.

AMENITIES: Restrooms, bike path, volleyball, showers.

ACTIVITIES: Swimming, surfing, biking, volleyball, basketball.

FOR MORE INFORMATION:

Los Angeles County Southern Section Lifeguard Headquarters—310-372-2166.

Los Angeles County Parks and Recreation—310-217-8361 or 310-217-8376.

FISHIN' THE COAST

The Chumash people fished freely along the coast back in the days of wooden ships, and fish was an important part of their diet. In the present, there are lots of places to fish for free. However, making these fish a staple in your diet could prove hazardous to your health.

In California, it is free to fish from any public pier or attached breakwater that is in ocean or bay waters. A license is necessary to fish from the beach or to fish for profit. Common coastal catches include mackerel, smelt, sardines, croakers, and various species of perch. A few lucky anglers wrangle in halibut, sand shark, barracuda, bonito, and yellowtail. Many piers have a bait shack that supplies fresh anchovies or squid bits and may even rent equipment.

While fish was a significant portion of indigenous coastal peoples' diets, care must now be taken when consuming fish. High pollution levels have forced public health advisories on fish consumption, which give suggested doses of certain types of fish. Yes, our oceans are that polluted. Guidelines for safe consumption are given in the "Sport Fishing Regulations" handbook published by the California Department of Fish and Game (www.dfg.ca.gov). The booklets, which include the state's fishing regulations, are available where licenses are sold. The info is supposed to be posted at the piers. Unfortunately the signs are often faded beyond legibility. If this is the case, call 562-590-5113 to inform the agency of the situation. Two things are pretty clear: Don't eat the white croaker, and pregnant persons need to be wary of all the fish. Almost all the fish can be consumed in varying amounts, especially if they are taken from different locations. The main trouble comes from long-term consumption. It's those who still depend upon the low-cost food source who are most directly affected

On the bright side, awareness of these problems is increasing. Next time you're dipping a line into the drink or see someone else doing so, think about the chemicals used to grow your food or to kill those pesky bugs or think about the wastewater plant that leaks sewage and claims how lucky it was that the leak was so "small." That's the stuff that heads downstream to the ocean. Those are the reasons we can't just eat the fish anymore.

REGION 11

MARINA DEL REY TO PACIFIC PALISADES

The wide, sandy coastline continues its course northward, where it thins in the shadows of the Santa Monica Mountains. A city the size of Los Angeles needs a huge patch of sand on which to play. This region provides this—often with space to spare.

Marina del Rey is the one gap in the sand-lined shore. This is a pleasure-boater's dream port, catering to the exclusive world of yachts. There is a waveless beach here, Mother's Beach, for those looking for a sheltered strand.

Venice's extremely wide platter of granular silica (sand) takes a backseat to the eclectic parade that proceeds down Ocean Front Walk, a wide strip of pavement running for about 0.75 mile along the beach. This is the place, seen in movies, where people perform bizarre acts from the deep recesses of society-rebelling minds. I saw what looked like the ghost of Jimi Hendrix, with his clothes still bearing the dirt of escaping the grave, rollerblading a serpentine path while attacking a helpless guitar whose strained screams were broadcast by a hip-borne amplifier. This apparition rolled by, shouting what must have been lyrics into the smiling faces of onlookers. This is part of the show that up to 150,000 people a day come to see. Ah, Venice. Unfortunately, the sand here is sometimes used as a litter box. The infamous Muscle Beach lies where the coastline blends into the shores of Santa Monica. This is pure L.A.: the beauty and the beast.

Santa Monica's vast expanse of sand sees more beach use than any other in the state. Fortunately it's big enough to do so. The Santa Monica Pier bisects the spacious strand, creating a platform of perpetual activity by hosting a plethora of amusements for all ages.

Pacific Palisades sits where the mountains start their fall into sea. This and private property have kept the coastline rather pristine. Three sandy miles of coast are available to the masses at Will Rogers State Beach, which connects to Santa Monica. The South Bay Bicycle Trail's northern terminus is here. The trail runs southward through this region and beyond to Torrance County Beach.

Access

Pacific Coast Hwy (Hwy 1) provides access to the entire region. Taking I-405 to I-10 westbound will connect with Hwy 1 in Santa Monica, the region's midsection. From this point northward, Hwy 1 provides a scenic, coastal drive that will access almost every beach northward.

MARINA DEL REY TO PACIFIC PALISADES

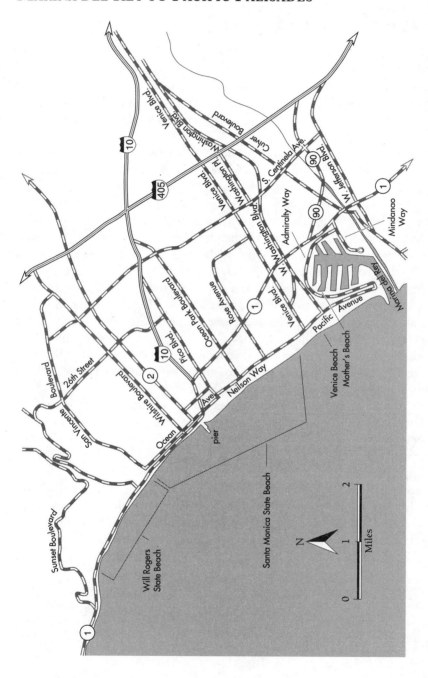

Beaches

Mother's Beach

Venice Beach

Santa Monica State Beach

Will Rogers State Beach

Camping

There is no camping available in this region. State-run facilities are available in both neighboring regions.

Venice Hostel—310-452-3052, 1515 Pacific Ave. at Windward Ave. The self-proclaimed "potion magique" (miracle cure) for travelers. Rates vary but remain very low. Possibly the best way to experience Venice.

Other points of interest

Venice's Ocean Front Walk—See Venice Beach.

Palisades Park—310-217-8376. A pleasant grassy bluff above Santa Monica State Beach offering ocean views, picnic tables, and shuffleboard with a senior center as well as many homeless people enjoying the warm sun and soft soil.

Venice Canal Historic District—310-827-2366, between Washington Blvd. and Venice Blvd. A quiet contrast to Venice's Ocean Front Walk. Strolling here takes in Venice's historic canals.

Museum of Flying—310-392-8822, 2772 Donald Douglas Loop North in Santa Monica. Get a glimpse of the wild blue ocean of air and the people and machines that play in it.

Third St. Promenade—310-393-8355, www.thirdst.com. Santa Monica's version of Venice's Ocean Front Walk. It's more sterile (and safer) than its southern cousin and offers more ways to spend money. In an impromptu, unofficial survey, I noted art galleries, book shops, forty-one clothing stores, an acting school, gift shops, salons, jewelry stores, dentists, music stores, a recording studio, and more than eighty restaurants, bars, or clubs.

Will Rogers State Historic Park—310-454-8212, off Sunset Blvd. in Pacific Palisades. He never met a man he couldn't like. The park is actually his old ranch and the ranch house an old museum. Tours, memorabilia, hiking and horseback trails all here from 8:00 A.M. to dark.

Ocean Discovery Center (University of California at Los Angeles)—310-393-6149, www.lifesci.ucla.edu/odc. Under the Santa Monica Pier, this educational center teaches that the ocean and the world as a whole are a living system. Staff strive to raise your environmental IQ. $5.

Hollywood—213-469-8311 or 213-689-8822. Starstruck? Check out the terrazzo-and-brass stars of the Hollywood Walk of Fame or the signatures, hand- and foot-prints in front of Mann's Chinese Theater, where you can often pick up free tickets for show tapings throughout tinsel town. Keep your eyes peeled for incognito actors.

Live viewing via the Internet

Santa Monica Pier Cam—207.155.120.13/piercam/index.html.

Venice Beach Cam—www.westend.net/beachcam/index.html.

Mother's Beach

Mother's Beach is a small corner of sand in Basin D of Marina del Rey. Its main feature is the lack of any semblance of ocean activity. Kayakers and windsurfers take advantage of the absence of waves and put their crafts in the water here. Volleyball nets for those not-quite-ready-for-Venice players and a picnic area round out this inland beach. The showers are a necessity for those who brave the stagnant, er, uh, still waters of Basin D.

Marina del Rey, literally a floating city, is the world's largest small-craft harbor with more than 6,000 yachts in the water.

Access: From Hwy 1 (Lincoln Blvd.), turn into the marina on Mindanao Way, then turn immediately right onto Admiralty Way. Follow this road around and turn left onto Palawan Way. The Marina del Rey visitor center is on Mindanao and Admiralty Way.

Parking: There's a lot on Palawan Way.

Hours/Fees: 8:00 A.M. to 9:00 P.M. $5 to park.

Amenities: Lifeguard, picnic tables, showers, restroom.

Activities: Swimming, picnicking.

For more information:

Los Angeles County Central Section Lifeguard Headquarters—310-394-3261.

Los Angeles Department of Harbors and Beaches—310-305-9503.

Marina del Rey Chamber of Commerce—310-821-0555.

Marina del Rey Visitor's Information Center—310-305-9547.

VENICE BEACH

Ah, Venice. The wide sands of Santa Monica continue southward through Venice as does the South Bay Bicycle Trail. However, the ambiance is a 180-degree switch. Instead of the thong-bikini-wearing rollerblader who seems to have stepped directly from the silver screen, change the vision by keeping the rollerblades but making the person a man and give him a guitar, loud voice, and an overcoat and have him skate circles around people while singing (his name is Harry Perry). After he passes, you may see that bikini-wearing lady, but she's probably swallowing swords and eating fire. It's a crapshoot as to what you'll see. Known as one of the funkiest places on earth, Venice's Ocean Front Walk draws spectators daily to witness a street fair without parallel. The painted lifeguard towers are known as "The Official Open Air Art Museum of L.A. County Beaches."

Jim Morrison and the Doors were born on these sands. They used to play on the pier at the Cheetah. A mural of Jim, who lived in a house along one of the canals, stares down Ocean Front Walk at the society that fueled his fire.

A few visitors actually use the beach, which is extremely wide, gently arcing 3 miles from the mouth of Marina del Rey northward to Santa Monica. There are two paved paths here. The bike path is for wheeled vehicles. Tickets are given to bikers who don't dismount when they switch to a sidewalk. The playground's basketball courts, complete with viewing stands, are worthy of TV coverage, and you may catch a glimpse of the next Conan working out here at Muscle Beach alongside his well-endowed prize.

Keep in mind that these funky entertainers need to eat. Put something in their hats if you enjoyed their shows. On that note, keep your valuables at home and your wallet where you can feel it. Nonentertaining types sometimes work the crowds too: purse snatchers and pickpockets. Ah, Venice.

The pier here is closed and slated for demolition. It seems the times of entertainment over the waves have receded.

ACCESS: From Hwy 1 turn seaward on Venice Blvd. Flip a coin and turn right or left on Pacific Ave., which runs the length of the beach. Continue straight on Venice Blvd. to reach the pay lot.

PARKING: Park as soon as you see an empty spot with a meter. The pay lot fills up fast during the summer. If you dare, park inland about 0.5 mile away and save the headache. That's not advised with a high-dollar vehicle.

HOURS/FEES: 6:00 A.M. to 10:00 P.M. 50 cents per hour.

AMENITIES: Volleyball, basketball, bike path, restrooms, showers, playground.

ACTIVITIES: Partying, swimming, sunbathing, volleyball, basketball, weight lifting, platform tennis, handball.

FOR MORE INFORMATION:

Surf/weather report—310-457-9701.

Los Angeles County Central Section Lifeguard Headquarters—310-394-3261.

Los Angeles Department of Harbors and Beaches—310-305-9503.

Venice Chamber of Commerce—310-396-7016.

Venice Visitor's Bureau—310-827-2366.

Venice Boardwalk Association—310-392-4687, ext. 6.

SANTA MONICA STATE BEACH

A quarter-mile-wide band of sand wraps around the base of the oldest pleasure pier still standing on the West Coast. The Ferris wheel and roller coaster of the Pacific Park midway are visible for miles in both directions. An antique carousel spins away the troubles of its riders, though many are too young to have troubles. Fishing platforms are set below the main walkway, allowing more room for anglers. An information station at the pier's ocean end enlightens readers to Santa Monica's past. The original Muscle Beach, birthplace of the 1970s fitness boom is in the pier's south shadow. An erector-set-like array of metal-tubed structures give men a place to flex. Also left of the pier are the volleyball pits, a playground, and the Santa Monica International Chess Club. While it's not the scene from the movie *Searching for Bobby Fisher*, it is a refreshing display of chess. The South Bay Bicycle Trail runs along the inland side of the broad sands curving its way toward Torrance. Shapely men and women strut their stuff while traveling down the path on a variety of wheeled devices. Speaking of strutting, Santa Monica's nearness to Hollywood seems to bring out the exhibitionism in people. Thong bikinis, pumped muscles, and requisite dark shades (sunglasses) to complete the "I know you're looking, but I'm above noticing" look. The TV show *Pacific Blue* is based on the Santa Monica Beach Police, who are seen cruising the area. While a lot of the show is shot in Venice, the cops here do wear shorts and ride bikes.

ACCESS: Hwy 1 southbound runs along the northern portion of the beach.

From southbound Hwy 1—To reach the south side of the pier, exit onto Ocean Ave. as Hwy 1 turns left to briefly join up with I-10. From Hwy 1 northbound (Lincoln Blvd.), turn left on Pico Blvd. and then right onto Ocean Ave. to reach the southern side of the pier. Otherwise, continue on Hwy 1 by turning right off Lincoln Blvd. where Hwy 1 rejoins the coast.

From I-405—Exit onto I-10 and follow it straight to the coast.

The Tide Shuttle (310-451-5444) offers service along Ocean Ave., looping around on Main St. and Fourth St. It costs a quarter and runs from noon to 10:00 P.M.

PARKING: A large lot is on Ocean Ave at Hwy 1. More lots line the highway on the north side of the pier. Metered parking lies to the south of the pier on Ocean Ave. There are three parking structures on 2nd St. between Wilshire and Broadway. Three more parking structures lie between Wilshire and Broadway on 4th St.

HOURS/FEES: Metered parking is 50 cents per hour. Lots are $6, except on the parking pier where it's only $5.

AMENITIES: Pier, snack shack, volleyball, lifeguard, restrooms, showers, workout area, bike path, playground, picnic area.

ACTIVITIES: Everything under the sun, including chess.

FOR MORE INFORMATION:

Surf/weather Report—310-457-9701.

Los Angeles County Central Section Lifeguard Headquarters—310-394-3261.

Los Angeles Department of Harbors and Beaches—310-305-9503.

California State Parks, Angeles District Headquarters—818-880-0350.

Santa Monica Chamber of Commerce—310-394-4977 or 310-393-9825.

Santa Monica Convention and Visitors Bureau—310-319-6263.

Pacific Park—310-260-8744.

WILL ROGERS STATE BEACH

The long, gentle arc of sandy shore known as Will Rogers State Beach runs beneath the low bluff on which Pacific Coast Highway sits. While I've never found a beach I couldn't like, this one requires little effort to love. There's plenty of room on these flat sands for all, including hordes of volleyballers. Smiles are seen everywhere you look. The South Bay Bicycle Trail starts—or ends—here, depending upon your perspective, but then an optimist knows that endings are really beginnings.

ACCESS: Hwy 1 runs along the entire beach. Reach it from the south by taking I-10 from I-405. Will Rogers State Beach begins at Sunset Blvd. to the north and West Channel Rd. to the south.

PARKING: Parking lots line the ocean side of the highway. The closer to Santa Monica, the more expensive and full they are.

HOURS/FEES: $5 and $2 lots.

Amenities: Lifeguards, restrooms, showers, bike path.

Activities: Surfing, swimming, biking, sunbathing.

For more information:

Surf/weather Report—310-457-9701.

Los Angeles County Central Section Lifeguard Headquarters—310-394-3261.

Los Angeles Department of Harbors and Beaches—310-305-9503.

California State Parks, Angeles District Headquarters—818-880-0350.

Pacific Palisades Chamber of Commerce—310-459-7963.

He'e nalu (Hay-ay NA-lu) = "Wave Sliding" in Hawaiian

It started like any other surf session. I filled my old laundry-detergent jug with hot water, tossed it into a five-gallon plastic bucket with my wet suit, booties, and wax, shoved my board into the car, and headed for the surf. The little voice in my head that keeps things organized was silent. I had more things that "needed" to get done than time to do them...and here I was going surfing, but knowing my priorities, that little voice stayed silent.

The surf was probably going off at County Line, the Strand (Silver Strand Beach), Rivermouth (Surfer's Knoll), Stables (Ventura Fairgrounds), and Rincon, but I was looking more for solitude than great waves. I pulled onto the 101, headed north to Old PCH, and started hunting. I passed a group of people at Overheads (Emma Wood State Beach). The wind was making things pretty mushy. Still, about ten guys were out in the line-up. Passing a sloppy Solimar (Beach), I continued down the road. By this time I was driving on instinct, waiting for the "Stop here!" alarm to go off inside my head.

Things were looking pretty bleak when the mental chimes sounded and I pulled off the road. I was at a place where the waves are small and forgiving. I wondered why I stopped here, but I got out and suited up anyway. A nearby hill sheltered the water from the brunt of the day's wind and a handful of neoprene-clad wave riders were bobbing in the water. I squinted and looked up the coast. Another handful were out at the point, but, in between was a nice little peak (wave) without any company. I grabbed my 9'10" Stan Fujii custom longboard and started the long walk down the beach. Looking for a spot to go out, I notice several dolphin fins and decided this is the place. I put my board down on the sand, stretched out some of my body's kinks, strapped on my leash, and headed toward the water.

"Hi, Ma," I said aloud to the ocean, long over the self-conscious concern that others would hear my oceanic greeting. "How're ya doin?" I chuckled while wading into the water. The breeze was light and an offshore kelp bed smoothed the surface. Lying atop the board I started to stroke outside past the breaking waves.

Not quite past the impact zone (where the waves break), I saw a set wave rolling my way with three California brown pelicans surfing the air currents in front of it. They held formation, skimming the water, their wingtips feeling the wave's face. I watched them pass a few feet in front of me, then I turtled (rolled over) to avoid being pushed back toward shore by the breaking wave. Feeling the wave's energy pass by, I climbed back on my board and continued to paddle.

Outside (the breaking waves), I sat up. The wind had died down, but so had the waves. It didn't matter. My body was free of stress as I soaked up the sun and continued to scan the horizon for signs of another set. Noticing some action up the coast, I paddled into position. A nice wave was rolling my way. I turned and stroked into it. My board broke the water's grasp and began to plane as I stood. A quick bottom turn and I was angling along the wave. It didn't have much power, but I started climbing and dropping on the wave's face when I saw something that will forever be etched in my mind. There's a pair of dolphins surfing the same wave!

Their arched bodies glided effortlessly beneath the water, pushed by energy that was transferred to the water days ago by winds that were hundreds, maybe thousands, of miles away. I held my board's line (path) midway up the wave's face, managing to keep my excitement from spoiling my balance. For a few fleeting seconds I basked in the warmth of cross-species coexistence before the dolphins pulled out of the wave. I turned my head to watch, dug my rail into the wave's rapidly collapsing wall, and wiped out.

Reflecting back on those fifteen seconds, the warmth is still with me. I tell myself I was looking for solitude when in fact I was looking for unconditional acceptance. Unfortunately, surfers often compete and maneuver for position, attempting to score the best wave, but when you're surfing with others instead of against them, every wave is the sacred "wave of the day."

Today's line-ups see an assemblage of individuals representing diverse demographics. Women are more prevalent than at any time in surfing history. Others, who had left the sport while pursuing careers, are coming back to the water and rediscovering wave magic. This has the line-up crowded with old and new alike, which makes board control more important than ever.

Unfortunately, before anyone can really learn this, they need to spend some time in the water. Find a board about 2 or 3 feet longer than yourself that is very buoyant. Short, thin boards are hard to learn on. Next, grab a wet suit and head for the beach. A 3.2-mm full suit from fall through spring is popular around Ventura. The suits get thicker farther north and thinner to the south.

Spend time learning to move the board around and observe the dynamic environment. Being able to distinguish "inside" and "outside" is key to learning how to keep from obstructing other surfers. Also, note where other surfers are heading out. They find an easier way out that isn't in the way of those who are riding waves. Remember, everyone in the water was once a beginner. Smile a lot, be safe, try not to get in the way of a riding surfer, and the rest should take care of itself.

Finally, the surf shop is there to help. Staff can help pick a board that suits your style and ability or simply keep you stoked about the entire experience. Visit them often.

Hang loose, Brah.

REGION 12

MALIBU

Malibu. The word alone conjures up visions of bikini-clad maidens frolicking in an aquamarine playground while men with chiseled physiques slide down perfect waves. Well, in reality, the people frolicking are a cross section of Americana, the aquamarine playground is a bit dingy, and the wave riders are a healthy mix of men and women. Justified or not, the reputation stands, and Malibu remains the standard by which other California beach towns are measured.

The shoreline is a rugged ribbon of sand and rock winding beneath the Santa Monica Mountains as they plunge into the Pacific. This leaves little room for a highway, let alone a town. Mother Nature seems bent on spicing up the worry-free lives of celebrity residents, sending fires to strip the hills of vegetation and rain to saturate the ground, causing the soil to seek a new home in the ocean, often carrying man-made structures with it.

This very struggle is what makes Malibu unique. Despite man's attempts to tame it, nature's presence is here, casting her aura over the entire region. The beaches cover the spectrum from long, sandy strands to rocky coves mostly suited to underwater sports and tide-pool explorations. As you travel north up Highway 1, crowds and development diminish.

At first glance the town of Malibu seems like a series of strip malls between expansive, gated communities. Given time to explore, there is still plenty of charm in the mom-and-pop shops that coexist with the big-name chains. Adding excitement to any activity in Malibu is the possibility of bumping into one of the celebrity residents. The beach at Paradise Cove is where some of the famous folk get their coastal jollies unless they own an estate along Broad Beach.

Access

The region's mudslides and fires can close all access routes at any time.

From the north—Pacific Coast Hwy (PCH/Hwy 1) runs along the coastline from north to south beneath the Santa Monica Mountains. During the rains of winter, it is often closed from mudslides. To access Hwy 1, take State Hwy 27 (Topanga Canyon Blvd.) south from Hwy 101. This road winds through Topanga Canyon beside Topanga State Park and reaches Hwy 1 on the coast. Turn right and follow PCH (Hwy 1) into Malibu. Malibu Canyon Rd., Kanan Dume Rd., and Decker Rd. take similar paths to Hwy 1. The Mulholland Hwy connects these routes and makes for a scenic driving tour of the region's mountains.

From the south—Take I-405 northbound to I-10 westbound. Follow I-10 to northbound Hwy 1 and follow it into Malibu.

MALIBU

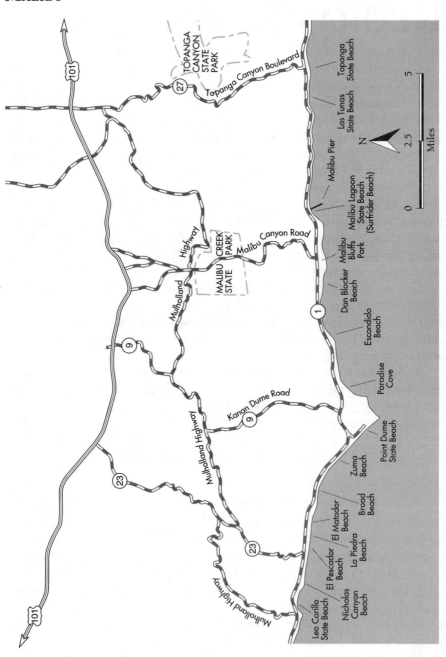

Beaches

Topanga State Beach

Las Tunas State Beach

Malibu Lagoon State Beach (Surfrider Beach)

Malibu Bluffs and Stairways

Dan Blocker Beach (Corral Beach and Solstice Beach)

Escondido Beach

Paradise Cove

Point Dume State Beach

Zuma Beach

Broad Beach

Robert H. Meyer Memorial State Beaches— Nicholas Canyon, El Pescador, La Piedra, El Matador

Leo Carrillo State Beach

Camping

Malibu Creek State Park—800-533-7275 or 818-880-0350. 60 sites, pets allowed, water, restrooms, picnic tables, showers.

Leo Carrillo State Beach—818-880-0350.

Sequit Canyon—138 sites with water, picnic tables, barbecue grills, showers, restrooms, and a dump station.

North Beach—32 sites on an old parking lot.

Malibu Beach RV Village—310-456-6052. 160 sites most with full hookups. Playground, laundromat, food store, showers, restrooms, and a dump station.

Topanga State Park—310-455-2465 or 310-454-8212. 1-mile hike, bike, or horseback ride into camping area. Water, restrooms, hitching rails, and water troughs for equestrian use.

Other points of interest

Topanga State Park—310-455-2465 or 310-454-8212. Mountain biking on fire roads and horseback riding on trails are popular in this park, presenting a cross section of the diverse coastal mountain habitat.

Charmlee County Park—A pleasant day-use park with multiple-use trails. There's an informative nature center that offers guided hikes.

Malibu Creek State Park—818-880-0367 or 818-880-0350. In addition to the campground (see above), the trails, picnic areas, and visitor center set among the striking natural beauty of creeks and canyons make this a spectacular park. A special Braille trail gives a unique opportunity for blind visitors touring the park. You may recognize the area from the TV series M*A*S*H.

Solstice Canyon Park—310-456-7154. A picturesque stream surrounded by tall trees runs through this park, which offers horse and hiking trails.

Adamson House—310-456-8432, just north of Malibu Lagoon State Beach. This national historic site highlights the tiles made by Malibu Potteries during the late 1920s. The 13-acre beachfront estate of a Moorish-Spanish Colonial Revival residence, built in 1929, is the base for this museum. There's even a 20-foot-long Persian rug made from tiles.

Santa Monica Mountains Conservancy—310-858-7272.

Santa Monica Mountains National Recreation Area—818-597-9192.

Mulholland Drive—named after William Mulholland, who made Los Angeles possible by creating the city's water system—connects Hollywood to Leo Carrillo State Beach. Along the way, overlooks of Hollywood Bowl and "the sign" are granted. A 7-mile dirt section makes for good mountain biking and is a surreal mix of wild within civilized walls. The stretch between Topanga State Park and the ocean connects to a variety of nature-laden places like Cold Creek Canyon Preserve (818-346-9675).

Paramount Ranch—818-597-9192. Ever watch *Dr. Quinn: Medicine Woman* and see the train pull into picturesque Colorado Springs? Well, that was up in the Santa Monica Mountains off Cornell Rd. near Mulholland Dr. It's a nice picnic area with an Old West set and a nature trail.

Peter Strauss Ranch—818-597-9192. Picnicking, trails, and a nature center accent the offerings of summer concerts in an outdoor amphitheater.

Elysium Fields—310-455-1000. A "clothing optional resort" in Topanga with pool, sauna, hot tub, tennis courts, and meeting rooms.

TOPANGA STATE BEACH

There are some who say that Topanga is a Chumash word for "where the mountains meet the sea." Others insist the name means "place of green water." Either of these is an apropos description of the beach. The Santa Monica Mountains rise out of the Pacific as the sand clings to the rocky embankment, which protects Pacific Coast Highway from the ocean's green waters. While the green seems to signify life, the waters of Santa Monica Bay are often fouled. A local group is making strides to inform an ignorant public of the ocean's plight, which means some bad press to those who pollute, which means the situation has improved slightly. Someday maybe those upstream will realize what they are really doing.

Topanga's shore doesn't have much room for land-based activities. For those there is Topanga State Park, an 11,000-acre playground with trails and fire roads for hiking, horsing, and biking within a rejuvenated wildland. The area has been populated since about 6,000 B.C., when humans lived off the area's flora and fauna. The Tongva, a group of Native Americans known as Gabrielenos to westerners, once lived here. Their language would interpret Topanga as "the place of the Tongva." No matter how you name it, this beach has some good waves. From the highway, surfers can often be seen bobbing in the water waiting for the perfect wave.

ACCESS: From Malibu, head south on Pacific Coast Hwy (Hwy 1). From Region 11, head north on PCH. The beach's address is listed as 18500 Pacific Coast Hwy.

PARKING: A large pay lot sits along PCH.

HOURS/FEES: Dawn to dusk, free. $4 for parking.

AMENITIES: Lifeguard.

ACTIVITIES: Surfing.

FOR MORE INFORMATION:

California State Parks—Angeles District—818-880-0350.

California State Parks—Angeles District; Topanga Sector—310-454-8212.

Topanga State Park—310-455-2465.

Wildflower Report—818-768-3533.

Los Angeles County Lifeguard, Northern Division—310-457-9891.

Los Angeles Department of Harbors and Beaches—310-305-9503.

Surf/weather Report—310-457-9701.

Malibu Chamber of Commerce—310-456-9025.

LAS TUNAS STATE BEACH

A rugged ribbon of sand and rocks runs along Pacific Coast Highway. It is recognizable by the wide, dirt pull-over. Old groins, hunks of metal once thought to be beneficial in fighting beach erosion, are hidden under the waves and can be dangerous to swimmers or surfers who don't know the region. It's now well accepted that groins actually do more harm than good by interrupting the littoral flow of sand. These rusty reminders of how human intentions don't guarantee results are visible at minus tides and make good subjects for surreal black-and-white photographs.

ACCESS: The unimproved parking area is north of Topanga Canyon Blvd. on Pacific Coast Hwy (Hwy 1) and south of Las Flores Canyon Rd. at 19400 PCH. There are also stairs to the beach a few blocks north of the parking area at 19900 PCH.

PARKING: The parking lot is at 19400 PCH.

HOURS/FEES: Dawn to dusk, free.

AMENITIES: Picnic tables, lifeguard.

ACTIVITIES: Diving, surfing.

FOR MORE INFORMATION:

Los Angeles County Lifeguard, Northern Division—310-457-9891.

Los Angeles Department of Harbors and Beaches—310-305-9503.

Surf/weather Report—310-457-9701.

Malibu Chamber of Commerce—310-456-9025.

MALIBU LAGOON STATE BEACH (SURFRIDER BEACH)

Malibu Lagoon State Beach is the Malibu that surfers made famous. Up the coast from the wooden pier is the area known as Surfrider Beach. Most days dawn to an ocean full of surfers spread over three places where the waves break with consistency. The sand then fills up with surf watchers. The Malibu Lagoon lies upshore of the beach. Its pungent waters are rumored to be the source of bizarre diseases caught by surfers. Recent efforts to save the bay have helped, but after a heavy rain, runoff makes the water downright dangerous. The lagoon's park has nature trails. picnic tables, and the Malibu Lagoon Museum, which has exibits relating to the area's Native American past.

The surfing action takes place at the Point, which includes First, Second, and Third Point, with the latter being farthest from the pier. With the right conditions it's possible to ride a quarter mile from Third through First Point. Second Point (also known as Kiddy Bowl) tends to see faster waves and performance shortboard surfing.

ACCESS: North of Las Flores Canyon Blvd. and south of Malibu Canyon Rd.on Hwy 1. The beach is accessed just north of Malibu Pier or from a trail by the lagoon, 23200 Pacific Coast Hwy.

PARKING: There are parallel parking spaces along Hwy 1 and a parking lot at Malibu Lagoon. There aren't many spaces, so arrive early.

HOURS/FEES: Sunrise to sunset, free.

AMENITIES: Pier, restrooms, showers, lifeguard, wildlife area, snack shack, volleyball nets.

ACTIVITIES: Hang 10, volleyball, sunbathing, fishing.

FOR MORE INFORMATION:

Los Angeles County Lifeguard, Northern Division—310-457-9891.

Los Angeles Department of Harbors and Beaches—310-305-9503.

Malibu Lagoon Museum—310-456-1770.

Surf/weather report—310-457-9701.

Malibu Chamber of Commerce—310-456-9025.

Malibu Lagoon State Park—310-456-8432.

MALIBU BLUFFS AND STAIRWAYS

Malibu Bluffs is a county park complete with picnic tables, ball fields, restrooms, and parking. The sandy beach at the bottom of the steps is uncrowded.

ACCESS: Take Hwy 1 to Malibu Canyon Rd. Turn right and park in the free lot across the field from Pepperdine University. It's over a mile to the beach. To reach the beach, follow the path to Malibu Rd., where a series of five stairways grants access to the beach. 24602 Malibu Rd. marks the middle staircase, all of which should be indicated with a "Coastal Access" sign.

PARKING: The park has a fee-free lot.

HOURS/FEES: Sunrise to sunset. The beach has no hours. Both are free.

AMENITIES: Picnic area, playground, hiking trail, restrooms.

ACTIVITIES: Picnicking, surfing, sunbathing, tide pool.

FOR MORE INFORMATION:

Los Angeles County Lifeguard, Northern Division—310-457-9891.

Los Angeles Department of Harbors and Beaches—310-305-9503.

Surf/weather Report—310-457-9701.

Malibu Chamber of Commerce—310-456-9025.

Dan Blocker Beach (Corral Beach and Solstice Beach)

We chased lady luck 'til we finally struck Bonanza.
With a gun and a rope and a hat full of hope we planted our family tree.
We got a hold of a pot full of gold, Bonanza!
With a horse and a saddle and a ring full of cattle, how rich can a fella' be?!
On this land we put our brand. Cartwright is our name.
Fortune smiled the day we filed the Ponderosa claim!
Here in the West we're living in the best Bonanza.
If anyone fights anyone of us, he's gotta fight with me!
—*as sung by Lorne Greene to the theme music of* Bonanza!

Perhaps they should've called this narrow band of sand beneath a rugged bluff Bonanza Beach. Maybe that would have quelled the beach's identity crisis. It was once called Solstice Beach, then Corral Beach, and now Dan Blocker Beach. Well, Dan Blocker Beach is correct. Dan was the guy who played Hoss Cartwright on television's *Bonanza*. Seems Lorne Greene (Daddy Cartwright), Michael Landon ("Little Joe" Cartwright), and some non-Cartwrights owned this land. The state was buying up shoreline for recreational use but couldn't afford the land, so the group gave 'em a break on price in exchange for memorializing the beach in their costar/friend's name.

Facilities are minimal. However, rumors of future improvements are circulating. For now there are water and restrooms.

Access: Take Pacific Coast Hwy (PCH/Hwy 1) north from Malibu Canyon Rd. or south from Kanan Dume Rd. The beach is accessed from PCH.

Parking: Park along PCH and obey the regulatory signs.

Hours/fees: Sunrise to sunset, free.

Amenities: Drinking water, restrooms.

Activities: Surfing, swimming.

For more information:

Los Angeles County Malibu Bluffs Park—310-317-1364.

Los Angeles County Lifeguard, Northern Division—310-457-9891.

Los Angeles Department of Harbors and Beaches—310-305-9503.

Surf/weather Report—310-457-9701.

Malibu Chamber of Commerce—310-456-9025.

Escondido Beach

Escondido Beach offers scuba diving and surfing to those brave souls who leave their cars unattended along Pacific Coast Highway (PCH). Walkways and stairs lead from PCH and over private property before coming to the slender beach. There aren't any facilities, but there aren't crowds either. Snorkeling, diving, and tide-pool exploring rule.

ACCESS: This beach is hard to find. The access options are marked with "Coastal Access" signs. Look for a group of three or four cars parked on the northbound side of PCH, which usually marks the entrance. The state lists the address for the stairs as 27150, 27400, and 27420 Pacific Coast Hwy. One staircase is near Malibu Cove Colony Dr. Another is next to the Seacliff condos. The other is in Geoffrey's (a restaurant) parking lot. The beach is south of the big Paradise Cove sign and north of Latigo Canyon Rd.

PARKING: Along PCH.

HOURS/FEES: 6:00 A.M. to sunset. Free.

AMENITIES: Restrooms, trail.

ACTIVITIES: Snorkeling, tide pool, hiking.

FOR MORE INFORMATION:

California Department of Parks and Recreation, Angeles District, Malibu Division—310-457-8140.

Surf/weather Report—310-457-9701.

Malibu Chamber of Commerce—310-456-9025.

Paradise Cove

This is the most exclusive of the public beaches partly because it isn't really public. The parking will set you back $15 at last check and can fluctuate. Why pay this much? Well, it keeps out the riffraff. Paradise Cove offers the best chance to see a star who's famous enough to live in Malibu but not famous enough to own a private beach. We ordinary people stroll the sands looking for someone famous while a few unrecognizable folk enjoy the relative seclusion that high prices bring. The television literate may recognize the *Rockford Files* setting. Sorry, he moved his trailer, but the pier is still here.

ACCESS: Take Hwy 1 to the big Paradise Cove sign and enter the private road that leads to the parking lot. This road is south of Kanan Dume Rd. and north of

Latigo Canyon Rd. It'd be legal to hike in from Escondido Beach as long as the hiking was done below the mean high-tide line and the hiker remained beneath this line at the beach.

PARKING: The only place to park is in the private lot.

HOURS/FEES: Sunup to sundown. $15.

AMENITIES: Restaurant, pier.

ACTIVITIES: Pier fishing, sunbathing, star searching.

FOR MORE INFORMATION:

Paradise Cove—310-457-2511.

Los Angeles County Lifeguard, Northern Division—310-457-9891.

Malibu Chamber of Commerce—310-456-9025.

POINT DUME STATE BEACH (WESTWARD BEACH)

This state beach starts where Zuma Beach turns southward and ends at rocky Point Dume (pronounced Doo may). This beach seems more exclusive than Zuma as the bluff is closer to the beach and the free parking is harder to come by. Californians pride themselves on beating the system, so sitting on the beach while others scan for empty parking spaces is cause to gloat. So how do you score a space at this wide stretch of golden-grained sand? Either by being early, lucky, or using the pay lot.

The sand closest to Zuma Beach is known as Westward Beach. The area in front of the state-run parking lot is Point Dume State Beach.

ACCESS: From Hwy 1, turn toward the ocean onto Westward Beach Rd. The road ends at the pay lot.

PARKING: Either parallel park along Westward Beach Rd. or continue into the pay lot.

HOURS/FEES: Parking is $5; open sunrise to sunset.

AMENITIES: Restrooms, showers, parking lot, lifeguard.

ACTIVITIES: Surfing, snorkeling, swimming, tide pool.

FOR MORE INFORMATION:

Los Angeles County Lifeguard, Northern Division—310-457-9891.

Los Angeles Department of Harbors and Beaches—310-305-9503.

Surf/weather Report—310-457-9701.

California State Parks, Angeles District, Malibu Sector Headquarters—
310-457-8143.

Malibu Chamber of Commerce—310-456-9025.

ZUMA BEACH

Zuma Beach is by far the most accessible of Malibu's shores. This strand's paid parking, restrooms, and snack shacks parallel Pacific Coast Highway for 2 miles between Point Dume State Beach and Broad Beach. In true California fashion, there is almost an equal amount of free parking along PCH. The scene is stereo-typical California with settlements of Barbies and Kens working on their bronze tans and practicing the social skills they will need to survive in Malibu or Hollywood. With the convenience of free parking, this beach is family friendly, and plenty of families spread out on these sands. Surfers call this the "Two-mile Close-out" in reference to the waves that hit the shore straight on, which causes them to break all at once. The result is a loud, thundering wave that isn't ridable. This same phenomenon makes for wicked rip currents. Watch the kids!

ACCESS: Hwy 1 runs the length of this beach. To reach the pay lots, turn on West-ward Beach Rd. at the south end of Zuma Beach. The big Zuma Beach sign is visible here. Immediately turn right onto Zuma Bay Way and into the lots.

PARKING: Either park in the lot described above or along Hwy 1 beside the beach's fence.

HOURS/FEES: Sunrise to sunset.

AMENITIES: Restrooms, showers, snack shacks, volleyball, playground, lifeguard.

ACTIVITIES: What don't they do here?! Well, they don't do much fishin' here.

FOR MORE INFORMATION:

Los Angeles County Lifeguard, Northern Division—310-457-9891.

Surf/weather Report—310-457-9701.

Malibu Chamber of Commerce—310-456-9025.

Los Angeles Department of Harbors and Beaches—310-305-9503.

California Department of Parks and Recreation, Angeles District, Malibu Division—310-457-8140.

Broad Beach

"Malibu" and "Beach" are almost synomymous. Broad Beach is yet another gem in the Malibu crown. With a name like Broad Beach you'd expect it to be wide, and it is. These golden sands lie near a point of land dubbed Trancas Point by surfers. The homes and land that face the beach are all private and parking is scarce, which keeps the crowds away. Of course, local landowners have their own steps and frequent *their* beach. It's a quiet change from the nearby party at Zuma.

Access: From Pacific Coast Hwy (PCH/Hwy 1), turn toward the ocean on Broad Beach Rd. "Coastal Access" signs denote the stairs to the beach at 31344 and 31200 Broad Beach Rd.

Parking: Some parking is allowed on the street. Obey all signs and don't block any of the driveways.

Hours/fees: Sunrise to sunset. Free.

Amenities: None.

Activities: Sunning, strolling, anonymity.

For more information:
Malibu Chamber of Commerce—310-456-9025.

Robert H. Meyer Memorial State Beaches (Nicholas Canyon, El Pescador, La Piedra, El Matador)

Nicholas Canyon, El Matador, La Piedra, and El Pescador all share a common set up: a gravel, self-pay parking lot atop a bluff connected to the shore via long steps or a dirt path. The scenery that awaits is also similar. Tall eroding cliff sides descend to sandy coves deposited between rocky points. The $2 fee and long walk keep the number of visitors down on most days. Sunbathing, strolling, and basic oceanic meditating are the forte here. Some die-hard surfers cart boards the half-mile to the breaks below.

Access: These areas each have a small, signed, fee parking area to the ocean side of Hwy 1. The addresses are 33150 Pacific Coast Hwy (PCH) for Nicholas Canyon, 32900 PCH for El Pescador, 32700 PCH for La Piedra; and 32350 PCH for El Matador.

Parking: Each area's lot is dirt and rutted. Parking along PCH is allowed.

HOURS/FEES: The lots cost $2 and gates close at sunset.

AMENITIES: Restrooms at the parking areas.

ACTIVITIES: Surf, private sunbathing.

FOR MORE INFORMATION:

Robert H. Meyer Memorial State Beaches—805-986-8591.

California State Parks, Angeles District, Malibu Sector Headquarters—310-457-8143.

Surf/weather Report—310-457-9701.

Malibu Chamber of Commerce—310-456-9025.

LEO CARRILLO STATE BEACH— NICHOLAS CANYON COUNTY BEACH

A "Giant Rock" sits in the small bay east of Sequit Point with gently peeling waves making their way to the horseshoe of sand that is Leo Carrillo State Beach. Its wide, inviting sands and developed amenities make this beach popular. Visitors from the north will notice the first signs of Los Angeles crowding as cars line Pacific Coast Highway and fill the parking lot. It's also the northernmost sample of the rugged shores and wide sands of Malibu. There are 150 camping sites here if a day at the beach isn't enough.

ACCESS: Drive north on Hwy 1 through Malibu and continue heading north. About 2 miles past Decker Rd. (Hwy 23), Hwy 1 descends a hill. The beach and its large, waterbound rock are visible in the valley. Turn right to enter the pay lot.

PARKING: Use the pay lot or find a space along the southbound side of Hwy 1.

HOURS/FEES: 6:00 A.M. to 10:00 P.M. $5 day use, $16 en-route camping.

AMENITIES: Snack shack, restrooms, showers, picnic area, trails, lifeguard, RV parking.

ACTIVITIES: Surfing, swimming, sunbathing.

FOR MORE INFORMATION:

Leo Carrillo State Park Ranger Station—805-986-8591.

Los Angeles County Lifeguard, Northern Division—310-457-9891.

Los Angeles Department of Harbors and Beaches—310-305-9503.

Surf/weather Report—310-457-9701.

CAMPING

The crescendo of the cricket chorus outside the nylon walls of the tent creates a deafening silence, which allows the mind to wander into corners of thought that have gathered cobwebs during a "civilized" existence. The sound of a twig's crack floods the brain with warm memories of a child terrified of what lurked beyond the tenuous security of the tent's walls. As an adult, the terror of the great unknown comes late during sleepless nights while locked safely behind thick walls and locked doors. The fear of a drooling, snarling beast lurking in the dark doesn't keep adults awake: It's the knowledge that the future is entirely in their hands. For some reason, that freeing knowledge can be paralyzing. Yet while camping beneath the immense sky, that same freedom to choose one's life path empowers. Camping frees the brain of society's stranglehold in the form of "should do this" and "have to do that." Living simply, even if for one fleeting moment, can help keep things in perspective. Southern California has a number of places to set up camp and get away from it all.

Camping along the Southern California Coast is generally oriented toward the recreational vehicle (RV) crowd. Many of the campgrounds consist of asphalt or cement parking areas nestled between grassy or dirt picnic areas. During the summer these fill up and RVs are packed in like sardines. In addition to the RV-motels, some lesser-known campgrounds still deliver a feeling of seclusion. A few campgrounds have separate sites designated for tents only. However, a tent is often treated just like an RV and given a parking space.

Currently campsites are reserved via the National Park Service's automated reservations system for most campgrounds. There is a seven-month window to book a space. At the start of any month, spaces become available seven months hence. Just showing up is a risky proposition and may lead to a stay in a hotel. A major credit card helps in the reservation process, but it is possible to pay via check or money order if the reservation is made far enough in advance. How far in advance is one of those funny mysteries in life. For reservations or to have specific questions answered, call 1-800-444-PARKS between the hours of 8:00 A.M. and 5:00 P.M., seven days a week.

A few campgrounds seem to stand out from the rest. Book far in advance to have any chance of getting a spot at one of them.

El Capitán State Beach—In addition to its secluded locale, the campground is well designed. Despite the crowds that use this area, it still feels quaint and cozy.

McGrath State Beach—The campground is set behind an extensive series of sand dunes and alongside a well-established estuary habitat. The beach here is uncrowded as is the nature trail.

Montaña de Oro—Spectacular flowers coat the coastal hill here in the summer. The rustic campground offers pit toilets, no amenities, and no crowds. This well-kept secret isn't on the park reservations system.

San Onofre State Beach—This popular area sits atop a bluff, providing a pleasant perch to view the sun setting into the Pacific, and it's near good surf, San Clemente, and Oceanside. The only drawback is the nearby nuclear power station. Odds are it won't have a meltdown when you're there.

Thorne Broomhill—This place is smack dab on the beach, so expect some wind along with sand in the food. It's nostalgic beach camping reminiscent of a time when camping on the beach meant camping on the beach.

Emma Wood State Beach—Clinging to a small section of coast between an extremely steep coastal hill and the ocean, Emma Wood State Beach offers camping right on the rocks. High tides paired with high surf can close this campground down. The group camping area is farther from the ocean and has grassy areas for those group activities.

Jalama County Beach Park (not on state reservation system)—805-736-3504. This is an excellent all-around campground. Located 14 miles from Hwy 1 and 25 miles from civilization, it is a self-contained campground with food available. This is the ultimate way to enjoy Jalama Beach.

Pismo Beach (North Campground)—Camping sites beneath eucalyptus trees that scrape the sky filled with orange and black Monarchs that flutter among the branches like pixies—and there is a wide sandy beach. The butterflies show up in November and stick around into the new year. A trail through the main eucalyptus grove is available to campers and noncampers for free.

STATE PARKS RESERVATION INFORMATION:

Camping Reservations—800-444-7275.

Reservations Outside the United States—916-638-5883.

Cancellations—800-695-2269.

TDD—800-274-7275.

Reservations are recommended for summer and holiday visits. Family campsites may be reserved up to seven months in advance but no less than 48 hours before you wish to arrive. Group campsites may be reserved up to six months in advance.

All major credit cards and traveler's checks are accepted to reserve campsites and tours. If reservations are made far enough in advance, payment can be made with a money order or a check, following your reservation confirmation by phone.

Reservation charges include a $7.50 processing fee in addition to the camping fees shown for each California State Park campground.

REGION 13

VENTURA COUNTY LINE TO OXNARD

The Santa Monica Mountains dive into the ocean, creating a rugged twisting coastline as they fall into the sea. Pacific Coast Highway (Hwy 1) winds along a shoreline shelf beneath the steep slopes of the mountains, a popular spot for Sunday drives. Sandy, pocket beaches, developed as camping and coastal play areas, break up the rocky cliffs. At Point Mugu, civilization returns with a navy base then the towns of Port Hueneme and Oxnard.

The region's southern beaches offer scarce amenities. The lifeguards, provided on a seasonal basis, can provide information on the tricky currents. Hiking, mountain biking, and camping are available at Point Mugu State Park.

Port Hueneme's beaches are divided by what was once a T-shaped pier. It became an L after some strong storms. It became a straight pier following a strong El Niño-driven storm in 1998. Port Hueneme was a crucial link in the Pacific Fleet's World War II role as the first deepwater harbor south of San Francisco. When Juan Rodriguez Cabrillo stopped by in October of 1542, he saw the Canalinos Indians, a Chumash tribe, in the area they called Hueneme, meaning "resting place" or "halfway," representing the stopping-off point for trips between Mugu and Ventura. The word is probably an attempt to make a Chumash word into a Spanish one. It's also been found as "Wynema" and "Y-nee-ma." I personally think it should be pronounced "Hwahy-nee-meh" with the "H" pronounced like the "H" in Hawaii.

Oxnard's coast starts with Channel Islands Harbor, followed by the return of sandy shores. Oxnard is actually situated on a dune plain that has been reclaimed by humans. Luckily, wide swaths of dunes still exist here in Mandalay and McGrath Parks, which also sport wide, uncrowded beaches. Oxnard built itself on the success of the port in Hueneme and capitalized on that harbor's success by shipping sugar beets. Meanwhile, the City of Oxnard realized another asset in its sandy shores. Hollywood was booming and needed shooting locations. Rudolph Valentino and Agnes Ayers were placed on the sand with a few hundred fake palm trees and *The Shiek* was filmed. Its success led to a flood of people who were surprised to find a land of swamps and sand dunes. Build it and they will come. Shrewd developers came up with three shoreside developments: Hollywood Beach, Silver Strand, and Hollywood by the Sea. The area filled up with a group of people with enough money to have pleasure boats, and these boats needed a place to park, which led to the digging of Channel Islands Harbor.

The region's northern beaches are the wide, dune-backed variety. While the harbors interrupt the natural flow of sand, dredging and relocating have helped

Ventura County Line to Oxnard

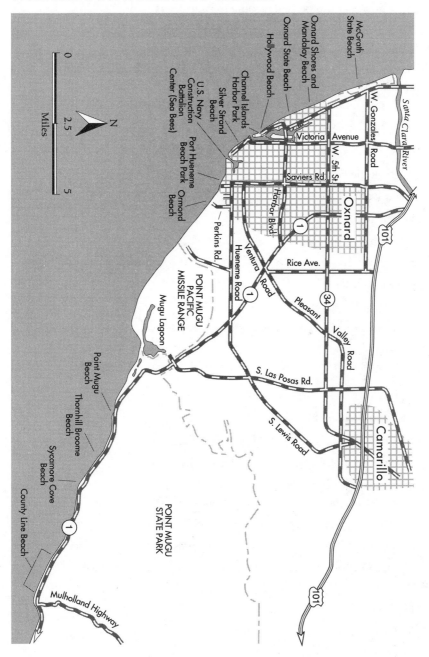

McGrath State Beach

Oxnard Shores and Mandalay Beach

Oxnard State Beach

Hollywood Beach

Channel Islands Harbor Park

Silver Strand Beach

U.S. Navy Construction Battalion Center (Sea Bees)

Port Hueneme Beach Park

Ormond Beach

W. Gonzales Road

Santa Clara River

W. 5th St.

Victoria Avenue

Saviers Rd.

Harbor Blvd.

Oxnard

101

Rice Ave.

Perkins Rd.

Hueneme Road

Ventura Road

POINT MUGU PACIFIC MISSILE RANGE

Mugu Lagoon

Pleasant

Valley Road

34

S. Las Posas Rd.

S. Lewis Road

Camarillo

Point Mugu Beach

Thornhill Broome Beach

Sycamore Cove Beach

County Line Beach

POINT MUGU STATE PARK

101

Mulholland Highway

0 2.5 5
Miles
N

restore the local shoreline. As the dunes point out, the region often has strong, afternoon winds that can be bothersome to sunbathers.

Access

Hwy 101 provides access to the entire region. The southern portion is accessed via Pacific Coast Hwy (Hwy 1), which can by reached by taking Las Posas Rd. south from Hwy 101 in Camarillo.

Beaches

County Line Beach (Staircase Beach)

Sycamore Cove Beach

Thornhill Broome Beach

Point Mugu Beach

Ormond Beach

Port Hueneme Beach Park

Silver Strand Beach

Hollywood Beach

Oxnard State Beach

Oxnard Shores and Mandalay Beach

McGrath State Beach

Camping

Camping Reservations—800-444-7275, cal-parks.ca.gov/travel/reserve/index.htm.

McGrath State Beach—805-654-4610. 175 sites.

Point Mugu State Park (see Point Mugu State Park below).

Camping without Reservations—916-653-6995.

Sycamore Canyon Campground—818-880-0350. 55 sites for tents and RVs, pay showers, restrooms, picnic tables w/ barbecue.

Danielson Ranch Group Camp—805-986-8484. A hike-in group site.

La Jolla Valley—818-880-0350. Hike-in campsites in the backcountry.

Thornhill Broome Beach—818-880-0350. 60 sites right on the beach, restrooms, picnic tables with barbecue grill.

Other points of interest

Point Mugu State Park—818-880-0350.

Sycamore Cove—805-986-8591. Hiking and biking among tall sycamore trees and rugged coastal canyons. La Jolla Valley, open to hikers, offers primitive camping in a wilderness setting. The hikers have 200 miles and horseback or bike riders have 65 miles of trails to explore.

Channel Islands Harbor—Visitor center, 800-994-4852 or 805-985-4852; harbor patrol, 805-382-3007; fuel dock, 805-984-1081. Sportfishing, whale watching, picnic area, dining, and shopping. Farmer's market every Sunday. Check out the Parade of Lights near Christmas.

Oxnard and Port Hueneme Visitor Information—800-269-6273 or 805-385-7545. Museums and numerous historic areas dot these two towns.

Carnegie Art Museum—805-385-8157.

Gull Wings Children's Museum—805-483-3005.

Port Hueneme Museum—805-488-2023.

Seabee Museum—805-982-5163.

Heritage Square—805-483-7960.

Ventura County Maritime Museum—805-984-6260. A model-ship enthusiast's dream. Exhibits include a model-ship builder's workshop and an extensive display on the local harbor's history. The history of the pleasure ship *La Jenelle*, a wreck that constitutes the southern jetty for Silver Strand Beach, is captured here in pictures and artifacts.

Oxnard Factory Outlet Stores—Outlet Center Dr. off Hwy 101. Big names in the retail world selling stuff at a discount.

County Line Beach (Staircase Beach)

Visible to passengers of vehicles on southbound Pacific Coast Highway, this spacious sandy coast alongside cliffs almost always has surfers sitting offshore. A kelp bed lies off County Line Beach and keeps the water smooth and glassy. This same submarine forest brings fishermen to the beach's northern end. Getting to the sand requires a dexterous jaunt down one of many eroded trails. Perhaps this explains the scarcity of non-surfing-and-fishing folks.

ACCESS: Pacific Coast Hwy (Hwy 1) is the only way to get to this beach.

From Santa Monica or Malibu—Follow Hwy 1 northbound. The beach is just up the hill from Leo Carrillo State Beach.

From Hwy 101 in Camarillo—Exit at Las Posas Rd., turn toward the ocean (right if southbound, left if northbound), and follow it to Hwy 1 southbound. It's about another 10 miles to the beach. Look for cars lining the wet side of Hwy 1 at the top of a hill. There is a small sign marking the county lines of Ventura County and Los Angeles County.

PARKING: Park along the ocean side of PCH. No overnight parking.

HOURS/FEES: Sunrise to midnight. Free.

AMENITIES: Porta Potty.

ACTIVITIES: Surfing, fish, sunbathing.

FOR MORE INFORMATION:

California State Parks, Angeles District—818-880-0350.

Water-quality Hotline—805-662-6555.

Water Testing Results—www.ventura.org/env_hlth/ocean.htm.

SYCAMORE COVE BEACH

The campsites in this coastal valley sit among tall, old trees inland of Sycamore Cove's horseshoe-shaped beach and are hot commodities. The beach is on the boundary of the Santa Monica Mountains' Point Mugu State Park and its hiking, biking, and equestrian trails. The ocean here is relentless with a powerful shore break and strong currents. Experienced bodyboarders (and kids whose parents don't know about the rip currents) are often the only ones in the water.

ACCESS: Located on Hwy 1, 4 miles south of Point Mugu Rock and 4 miles north of Leo Carrillo State Beach.

From Santa Monica or Malibu—Follow Hwy 1 northbound.

From Ventura or Inland Los Angeles—Take Hwy 101 to the city of Camarillo, exit at Las Posas Rd., turn toward the ocean (right if southbound; left if northbound), and follow it to Hwy 1 southbound.

PARKING: Both sides of Hwy 1 have some room to pull over and park. A pay lot is located east of Hwy 1 in Sycamore Canyon.

HOURS/FEES: 9:00 A.M. to sunset. $6 day use, $18 to camp.

AMENITIES: Lifeguard, picnic area, restrooms, showers, barbecue grills, trails.

ACTIVITIES: Sunbathing, hiking, biking, picnicking.

FOR MORE INFORMATION:

California State Parks, Angeles District—818-880-0350.

Camping Reservations—800-444-7275, cal-parks.ca.gov/travel/reserve/index.htm.

Camping without Reservations—916-653-6995.

Water-quality Hotline—805-662-6555.

Water Testing Results—www.ventura.org/env_hlth/ocean.htm.

THORNHILL BROOME BEACH

Once upon a time there was simply Pacific Coast Hwy (PCH) passing a wide, sandy beach. Humans came along, put in another road with a parking place, and put up a fence, thus establishing Thornhill Broome Beach. Now winds carry sand to cover up the "improvement" like a cat in a litterbox. The result is a line of cars parked on both sides of a fence and a broad patch of sand. The campground is right on the beach. Count on getting sand in the sleeping bags. Day users park along PCH and walk through one of the many holes in the fence.

ACCESS: Located on Hwy1, 4 miles south of Las Posas Rd. and 3 miles north of Sycamore Cove

PARKING: Along the west side of Hwy 1 or in the campground/day-use parking lot.

HOURS/FEES: 9:00 A.M. to dusk. $5 to enter the parking lot. It's free to park along Pacific Coast Hwy.

AMENITIES: Restrooms, showers, lifeguard, picnic tables, campground.

ACTIVITIES: Camping, picnicking, sunbathing, surfing.

FOR MORE INFORMATION:

California State Parks, Angeles District—818-880-0350.

Camping Reservations—800-444-7275, cal-parks.ca.gov/travel/reserve/index.htm.

Camping without Reservations—916-653-6995.

Water-quality Hotline—805-662-6555.

Water Testing Results—www.ventura.org/env_hlth/ocean.htm.

POINT MUGU BEACH

Point Mugu Rock is recognizable to car-advertisement watchers. Pacific Coast Highway passes precariously between the monolithic boulder and its big brother, the mountain. Below the rock and to the north is narrow, sandy Point Mugu Beach. Climbers who haven't found a less crumbly rock on which to practice flock here on weekends and are seen cooling off in the Pacific, then sprawling on the sand like the marine iguanas of the Galapagos Islands.

The name Mugu is a westernization of a word in the language of the Chumash, the area's early inhabitants. Their word, "Muwu," is said to mean beach.

ACCESS: Hwy 1 provides access to this beach. Take the Las Posas Rd. Exit from Hwy 101 and head toward the ocean. Join Hwy 1 southbound and travel 2.5 miles to Point Mugu Rock.

PARKING: Park on the ocean side of the road in the dirt on either side of Point Mugu Rock.

HOURS/FEES: 8:00 A.M. to sunset. Free.

AMENITIES: None.

ACTIVITIES: Fishing, tide pools, climbing.

ORMOND BEACH

The sands of Ormond Beach arc slightly from the ocean as they reach inland toward a series of dunes. Unfortunately, the rest of the surroundings show the industrialization that made Port Hueneme so important during World War II. This beach doesn't make it onto postcards, but it's clean and uncrowded. Graffiti marks the southern access point and a paper mill bounds the beach on the north. As a result it is difficult to enjoy the solitude.

ACCESS: From Hwy 101, take Pleasant Valley Rd. toward the ocean (that's left after the exit if northbound). Follow this road for 12 miles as it heads to Port Hueneme. Turn left on Perkins Rd. and drive another mile to the parking lot. A path leads past the dunes to the beach.

From Hwy 1, take Hueneme Rd. toward the ocean and turn left at Perkins Rd. Arnold Rd., off Hueneme Rd., leads to the beach's south end.

PARKING: Parking lot at the end of Perkins Rd.

HOURS/FEES: Always open

AMENITIES: None. Established dunes.

ACTIVITIES: Walking, surfing, being alone.

FOR MORE INFORMATION:

Oxnard Recreation Department—805-385-7995.

Oxnard Parks Division—805-385-7950.

Water-quality Hotline—805-662-6555.

Water Testing Results—www.ventura.org/env_hlth/ocean.htm.

PORT HUENEME BEACH PARK

The main focal point of Port Hueneme Beach Park is the pier. Unfortunately, it's been through some rough times of late. It used to be a T-shaped pier until an angry storm lopped off one of its arms, making it an L-shaped pier. Then the famed El Niño of 1998 lopped off the other arm. Not to worry: It is but a flesh wound to this 24-hour, lighted stalwart of a fishing platform, complete with cleaning sinks. The wide beach is but part of the park's popularity. There is a picnic area with tables, grills, and a grassy play area. All this is in uncrowded and unknown Port Hueneme (commonly pronounced Why-nee-mee).

The beach's sand disappeared after Port Hueneme Harbor was built in 1939. The new harbor interrupted the flow of sand to the south and Hueneme and Mugu soon lost their beaches. It rapidly became apparent that something had to be done if the town was to remain on dry land. Now sand is transported around the subter-ranean canyon that makes the harbor so useful.

ACCESS: From Hwy 101 exit onto Ventura Rd. and head toward the ocean. Drive through Oxnard and into the city of Port Hueneme. The road continues into Surfside Dr. Turn left and follow the road to parking.

PARKING: The lot here is self-pay. Some limited, streetside parking is available. The town rigorously enforces parking regulations.

HOURS/FEES: Sunup to 10:00 P.M. $2 for parking.

AMENITIES: Pier, volleyball, restrooms, picnic tables, grills, playground.

ACTIVITIES: Volleyball, surfing, picnicking, sunbathing.

FOR MORE INFORMATION:

Port Hueneme Recreation Administration—805-986-6555.

Water-quality Hotline—805-662-6555.

Water Testing Results—www.ventura.org/env_hlth/ocean.htm.

SILVER STRAND BEACH

Known by locals simply as the Strand, Silver Strand Beach is a half-mile of wide, gray-white and tan beach between two breakwaters. The east jetty has large, rusty metal outcroppings. Actually, it's an old ship that was immortalized as a breakwater. The *La Jenelle*, a 465-foot pleasure ship weighing 12,500 tons, was anchored offshore to avoid the fees in the harbor. It had recently had its name changed from the *Bahama Star*. Prior to that it was *The Arosa Star*, after it was the *Porto Rico*. The ship started life as *The Borinquen*. Sea superstitions say that renaming a ship is bad luck. Not to disappoint, a storm blew *La Jenelle* into the rocks on April 13, 1970, and the two crew members, unable to start the ship in time to save her, had to be rescued by helicopter. The ship's stern hit the harbor's north jetty, filled with water, and rolled onto her port side. The wreck lay on the jetty to be picked apart. Later, part of her hull was cut into sections, pulled seaward, and sunk to become an artificial reef. The remainder of the hull was rocked over and remains in the jetty at the south end of Silver Strand Beach. The parking lot there has a plaque memorializing the event.

The waves here are thought to be "always bigger" than anywhere nearby. It is also known to suffer from "localism," a self-governing technique surfers use to keep crowds to a minimum. Usually localism is simply rumors and innuendo. However, here it was guerilla warfare. Cars were stolen and nonlocal surfers (unlocals) beaten up. Nowadays things are pretty mellow. Nonsurfers wouldn't notice a thing and are free to happily enjoy the Strand. Nonlocals will still feel uncomfortable on a crowded day when the waves are good. However, it seems the police have the major source of trouble controlled: "Incidents" have declined significantly. One of the best parts of the Strand is Pepe's taco stand at Rossmore Drive and Roosevelt Boulevard. His fish tacos could be the best on the coast.

ACCESS: From Hwy 101, exit on Victoria Ave. and head away from the hills. Follow Victoria Ave. into Channel Islands Harbor. Victoria ends at an irregular four-way intersection. Turn right on San Nicholas Ave., which runs along the harbor and ends in a parking lot. Ocean Dr. runs the length of the Strand.

PARKING: The lot at the end of San Nicholas Ave. Another lot sits at the end of Ocean Dr. However, wind sometimes blows sand across the road, closing it.

HOURS/FEES: 5:00 A.M. to 10:00 P.M. Free.

AMENITIES: Jetty, restrooms, lifeguard, volleyball, parking lot.

ACTIVITIES: Surfing, sunbathing, volleyball.

FOR MORE INFORMATION:

Oxnard Recreation Department—805-385-7995.

Oxnard Parks Division—805-385-7950.

Water-quality Hotline—805-662-6555.

Water Testing Results—www.ventura.org/env_hlth/ocean.htm.

HOLLYWOOD BEACH

Hollywood Beach's sand creates a wide boundary between fancy beach homes and the ocean as it reaches from the harbor's western shore to Oxnard State Beach. Parking is plentiful but requires a short walk to reach the beach. Of course, for many, that beats paying to play at Oxnard State Beach. A massive dune structure has settled in at the east end of the beach behind the harbor's breakwater. This end also has the volleyball nets placed strategically outside a small tavern. The facilities on the beach are often locked, making necessary a journey to the harbor's buildings a couple blocks inland. The west end of the beach contains additional volleyball poles. The northern Ventura County coast and the Channel Islands are visible on clear days. Kite aficionados take note: It's often windy here and the beach has plenty of space to fly. At the end of Ocean Drive and Harbor Boulevard is a small grassy picnic area, Channel View Park.

ACCESS: From Hwy 101, exit onto Victoria Ave. and head south, away from the hills of Ventura. Turn right on Channel Islands Blvd. just before Victoria Ave. enters the harbor. The road crosses a bridge. Immediately after the bridge turn left. A Y-intersection is next. Left takes you along Harbor Blvd. to the large parking lots of the harbor; right leads to the beach's frontage road, Ocean Dr.

PARKING: On-street parking is sometimes available along Ocean Dr. If not, park in the harbor's lots. Be sure not to park in the permit-only spaces that surround the yacht club. There are thirteen spaces at Channel View Park at the junction of Ocean Dr. and Harbor Blvd.

HOURS/FEES: Always open, no fee.

AMENITIES: Volleyball nets.

ACTIVITIES: Sunbathing, surfing, volleyball.

FOR MORE INFORMATION:

Oxnard Recreation Department—805-385-7995.

Oxnard Parks Division—805-385-7950.

Water-quality Hotline—805-662-6555.

Water Testing Results—www.ventura.org/env_hlth/ocean.htm.

OXNARD STATE BEACH

The broad sands of Oxnard State Beach beach connect to Hollywood Beach on the east and Oxnard Shores Beach on the west. A series of smooth, cement paths (and a couple not-so-smooth ones) dodge the dunes and end up in a large grassy park and picnic area, making this a popular place with in-line skaters. The paths include benches from which to watch the ocean. The pay lot keeps crowds down as the beaches on either side are free.

ACCESS: From Hwy 101 exit onto Victoria Ave. and head south, toward the ocean. After 4 miles turn right on 5th St. Turn left on Harbor Blvd. and travel to the signed entrance at Mandalay Beach Rd. on the right.

PARKING: Park in the self-pay lots along Mandalay Beach Rd.

HOURS/FEES: Sunrise to sunset. $2 to park.

AMENITIES: Restrooms, bike path, picnic area, handicapped-accessible boardwalk through dunes.

ACTIVITIES: In-line skating, biking, surfing, sunbathing.

FOR MORE INFORMATION:

California State Parks, Channel Coast District—805-899-1400.

California State Parks, Channel Coast District, Ventura Sector—805-654-4610.

Water-quality Hotline—805-662-6555.

Water Testing Results—www.ventura.org/env_hlth/ocean.htm.

OXNARD SHORES AND MANDALAY BEACH

Oxnard Shores and Mandalay Beach are about 50 yards of light tan sand that stretches between two breakwaters. The facility-free beach is backed by a row of homes awaiting the eventual storm that will flood them. The Ventura coast, westward to Rincon, is visible as are Anacapa Island and Santa Cruz Island. The surf here moves around with the sand but can be a fun beach break for local surfers during "morning glass." Neptune Square, at Neptune Place and Mandalay Road, has a swing set and a basketball goal. A wide set of dunes sits off the end of Amalfi Way.

ACCESS: From Hwy 101 exit onto Victoria Ave. and head south, toward the ocean. After 4 miles turn right on 5th St., which ends at the beach. Mandalay Beach Rd. runs the length of the strand with a few minor detours.

PARKING: On-street parking along Mandalay Beach Rd.

HOURS/FEES: No hours. No fees.

AMENITIES: None.

ACTIVITIES: Swimming, surfing, sunbathing, fishing.

FOR MORE INFORMATION:

Oxnard Recreation Department—805-385-7995.

Oxnard Parks Division—805-385-7950.

Ventura County Parks Department—805-654-3963.

Ventura County Parks, Operations Department—805-654-3934.

Water-quality Hotline—805-662-6555.

Water Testing Results—www.ventura.org/env_hlth/ocean.htm.

McGrath State Beach

This is one of my favorite campgrounds in Southern California. The coastal dunes are relatively healthy and wide, thanks to a consistent effort by officials to educate visitors. A nature trail into the Santa Clara Estuary Natural Preserve touches on the diversity and importance of our coastal resources. The beach, wide and sandy, is at the end of a long trail. The effort is rewarded with a pristine shoreline where birds dart back and forth in search of lunch. Anacapa Island and Santa Cruz Island are sometimes visible straight offshore, to the south.

Migratory birds flock to freshwater McGrath Lake, accessible by a dune-crossing path. A self-guided tour on the park's nature trail affords access to the estuary, which is known to deliver some of California's best birding.

ACCESS: From Hwy 101 exit onto Victoria Ave. and head south, toward the ocean. Turn right on Olivas Park Rd. Pass by the historic Olivas Adobe to Harbor Blvd. and turn left. The park's signed entrance is a mile down the road on the right.

PARKING: Day-use parking lot in the park.

HOURS/FEES: 8:00 A.M. to 8:00 P.M. $5 for day use, $18 for camping.

AMENITIES: Lifeguard, nature trails, camping.

ACTIVITIES: Swimming, boogie boarding, birding, kite flying, beachcombing, sandcastle building.

FOR MORE INFORMATION:

McGrath State Beach—805-654-4744.

Camping Reservations—800-444-7275, cal-parks.ca.gove/travel/reserve/index.htm.

California State Parks, Channel Coast District—805-899-1400.

California State Parks, Channel Coast District, Ventura Sector—805-654-4610.

Water-quality Hotline—805-662-6555.

Water Testing Results—www.ventura.org/env_hlth/ocean.htm.

BENEATH THE SURFACE

The ocean surface undulates to a rhythm whose beat goes unheard in the civilized world. It rises and falls in time with the phases of the moon as the lovelorn stare out over it. With the dying light of the day, it takes on a metallic quality, looking like a flag made of mercury that flaps in the breeze. Surely the ocean is beautiful on the surface. Whoever said beauty is only skin deep didn't understand beauty, for beauty can be found at the greatest of depths.

Scuba diving allows humans to break the bonds of land and experience the weightlessness of submarine living. Many nondivers consider the sport difficult, dangerous, and expensive. In truth, diving is easily learned, safe, and reasonable on the purse strings. What other sport teaches you proficiency for under $300? Scuba, taught to people from twelve years old on up, is a sport that knows no age limits. Some people, bound by wheelchairs on land, have trained to become great divers. Diving does require a buddy, which can be difficult for the soloist. Not to fear! A number of dive clubs exist. These are great places to link up with like-minded aquanauts, as are the frequent dive trips offered by dive shops. For those without the time, money, or desire to get certified for scuba, snorkeling provides a similar experience.

Once in this alien underwater environment, a whole world of possibilities opens up. Some divers take to celluloid endeavors and photograph the sights. Others seek "bugs" (lobsters) for their dinner plates. Spear fishing has a big following, too. (Keep in mind that these last two activities are regulated.) The best places to dive are often in reserves or sanctuaries and thus closely monitored. The precautions for handling sea creatures in tide pools apply underwater, too.

The Channel Islands National Marine Sanctuary and Catalina Island make up one of the world's most desirable diving areas. A variety of habitats can be seen on one dive without traveling long distances. No doubt you'll be mesmerized by the kelp forests, reefs, and wrecks abounding with life, but don't forget to surface.

REGION 14

CHANNEL ISLANDS NATIONAL PARK

Endangered wildlife seeks sustenance on thin-soiled islands of rock, which stand defiantly against pounding waves and howling winds just 14.5 miles across the Santa Barbara Channel from the coast of Ventura. These are the wild shores of Channel Islands National Park's five islands: Santa Barbara, Anacapa, Santa Cruz, Santa Rosa, and San Miguel. The Channel Islands actually consist of eight islands. However, the islands of San Nicholas and San Clemente are off-limits to we mere mortals as they are military reservations. Santa Catalina, technically one of this chain, is covered elsewhere. The National Park Service shares custody of Santa Cruz Island with The Nature Conservancy's Santa Cruz Island Preserve.

Each island in the chain, sometimes called the Galapagos of California, is unique and worthy of extensive exploration by nature enthusiasts. The elusive island fox, only found here, and numerous pinnipeds are common attractions. The park contains the largest elephant seal rookery in the world.

Every island here has suffered indignities from humans and is at a different stage of recovery. Having been used as ranches and even artillery ranges, the islands now lick their wounds while endemic plants stuggle to regain their hold on the land. The endemic animals face long odds. However, staff are diligent in their efforts to restore the park's environment and health to a survivability level.

Channel Islands National Park is in charge of protecting its islands and the water surrounding them. The liquid portion of the park is called Channel Islands National Marine Sanctuary. Recreational fishing is allowed with a license. Scuba divers flock to the sanctuary, which consists of 125,000 submerged acres and 1,252 square nautical miles surrounding the islands that comprise one of the top fifty dive locations in the world. The visitor center offers informative and entertaining lectures, an indoor tide pool, permits for camping, and other park information at its location in Ventura Harbor (805-658-5730).

This pristine solitude lies a short distance across the channel and is accessible only via boat or plane. Boat owners can make the trip themselves as each island offers public anchorage. The park's concessionaires, Island Packers and Channel Islands Aviation, can transport sightseers and campers who don't own boats.

Access

From the south—Take Hwy 101 northbound toward Ventura, exit on Victoria Ave., and turn left. Turn right on Olivas Park Dr. and cross Harbor Blvd. The road becomes Spinnaker Dr. Continue on Spinnaker Dr. to the visitor center and park headquarters.

From the north—Take Hwy 101 southbound toward Ventura, exit on Seaward, and turn left onto Harbor Blvd. Continue to Spinnaker Dr., turn right, and follow this road to the visitor center. From park headquarters, cross the parking lot to Island Packers' office. Island Packers also offers limited service from Channel Islands Harbor and Santa Barbara Harbor.

Island Packers—Reservations, 805-642-1393; recorded information, 805-642-7688. Ocean-going transportation to the islands. Tours and transportation available.

Channel Islands Aviation—805-987-1301, www.flycia.com. Access to Santa Rosa and Santa Cruz by air. Tours and transportation available.

National Ocean Survey Charts—Private boaters use charts 18720, 18729, and 18756. Check with the visitor center for required permits.

Parking

Island Packers has a small lot. If it's full, cross the road to the Peninsula Beach lot. Channel Islands Aviation leaves from the Camarillo Airport, which provides ample free parking.

Islands

Santa Barbara Island

Anacapa Island

Santa Cruz Island

Santa Rosa Island

San Miguel Island

Camping

Camping is available on each island with a permit. Call 805-658-5730 for information. When securing a permit, know the size of your group, the method of transportation, trip dates, and an emergency contact.

SANTA BARBARA ISLAND

Santa Barbara Island, the southernmost of the park's islands, lies 38 miles off the coast of Long Beach and has an area of about 1 square mile. When the coreopsis and goldfields are in bloom, the island looks like a bright yellow spot on an immense sea-blue canvas. The coreopsis, visible on all the islands, is a plant with thin, rubbery, green leaves; a thick stalk; and yellow blooms that grows in forestlike patches. While not a tree, it is the tallest plant on the island. In some places it is 10 feet tall. The rugged shoreline is dotted with caves, making for excellent kayaking. The area is also a rookery (birthing place) for seals and sea lions, which means you

Santa Barbara Island

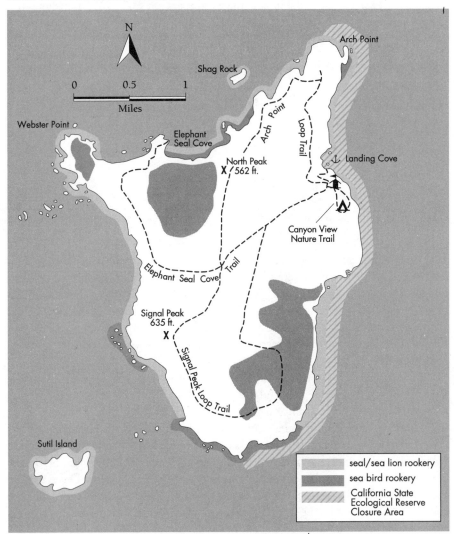

should call the park for current regulations and keep your distance from the animals. The largest nesting site in the world of the Xantus' murrelet, a seabird species, is on the island's cliffs. A number of other plants and animals, only found in the Channel Islands, live here. This is the only place in the park that the island night lizard, which looks positively prehistoric, is found.

Access: Island Packers schedules infrequent trips here, mostly in winter and spring. Package tours are available. The landing cove is the suggested anchorage for private boaters. There are no moorings.

HOURS/FEES: Call Island Packers for a schedule. The trip takes about 12 hours and the cost is $49 per adult and $35 per child. Campers pay $65 to $75 for round-trip shuttle service.

AMENITIES: Picnic tables, trails, campground, outhouse.

ACTIVITIES: Hiking, wildlife, photography, scuba diving, kayaking, snorkeling.

FOR MORE INFORMATION:

Santa Barbara Island Ranger (landing information)—VHF Channel 16.

Channel Islands National Park—805-658-5730, www.nps.gov/chis.

Island Packers—805-642-7688. Reservations, 805-642-1393.

ANACAPA ISLAND

Welcome to Anacapa Island. A bleached-white tower stands atop an isolated bluff, whose rocky cliffs are completely surrounded by water. California brown pelicans glide into their homes along the rocky cliffs beneath an island set ablaze by fields of magenta and orange iceplant blooms. Actually, the accessible portion of the island is known as East Anacapa. Middle Anacapa has some shoreline access, but West Anacapa is home to the recovering California brown pelican, which means the area is off-limits.

Anacapa, the closest island to Ventura, is sometimes visible from the mainland. However, the marine layer (also known as fog) often allows the island to play hide-and-seek with the California coast. This earned the name "Eneepah" from the Chumash, meaning "mirage island," which has evolved into Anacapa.

While the general public can't access the one beach here (Frenchy's Cove Beach) without a kayak or skiff, East Anacapa Island is an unforgettable excursion. This ocean-bound rock houses a number of birds on top and plenty of sea life below. Divers explore the kelp forest and kayakers check out the rocky shore's caves. Island Packers, the park concessionaire, combines the trip with whale-watching boats, and there's tent camping available that feels a bit like sleeping on the moon, except for all the birds.

Arch Rock, probably the most photographed site in the park, sits off the island's east end. After climbing the 154-step steel staircase to the island proper, a series of trails are available for hiking. The old lighthouse is off-limits due to the searing sound of the fog horn. However, a museum in one of the old Coast Guard buildings (officially called the East Anacapa Visitor Center) houses the beacon's lens, along with a brief history lesson.

Frenchy's Cove and East Fish Camp are anchorages provided for scuba divers and snorkelers. These are located on the north and south sides of Middle Anacapa Island respectively. Frenchy's Cove Beach is the only beach accessible without a permit.

ANACAPA ISLAND

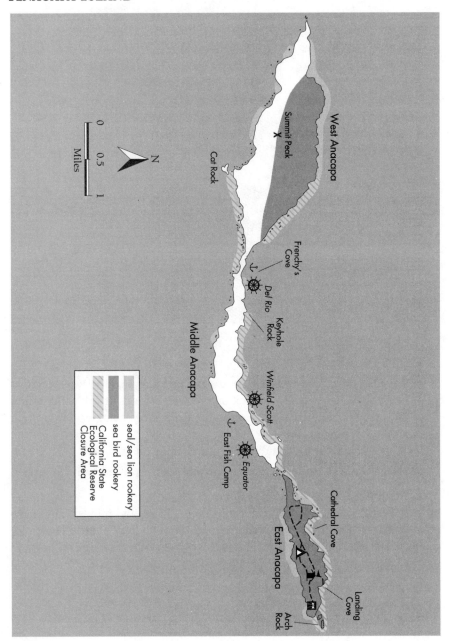

ARCH ROCK, OFF THE EASTERN END OF ANACAPA ISLAND, IS ONE OF THE MOST POPULAR PHOTOGRAPHIC SUBJECTS IN CHANNEL ISLANDS NATIONAL PARK.

Anacapa has more than 130 sea caves explorable by kayak. However, wildlife is very sensitive to human activity. Check over the regulations at the park's visitor center, and keep in mind that if the creature's behavior is being caused by your presence, then you're too close.

Don't forget to bring food and water. There's none on the island.

ACCESS: Island Packers makes frequent trips here from April through November.

PARKING: Not necessary.

HOURS/FEES: Island Packers' boats leave in the morning and midday and return around 5:00 P.M. $32 to $37 for adults and $20 for children. Shuttle service for campers is $48 for adults, $30 for children. It's free if you have your own boat.

AMENITIES: Restrooms, museum, fixed dock, two moorings.

ACTIVITIES: Hiking, wildlife, photography, scuba diving, kayaking, snorkeling.

FOR MORE INFORMATION:

Anacapa Island Ranger (landing information)—VHF Channel 16.

Channel Islands National Park—805-658-5730, www.nps.gov/chis.

Island Packers—805-642-7688. Reservations, 805-642-1393.

SANTA CRUZ ISLAND

This is a shared island. The Nature Conservancy owns the western 90 percent and the National Park Service controls Santa Cruz's eastern 10 percent. The park runs a campground and maintains a series of roads and trails that allow vistas of rocky shores, grassy hills, nearby Santa Rosa Island, and possibly an island fox.

Scorpion Ranch, founded in the late nineteenth century, is just inland of the pebbly beach that serves as the skiff landing for the island. Farther down the trail, nestled in the soft shade of a eucalyptus grove, sits the campground. While the eucalyptus trees are not native to the island, they offer the only substantial shade. However, the trees' shelter can be deceiving. Their root systems are shallow, which allows strong winds to topple the larger, top-heavy individuals.

Trails to Scorpion Bluffs, Cavern Point, Potato Harbor, San Pedro Point, and Smugglers Cove provide distinct island experiences. The latter two hikes take too long for those visiting only for the day. Smugglers Cove is another historic ranch site.

Santa Cruz's east end is now rid of the domestic sheep that helped perpetuate the persistence of nonnative grasses. It will be interesting to watch the progress of endemic flora as it returns to the island.

SANTA CRUZ ISLAND

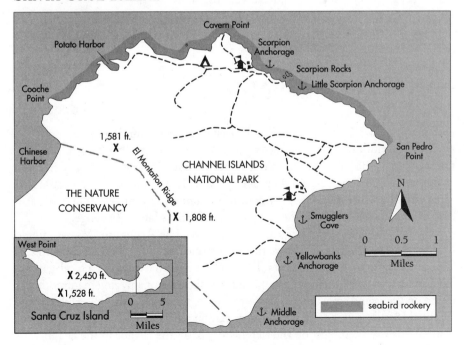

The remaining 90 percent of the island is The Nature Conservancy's Santa Cruz Island Preserve and requires a permit for visitation.

ACCESS: Island Packers provides year-round service to both east and west portions of the island. Package tours are available. Reaching the eastern side (National Park Service) of the island requires a skiff, which means prepare for your stuff to get wet. The existing moorings are for the Park Service and Coast Guard only.

Channel Islands Aviation services this island.

HOURS/FEES: Call Island Packers for schedule. The trip takes about 9 hours and the cost is $42 to $49 for adults and $25 for children (no children allowed on the West Santa Cruz trip). Campers pay $54 per adult and $40 per child for round-trip shuttle service. By air it's $85 per adult and $65 per child, or $150 for a camper shuttle. Air package tours are available.

AMENITIES: Restrooms, campground.

ACTIVITIES: Hiking, wildlife, photography, scuba diving, kayaking, snorkeling.

FOR MORE INFORMATION:

Santa Cruz Island Ranger (landing information)— VHF Channel 16.

Channel Islands National Park—805-658-5730, www.nps.gov/chis.

The Nature Conservancy—805-962-9111.

Island Packers—805-642-7688. Reservations, 805-642-1393.

Channel Islands Aviation—805-987-1301, www.flycia.com.

SANTA ROSA ISLAND

Listen to the wind. It speaks volumes. Listen for the sounds of the 5-foot-tall pygmy mammoth moseying along Santa Rosa's grasslands. Listen for the Arlington Woman as she gathers food in the Torrey pine forest. Listen for the Chumash as they enjoy life on the island they called Wima. Listen for the baying cattle that came with the white man. See how nature overcomes everything that humans dish out (or introduce). Watch as the land recovers from its latest challenge.

Santa Rosa is an archeological treasure trove. The Arlington Woman, found here in 1959 by Philip Orr, shows that our species has been interacting with this ground for more than 10,000 years. The lady seems to have died in a food-gathering accident. In 1994 the most complete fossil skeleton of a pygmy mammoth was found on the island's northeast side near Carrington Point. A small exhibit at the Channel Islands visitor center and a large exhibit at the Santa Barbara Museum of Natural History shed light on the rich history of all the islands in the channel.

SANTA ROSA ISLAND

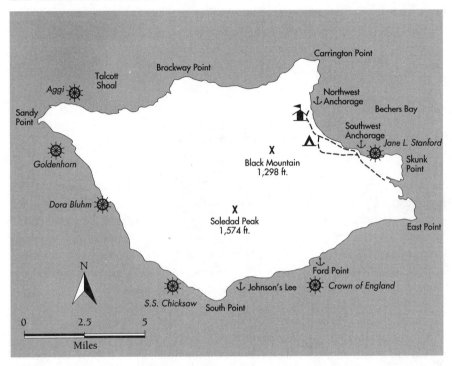

Recent history includes the Vail and Vickers Ranch, which raised cattle here until 1998, using a large wooden boat to "drive" the cattle to market at Port Hueneme. Unfortunately the ranch also encouraged the nonnative grasses that took root here. The National Park Service must now decide how to manage the situation.

Beach camping is allowed on portions of Santa Rosa's coast, providing you have a permit, and makes for an unforgettable kayaking excursion.

ACCESS: Island Packers schedules infrequent trips here, mostly in winter and spring. Package tours are available. Beach landings via skiff (read "wet") may be required, and pier landings require climbing up a steel ladder. The pier is not available to private boaters. Channel Islands Aviation services this island.

HOURS/FEES: Call Island Packers for schedule. The trip takes about 12 hours (7 of that on the boat) and the cost is $62 per adult and $45 per child. Campers pay $80 per adult and $70 per child for round-trip shuttle service. A park permit is needed for camping and for exploring past the beaches. Beaches between and including East Point and Southeast Anchorage are closed from March 15 to September 15 to help protect the snowy plover, an endangered bird. By air it's $129 per adult and $109 per child. Air package tours are available.

For more information:

Santa Rosa Island Ranger (landing information)—VHF Channel 16.

Channel Islands National Park—805-658-5730, www.nps.gov/chis.

Island Packers—805-642-7688. Reservations, 805-642-1393.

Channel Islands Aviation—805-987-1301, www.flycia.com.

San Miguel Island

On San Miguel Island's dirt and sand runway, beneath the full moon, a slight breeze carried elephant seals' grunting communication more than 2 miles to my ears. As I sat there playing my harmonica, a peregrine falcon came between me and the moon, its feathers glowing angelically. It hovered for a moment, perhaps wondering where the strange harmonics were coming from, then continued on its way. Ornithologists will say this didn't happen as peregrines don't hunt at night, but one checked me out on San Miguel Island during the full moon.

Situated a full day's boat ride from the mainland, San Miguel has few visitors. Private boaters anchor in the relative safety of Cuyler Harbor and skiff to shore. Those without boats arrive via Island Packers' camping shuttle service.

Camping on San Miguel Island is not for the timid. The campground (permit required) offers pit toilets, tables, and a windscreen for each of the nine sites. Food lockers are also provided to keep edibles from being snatched by the endangered island fox. There are no garbage or water facilities on the island. It is strictly pack in/pack out camping.

A spur off the campground's access trail leads through a forest of shoulder-high, yellow-topped coreopsis plants to Cabrillo Monument, dedicated to Juan Rodriguez Cabrillo, a character instrumental in the history of California. The monument, a few stairs off the main trail, overlooks the harbor and affords views of Prince Island, the good-sized bit of land that sits in Cuyler Harbor.

Lester Ranch lies farther up the main trail. This ruin was the ranch run by the Lester family in the 1940s.

Exploring the island past Lester Ranch requires a ranger's company. This ensures the protection of the environment while providing a knowledgeable and enthusiastic guide. Tell the Park Service before you leave the mainland that you'll need the ranger. This will help everyone make his or her plans.

Cardwell Point, Harris Point, and Point Bennett all require ranger accompaniment.

The trail to Cardwell is gentle and rolling with a few short hills. I sighted an island fox here. Look for telltale paths through the tall grass, little paw prints on

SAN MIGUEL ISLAND

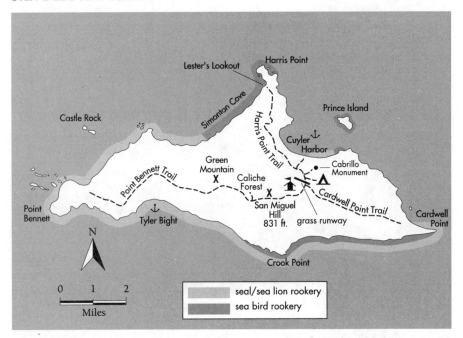

soft trail dirt, and insect- and fur-filled scat as signs of this endangered animal's presence. Keep your peripheral vision tuned for movement and you may see the elusive critter. The fox's numbers have fallen dramatically recently. The Park Service is trying desperately to keep this relative of the mainland's gray fox from becoming extinct.

Harris Point Trail is more strenuous and more diverse. Views of Simonton Cove, Cuyler Harbor, and Harris Point are breathtaking. The trail also passes a Chumash midden. These archeological sites give glimpses into the island's past. Please, don't touch.

Point Bennett is probably the most known area on the island. It's also the most difficult to reach. It's a 15-mile round-trip. Along the way is the caliche forest, an eerie gathering of spirelike stones that are the mineral remains of ancient trees. Point Bennett is home to thousands of seals and sea lions. To keep them happy and breeding, strict limits regulate proximity of people to these pinnipeds.

The toughest part of camping on San Miguel Island is leaving. As they say, all good things must come to an end. I'd like to know who "They" are.

Access: Island Packers schedules infrequent two-day and camper-shuttle trips here in winter and spring. Package tours are available. A difficult and often wet landing via skiff is required. Reaching the campground requires a 0.5-mile hike up a steep trail after hiking 0.5 mile on the beach, so pack lightly.

ON SAN MIGUEL ISLAND, BLOSSOMS ADORN A MONUMENT TO 16TH-CENTURY EXPLORER JUAN RODRIGUEZ CABRILLO.

HOURS/FEES: Call Island Packers for schedule. The boat ride is about 4 hours each way and costs $90 per adult and $80 per child. The two-day package is $235 per adult and $205 per child.

FOR MORE INFORMATION:

San Miguel Island Ranger (landing information)—VHF Channel 16.

Channel Islands National Park—805-658-5730, www.nps.gov/chis.

Island Packers—805-642-7688. Reservations, 805-642-1393.

GO FLY A KITE!

As the sun sinks behind the silhouette of Anacapa Island, the wind that has powered the afternoon dies down. The yellow, orange, and then pink of the setting sun light up the sky as a kite flyer finishes rolling up a kite, which was used to orchestrate its own symphony of color in the sky.

Dark blue, neon pink, and bright green nylon stretched over a fiberglass frame formed the delta-shaped stunt kite that tore through the evening breeze. Standing 75 feet away and gripping two handles that act as reins to control the kite, the pilot's mind was focused in on the dancing shape tethered to a body that felt the burn of an extended workout and the exhilaration of fresh air in the lungs. While flying, there is nothing else. The kite, the wind, and self.

Most of us remember flying a kite as a child. The memory usually includes a lot of running, untangling, and more running, but not much flying. Well, that was the good old days. Kites have successfully entered the space age. Lightweight materials and sophisticated designs have opened up new worlds of possibilities for kites.

Kites now fall, er um, climb into three categories: single-line, stunt or sport, and power kites. Single-line kites are traditional kites in the sense that they still have only one string between the flyer and the kite. These can be made in a number of fun shapes and are still the way for kids to fly. There's even a helicopter kite that really acts like a helicopter. Stunt or sport kites have two lines connected to handles, which are used to control the kite's flight path. Pushing or pulling on one line causes a turn. These nimble creatures can perform a wide range of seemingly impossible tricks when flown by experienced hands. Power kites are basically stunt kites with more pulling power. They are used to pull people on a variety of wheeled vehicles or to lift the flyer into the air—kind of a cross between windsurfing and parasailing.

There is a definite Zen-like state reached while flying. When the lines pull taut, so does your mind.

The sport's possibilities are expanding rapidly. Team and individual competitions are held in a variety of events such as ballet, precision flying, and freestyle. There's even talk of a future at the Olympics as new designs are pushing the envelope of what a kite can do.

One of the best parts of this sport is the quick learning curve. Kites are designed slightly differently to make them more suitable for beginners or experts. It's possible to buy a starter kit for under $60, which includes everything needed to get off the ground, plus a storage bag. A few tips make things easier. First, be sure that both lines are exactly the same length. The handles are designed to loop small bits of string to create equal lines. Second, don't flail your arms. The kite turns by pushing or pulling the handles, which effectively changes the length of one line and affects the kite's angle to the wind and thus makes it turn. Raising your arms or sticking them out to the sides doesn't affect the kite in the least and makes you look silly. You aren't guiding in planes on an aircraft carrier, so don't wave your arms around.

If you do much flying on the beach, the wax-coated lines will undoubtedly get dirty, which will shorten their life span. Not to worry! Since lines are constructed from manmade fibers, they can be lathered up with dishwashing detergent, rinsed, and dried, with the wax coating remaining intact.

Keep in mind that obstacles will cause turbulence. Of course you should always check for biological hazards before launch. People don't take kindly to being smacked in the head by a space-age flying machine doing 40 miles per hour. Remember that the kite's range extends in an arc on both sides. If you have 75 feet of line, you need at least 150 feet of space.

When the flags are flappin', go fly a kite!

REGION 15

VENTURA TO LA CONCHITA

Spacious sandy shores along with a laid-back city give way to thin ribbons of sand pressed between the ocean and coastal mountains. Surfers dot the waters off the numerous points, and RVs line up to absorb the ocean views.

San Buenaventura State Beach, nestled between two city parks, welcomes a large number of beachgoers to its thick slice of sand and still looks empty. State and county parks line the Old PCH (Highway 1) just seaward of Highway 101. These parks deliver camping and access to narrow sandy beaches, which are often covered at high tide.

Though only 62 miles away, Los Angeles is worlds from Ventura, whose official name of San Buenaventura was shortened by the railroad so it would fit on their printed schedules. The region was a Chumash village, called Shisholop, when Juan Rodriguez Cabrillo dropped anchor here in 1542 during the first known expedition to California. The Native American population declined dramatically following the establishment of the San Buenaventura Mission in 1782. Area museums as well as the mission offer insights to the region's rich history. Today the seaside portion of Ventura is a quiet, oceanfront town full of coffee shops while inland "east" Ventura is a generic suburbia whose main character is its lack of character. The historic downtown area, where the mission is, is undergoing renovation that the town leaders hope will rejuvenate business there. Unfortunately, it seems that the result will be more of the generic and less of the character. Hurry up and see it before they finish the "improvements."

Farther up the coast, Pacific Coast Highway (also Highway 1) parallels Highway 101. The Old Rincon Highway provides coastal access and links the small residential beach communities of Solimar Beach, Faria, and Seacliff. Between these housing tracts are open areas with narrow beaches, which often require a rock-climblike descent to reach the sand.

Access

Take Hwy 101 to Ventura. The Victoria Exit marks the region's southern border and the Seacliff Exit marks the northern border.

Beaches

Surfer's Knoll

Peninsula Beach

Marina Park

San Buenaventura State Beach

VENTURA TO LA CONCHITA

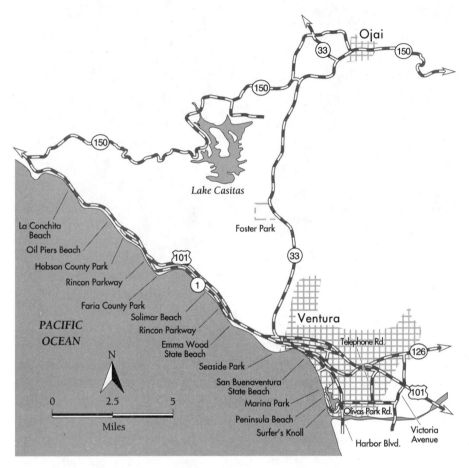

Seaside Park

Emma Wood State Beach

Solimar Beach

Faria County Park

Rincon Parkway

Hobson County Park

Oil Piers Beach and Mussel Shoals

La Conchita

THE TERRA COTTA HEADS OF TWO DOZEN FRIARS EMBELLISH CITY HALL IN VENTURA.

Camping

Ventura County Parks and Recreation—805-654-3951. The county runs fifteen campgrounds. The four below are right on the beach:

Emma Wood State Beach. 61 sites along a eroding seawall, chemical toilets, dump station, no water. $10.

Faria County Park. 42 sites facing the Pacific from behind protective rocks. Water, hot showers, restrooms, snack shack. $15.

The Rincon Parkway. 100 "self-contained" sites that equate to roadside parking along the shore. Chemical toilets. $10.

Hobson County Park. 31 sites situated on the ocean behind a rocky embankment. Water, hot showers, restrooms, snack shop. $15.

Emma Wood Group Camp—Operated by the state as an overflow campground available when everything else fills up. It sits just over the dunes from the ocean. Restrooms only. $10 to $16.

Ventura Beach RV Resort—805-643-9137. A large, 144-space RV park in the shadow of Emma Wood State Beach. Full hookups with cable TV, pool, laundry, showers, recreation room, path to the beach. $33.

Lake Casitas—805-649-2233. More than 800 sites ranging from $10 to $16 a night. The lake is a prime bass fishin' hole.

Other points of interest

Grant Memorial Park—805-658-4726. A large cross sits atop the hill, offering a view of the entire region. Erected in 1933, the cross represents the original one that the Franciscan monks put up with the mission. The hill was called La Loma de la Cruz, which means Hill of the Cross.

Mission San Buenaventura—805-643-4318. Founded in 1782 by an Italian Franciscan monk, Father Junipero Serra, the mission welcomes the public after a $1 donation. The mission's first church was never finished. It was deemed flawed and abandoned. The church standing today was built between 1805 and 1809. The entrance is at 225 East Main, where crosses, beads, and candles are sold to visitors who left theirs at home.

San Buenaventura City Hall—805-654-7850 or 805-658-4726. Twenty-four terra-cotta friar heads will beckon you inside to see a variety of artworks ranging from modern to an artist's rendition of Chumash cave paintings. The original building was completed in 1913 and the west wing, originally the sheriff's office and a jail, was added in 1932. The city bought the building from the county in 1971. It's truly one of Ventura's gems. 8:00 A.M. to 5:00 P.M. weekdays.

Historic Downtown Ventura—805-654-4723 or 805-658-4726. To help self-guide your own tour, Ventura's Revitalization Division (in the city hall building at 501 East Poli St.) provides a list of 76 historic landmarks in the downtown area. These sites lie mostly in the small area bordered by East Poli, Ventura Ave., Thompson, and Ann Sts. Many of the locations have information placards describing their historical significance. Keep in mind that most of these places are private property.

Ventura Harbor Village—805-642-2430 or 805-644-7001. A modern, bayside stroll with dining and shopping. The Channel Islands National Park's Visitor Center sits nearby.

Olivas Adobe Historical Park—805-644-4346. A 6-acre park around an adobe hacienda (house) built in 1847. The herb garden replicates the period's plantings. The park is open daily from 10:00 A.M. to 4:00 P.M. with tours on weekends.

Ortega Adobe Historic Residence—805-658-4728. This building, circa 1857, housed a variety of folks from the state's first canning company to the Ventura police department. It's been renovated to look like it did upon erection. 9:00 A.M. to 4:00 P.M. daily.

Albinger Archaeological Museum—805-648-5823. An excellent place to start a tour of downtown. Artifacts on display are more than 3,000 years old and were dug up in the area. 10:00 A.M. to 4:00 P.M., Wednesday to Sunday (shorter weekday hours in the winter).

Ventura County Museum of History and Art—805-653-0323. Another extensive collection of area artifacts and displays. A research library upstairs gives historians a true hands-on look into the past. 10:00 A.M. to 5:00 P.M., closed Monday.

Ojai—805-646-1872. This quaint town has an interesting mix of intellectuals, artists, and those who aren't quite either. Ojai is galleries and fine dining in a parklike setting with plenty of recreational areas nearby. Take Hwy 33 west from Hwy 101, then travel through Oakview and into Ojai.

Lake Casitas—805-649-2233. This lake offers a plethora of recreational opportunities, including camping. No swimming though, as it's Ventura's water supply. Take Hwy 33 west from Hwy 101 to Hwy 150 and turn left. It's 3 miles to the entrance station.

SURFER'S KNOLL

The Santa Clara River deposits its sediment load into the ocean off the wide sands of Surfer's Knoll, creating a sandbar that in turn creates a good wave. The beach's consistent winds keep sunbathers to a minimum, but kite enthusiasts come running. Stunt fliers and large dragons are seen aloft over the wide dunes. Currents here are strong and there is no lifeguard, making swimming ill-advised.

ACCESS: From the south—Take Hwy 101 north out of Los Angeles, exit after Oxnard on Victoria Ave., turn left, and continue for 0.7 mile before turning right on Olivas Park Rd. Continue straight, crossing Harbor Blvd., and enter the Ventura Harbor area. Surfer's Knoll is on the left as the road bends to the right.

From the north—Take Hwy 101 south from Santa Barbara and exit in Ventura on Seaward Ave. Turn left onto Harbor Blvd. Continue for 2 miles and turn right into the harbor on Spinnaker Dr. at Olivas Park Rd.

PARKING: A small lot at the beach's entrance often has room. Additional parking is available across Spinnaker Dr.

HOURS/FEES: Free.

AMENITIES: Restrooms, shower, nearby shops.

ACTIVITIES: Surfing, walking, flying kites.

FOR MORE INFORMATION:

Ventura City Parks and Recreation—805-652-4550.

Ventura Visitors and Convention Bureau—800-333-2989 or 805-648-2075.

Water-quality Hotline—805-662-6555.

Water Testing Results—www.ventura.org/env_hlth/ocean.htm.

Peninsula Beach

This dark-sand beach is protected from the ocean's rigor by Ventura Harbor's break-water, making Peninsula Beach a gentle place for kids and swimmers. A wide dune system separates the parking area from the beach, and a breakwater gives anglers a place to fish.

ACCESS: From the south—Take Hwy 101 north from Los Angeles, exit after Oxnard on Victoria Ave., turn left, and continue for 0.7 mile before turning right on Olivas Park Rd. Continue straight, crossing Harbor Blvd., and enter the Ventura Harbor area. Pass Surfer's Knoll as the road bends right and continue to the end of the road.

From the north—Take Hwy 101 south from Santa Barbara and exit in Ventura on Seaward Ave. Turn left onto Harbor Blvd. Continue for 2 miles and turn right into the harbor on Spinnaker Dr. at Olivas Park Rd.

PARKING: Parking is available in the lot on the wet side of the road's end. Additional parking is available near the retail stores in the harbor.

HOURS/FEES: Free.

AMENITIES: Lifeguard, jetty.

ACTIVITIES: Fishing, swimming, sunbathing.

FOR MORE INFORMATION:

Ventura City Parks and Recreation—805-652-4550.

Ventura Visitors and Convention Bureau—800-333-2989 or 805-648-2075.

Water-quality Hotline—805-662-6555.

Water Testing Results—www.ventura.org/env_hlth/ocean.htm.

Marina Park

Arg ye, mateys! This be a fine place ta' drop anchor. A big slab o' turf has the makins fer ye kite flyin' and there be a shipwreck for the little ones ta play pirate on. Bring out the dingy and let's hit the beach.

Known to locals as Pirate Ship Park, Marina Park is a grassy expanse with a small sandy beach. The waves are strong as is the current. The playground includes a cement mock-up of an old shipwreck that adults have been known to play on when the kids aren't looking. A sidewalk lined with eroded lampposts leads to a harbor breakwater and passes grassy dunes. The city's recreation department holds sailing classes at the marina at the park's eastern end. Anglers frequent the park's jetties, surfers try their luck with the waves, and stunt kites are flown in the park.

ACCESS: From the south—Take Hwy 101 north from Los Angeles, exit in Ventura on Seaward Ave., and turn left. Cross the highway and continue straight on Seaward, passing Harbor Blvd. Turn left at the stop sign (Pierpont Blvd.) and follow it to the park.

From the north—Take Hwy 101 south from Santa Barbara and exit in Ventura on Seaward Ave. Continue straight through the first stoplight and turn left at Pierpont Blvd., following it to Marina Park.

PARKING: A large free lot is provided by the park.

HOURS/FEES: Sunrise to 10:00 P.M. Free.

AMENITIES: Restrooms, picnic tables with grills, bike path, fishing jetty, playground, sailboat rental.

ACTIVITIES: Picnicking, flying kites, surfing, fishing, sailing.

FOR MORE INFORMATION:

Ventura City Parks and Recreation—805-652-4550.

Ventura Visitors and Convention Bureau—800-333-2989 or 805-648-2075.

Water-quality Hotline—805-662-6555.

Water Testing Results—www.ventura.org/env_hlth/ocean.htm.

SAN BUENAVENTURA STATE BEACH

The wide sands connecting Ventura Pier to Marina Park belong to San Buenaventura State Beach. The beach is naturally segregated into a couple of zones. A huge, rusted buoy sits in the sand along with those people visiting Pierpont Beach, the portion accessed at the end of Seaward Avenue. A couple of jetties further divide this area into little chunks. The jetties, built to keep the sand in place, actually have interrupted the natural littoral currents and probably done more harm than good. The end of San Pedro Street marks the start of the park proper. Picnic tables, a fitness court, snack shack, lifeguards, and a bike path, which runs along the coast to Emma Wood State Beach, are found here. As the beach encroaches on the pier, its dune backing is replaced with a parking lot and Harbor Boulevard.

Volleyballs see a lot of action at San Buenaventura State Beach. The courts next to Ventura Pier are where the hotshots play. The rest of us use the courts down by the end of San Pedro.

ACCESS: From the south—Take Hwy 101 north from Los Angeles, exit in Ventura on Seaward Ave., and turn left. Cross the highway and continue straight on Seaward, passing Harbor Blvd. Turn right at the stop sign (Pierpont Blvd.) and follow it to the entrance.

From the north—Take Hwy 101 south from Santa Barbara and exit in Ventura on Seaward Ave. Continue straight through the first stoplight and turn right at Pierpont Blvd., following it to the entrance.

PARKING: A large day-use lot is at the beach. Free parking is available along San Pedro St. or on San Jon St. San Pedro is the road crossed when entering the beach's parking lot from Pierpont Blvd. To reach San Jon St., turn right on San Pedro and then turn left on Harbor Blvd. San Jon is 1,050 yards up on the right. Parking is under the bridge. Parking for Pierpont Beach lies along the terminal block of Seaward Ave. If coming from Hwy 101 south, turn left on Pierpont to reach Seaward Ave. Northbound travelers just continue straight through the first stop sign.

HOURS/FEES: 8:00 A.M. to sunset. $5 for day-use lot.

AMENITIES: Restrooms, snack shack, volleyball, picnic area with grills, bike path, lifeguards.

ACTIVITIES: Volleyball, sunbathing, picnicking, surfing.

FOR MORE INFORMATION:

San Buenaventura State Beach—805-654-4610.

California State Parks, Channel Coast District, Ventura Sector—805-648-3918.

California State Parks, Channel Coast District—805-899-1400.

Ventura Visitors and Convention Bureau—800-333-2989 or 805-648-2075.

Water-quality Hotline—805-662-6555.

Water Testing Results—www.ventura.org/env_hlth/ocean.htm.

SEASIDE PARK

Adjacent to the Ventura County Fairgrounds, the city calls this area Seaside Park. However, it goes by many names: Fairgrounds Beach, Surfer's Point, C Street, the Promenade, and Pier Park. The thin, sandy beach starts at the Ventura River's mouth and continues eastward to Ventura Pier, where the beach widens. A wide promenade, garnished with flower islands that break the walkway into two busy lanes, starts at the pier and bends with the coast extending halfway to the river mouth, stopping after Surfer's Point. The bike path continues past the park and connects to Emma Wood State Beach. Surfer's Point lies in the middle of the park, where the beach makes a 30-degree turn and bends toward the pier. Longboard surfers flock here for the long "rights" that peel into the small bay.

The bike path has all but fallen into the ocean near the river mouth. Some planners want to solidify the area with seawalls or rocky banks. History has shown this is a sure path to further erosion and more beach loss. However, the city wants to save the bike path and parking lots that they spent so much money on, which may mean they spend even more money on structures that Mother Ocean will devour. She is very patient. For now, the beach is thin around the cobblestone point, with most sand activities happening by the pier.

Ventura Pier has the dubious honor of being the site where the world's first oil tanker burned and sank. There's no sign of that past. However, the pier is often damaged by strong winter storms. Luckily, the city cherishes this wooden icon and repeatedly repairs it.

ACCESS: From the south—Take Hwy 101 north from Los Angeles, exit in Ventura on California Ave., and keep left, crossing the highway and railroad tracks. Turn right on Harbor Blvd. and continue to Figueroa St. Turn left and follow the road past the fairgrounds parking. The pay lot is on the left along the shore.

From the north—Take Hwy 101 south from Santa Barbara and exit in Ventura on Ventura Ave. Turn right onto Thompson Ave. and right again on Figueroa St. Cross the railroad tracks and Harbor Blvd. and continue to the parking area.

Ventura Pier can be reached by turning left on Harbor Blvd. and following it to the pay lot on the right (see San Buenaventura State Beach).

PARKING: The pay lots mentioned above have sufficient space. Surfer's Point parking is free but reserved for those with surfboards. Additional pay parking is available in the fairgrounds parking lot.

HOURS/FEES: Sunrise to 10:00 P.M.

AMENITIES: Pier, promenade, playground, picnic area, restrooms, showers, lifeguard.

ACTIVITIES: Strolling, sunbathing, surfing, fishing off pier, biking, skateboarding.

FOR MORE INFORMATION:

Ventura City Parks and Recreation—805-652-4550.

Ventura Visitors and Convention Bureau—800-333-2989 or 805-648-2075.

Water-quality Hotline—805-662-6555.

Water Testing Results—www.ventura.org/env_hlth/ocean.htm.

EMMA WOOD STATE BEACH

Emma Wood State Beach looks a bit dilapidated. Highway 101 passes overhead, and the park's office is situated beneath a bridge. The ocean laps at the decaying cement seawalls and rocky embankments used to keep campers from washing out to sea. During big storms, the park closes and the area is evacuated. Trains race by within a few feet of the campsites and have claimed the lives of a railwalker or two. All that's missing is a brown bag and a bottle. Yet Emma Wood clings tenaciously to the hillside, continuing to give campers a front row seat to the Pacific's show.

Surfers herald this site as "Overheads" and say it's one of the best big wave breaks around. In the winter when the swell is just right, look out! The wave starts to break about a quarter-mile offshore and rolls in to give Emma Wood another headache.

The beach's only real sandy area lies near the Ventura River's mouth at the eastern portion of the state beach, which is now called Seaside Wilderness Park and was known as the Hobo Jungle when it housed a small villagelike community of homeless who were swept away by floodwaters. Now the area's trail visits vegetated dunes and a coastal copse. The park also contains the remains of a gun emplacement used for coastal defense in World War II. All that's left is the short, cylindrical wall of cement in the process of being reclaimed by the ocean.

ACCESS: From the south—Take Hwy 101 north and take the exit labeled "Beaches," immediately after cresting the hill out of Ventura. The road ducks under Hwy 101, then descends the hill parallel to the highway. At the hill's bottom, turn sharply left into the park's entrance road. The turn is over 120 degrees and easy to miss. If you pass it, simply pull into the Rincon Parkway parking (watch for bicyclists) and return.

From the north—Take Hwy 101 south from Santa Barbara and exit at Seacliff. Turn left onto Old Hwy 1 (Old Rincon Hwy) and follow it down the coast about 6 miles to the entrance.

PARKING: A small day-use lot is available in the park. Camp spaces have room for extra vehicles.

HOURS/FEES: Day use is $4 and camping costs $18.

AMENITIES: Showers, restrooms, camping, picnic areas with barbecue grills.

ACTIVITIES: Surfing, camping, biking, fishing.

FOR MORE INFORMATION:

California State Parks, Channel Coast District, Ventura Sector—805-648-3918.

California State Parks, Channel Coast District—805-899-1400.

Water-quality Hotline—805-662-6555.

Water Testing Results—www.ventura.org/env_hlth/ocean.htm.

Solimar Beach

While Solimar Beach officially lies seaward of a private community with the same name, for practical purposes it also represents the eastern section of the Rincon Parkway, which connects Solimar Beach to Emma Wood State Beach. Solimar Reef, a quarter-mile offshore, has a nice wave when conditions are right, though it is often peaky and mushy. The sand strand is so narrow here that strolling and jogging are the beach's main land-based activities. Road-weary drivers often pull off Highway 101 to get the blood flowing again with a walk on the beach or to be lulled to sleep for a short nap by the sounds of Mother Ocean.

ACCESS: From the south—Take Hwy 101 north and take the exit labeled "Beaches," immediately after cresting the hill out of Ventura. The road ducks under Hwy 101, then descends the hill to parallel the highway. At the hill's bottom is Emma Wood State Beach. Continue straight for about 1.7 miles and park on the left. Rincon Parkway's parking starts when the road reaches the bottom of the hill.

From the north—Take Hwy 101 south from Santa Barbara and exit at Seacliff. Turn left onto Old Hwy 1 (Old Rincon Hwy) and follow it down the coast about 4.3 miles (past the private-entrance sign for Solimar Beach) to the parking area on the right.

PARKING: On the wet side of the road. Pull over far enough to keep the biking lanes clear.

HOURS/FEES: 5:00 A.M. to 2:00 A.M. (in other words, "no camping"). Free.

AMENITIES: None.

ACTIVITIES: Biking, walking, surfing, meditating.

FOR MORE INFORMATION:

Water-quality Hotline—805-662-6555.

Water Testing Results—www.ventura.org/env_hlth/ocean.htm.

Faria County Park

This Ventura County park is on Pitas Point, a rocky outcropping that sends waves crashing against the barnacle-encrusted boulders that line the shore. The beach extends up the coast, bending slightly southward before melding into Hobson County Park. East (down coast), the shore is mostly algae-covered rock. During the summer more sand is deposited, creating a thin, sandy beach that widens at a cove about a half-mile east of the point. The park is mostly a dirt parking area, but it does have horseshoe pits and a small play area along with the campground's necessities.

ACCESS: Traveling north out of Ventura or south from Santa Barbara, exit at Seacliff and turn right toward Ventura. Follow this road (Old Rincon Hwy) 2.3 miles, passing Hobson County Park and Rincon Parkway, to the park's entrance on the right.

PARKING: A dirt, day-use lot is in the park. If it's full, park on the dry side of Old Rincon Hwy back up the road from the park's entrance.

HOURS/FEES: Day use (sunrise to sunset) is free. Camping costs $16.

AMENITIES: Restrooms, showers, horseshoe pit, playground, snack shack, campground.

ACTIVITIES: Surfing, fishing, camping.

FOR MORE INFORMATION:

Ventura County Parks—805-654-3951.

Water-quality Hotline—805-662-6555.

Water Testing Results—www.ventura.org/env_hlth/ocean.htm.

RINCON PARKWAY

From Emma Wood State Beach to Hobson County Park on the sea side of Old Highway 1, Rincon Parkway is basically a bike path and parking area beside a conglomerate of large boulders that form a seawall. At the base of this protective wall, a whisper-thin thong of sand is visible during low tide. Strong currents and waves splashing onto the road are fairly common events. Parking is free along the parkway except between Faria Park and a concrete seawall up the coast where a hundred spaces are reserved for recreational vehicle camping. The county plans to create more camping. However, locals are opposed to any further loss of coastal access. It seems wrong to take away residents' beach access to draw more business to the nationally owned gas stations and grocery stores, but Ventura's government has a history of strangely motivated initiatives, according to the folks at the city's numerous coffee houses.

ACCESS: Traveling north out of Ventura or south from Santa Barbara, exit at Seacliff and turn right toward Ventura. Follow this road (Old Rincon Hwy) 1.5 miles, passing Hobson County Park. The self-pay camping area is on the right.

PARKING: This area is one long parking zone. Just pull off to the wet side of the road.

HOURS/FEES: Open twenty-four hours, seven days a week all year. The noncamping spaces are free. Camping costs $12.

Amenities: Camping spaces, portable toilet.

Activities: Camping, surfing, fishing, biking.

For more information:

Ventura County Parks—805-654-3951.

Water-quality Hotline—805-662-6555.

Water Testing Results—www.ventura.org/env_hlth/ocean.htm.

Hobson County Park

Waves spill over an offshore reef, which lies hidden seaward of a small rocky point of land with narrow, sandy strands extending in both directions. Palm trees give a tropical look to Hobson County Park, a small campground and day-use area. The park is really just a parking lot with a restroom, snack shack, and stairs leading to the beach. It is very similar to Faria County Park, which is a mile down the coast.

The Channel Islands are visible on a clear day, as is an oil company's island, which has been dressed up with palm trees to hide its steel and pipe.

Access: Traveling north out of Ventura or south from Santa Barbara, exit at Seacliff and turn right toward Ventura. Follow this road (Old Rincon Hwy) about 1 mile to the park's entrance on the right.

Parking: A small, day-use lot is in the park. Extra spaces can be found along the Rincon Parkway.

Hours/fees: The day-use closes at 7:00 P.M. or sunset, whichever is later, after opening at dawn. Day use is free, and it's $17 to camp.

Amenities: Restrooms, showers, snack shack, picnic tables.

Activities: Surfing, camping, fishing, diving/snorkeling.

For more information:

Ventura County Parks—805-654-3951.

Water-quality Hotline—805-662-6555.

Water Testing Results—www.ventura.org/env_hlth/ocean.htm.

OIL PIERS BEACH AND MUSSEL SHOALS

Oil Piers Beach is now pierless. Not peerless, though it's silvery gray sand is nice and soft. Pierless. The old oil piers were dismantled. Surfers worry that without the structure the sandbar will disappear, taking with it one of the best beach breaks in Ventura County. Time will tell. For now the rock embankment here drops to a horseshoe-shaped beach that lies beside and below the highway as it arcs seaward, ending at a rocky point called Mussel Shoals, also known as Little Rincon to surfers.

ACCESS: Traveling north out of Ventura or south from Santa Barbara, exit at Seacliff and turn left toward Santa Barbara. Follow this road (Old Rincon Hwy) about 0.5 mile, then turn left under Hwy 101 to reach the parking area.

PARKING: Pull off to the dry-side shoulder.

HOURS/FEES: Free and always open.

AMENITIES: None.

ACTIVITIES: Surfing, fishing, Jet Skiing.

FOR MORE INFORMATION:

Water-quality Hotline—805-662-6555.

Water Testing Results—www.ventura.org/env_hlth/ocean.htm.

LA CONCHITA

Beneath a high rock wall that protects Highway 101 from the Pacific Ocean lies a beach that's thinner than a surfer's wallet. This is La Conchita Beach. The cars zooming by on 101 are a major hazard here. Parking along the southbound lanes is easy enough, but northbounders must zip across high-speed traffic either in a car or on foot. Either way isn't very safe. For the most part the area goes unused except by fishermen, surfers, and La Conchitites.

ACCESS: From the south—Drive north on Hwy 101 from Ventura. The first town you reach is La Conchita. If you're in the right lane, turn right and then turn around and wait until you can cross the highway. If you're in the left lane, use the left turn lane and wait patiently until you can cross the highway. Once parked, hop up on the rocks and climb down to the beach.

From the north—Drive south from Santa Barbara and look for the Bates Rd. Exit but don't take it. Pass the exit and descend the hill, remaining on Hwy 101. After

the highway bends right, slow down. When the road straightens out, park somewhere on the shoulder. Watch out for bikers.

PARKING: Park along Hwy 101. Pull far to the right, allowing room for bikes to pass.

HOURS/FEES: Always open, always free.

AMENITIES: None.

ACTIVITIES: Fishing, surfing.

FOR MORE INFORMATION:

Water-quality Hotline—805-662-6555.

Water Testing Results—www.ventura.org/env_hlth/ocean.htm.

SHELL COLLECTING

*I have a collection of sea shells. I keep it on the beaches around the world. Perhaps you've
seen it.*—Stephen Wright

Beachcombing is what it's called: the act of strolling up and down a beach with
your feet bare and your pants rolled up. Occasionally you should stoop over to
examine something. That's what it looks like from afar. To those who do the comb-
ing, it's a fascinating hobby with a heap of educational benefits and shelves of
nature's artwork.

Of course, a collector with a conscience only takes specimens from beaches
where the practice is allowed and then only specimens that they don't already have.
Humans have a way of assuming that other species litter like we do. Thus a spent
shell couldn't possibly have another use in the ecosystem. However, this is more
often than not a mistake, though I understand and accept that we are a species that
enjoys decorating our dens. Always keep in mind the impact of your actions and
make decisions from a base of knowledge. If you don't know, find out, but don't just
assume in any case. Always check the source of your knowledge.

The most ecologically friendly collection methods are photographs and memories. Some of the beaches are in or along underwater or ecological reserves, which
are "Look but don't touch" areas. *Please* obey their guidelines. With luck, the number of reserves will expand, thus preserving some of what we enjoy for generations
to come.

REGION 16

CARPINTERIA TO SANTA BARBARA

Ample amounts of white sand grace the gently sloping shores of Carpinteria and Santa Barbara. Between them lie the towns of Summerland and Montecito where a smattering of tall cliffs separate cove beaches. Heading westward up the coast, the mountains, while still casting early morning shadows, move back to give more room to the ocean.

Carpinteria brags about having the coast's safest beach. An offshore shelf helps keep rip tides from forming and protects the sandy shore. There are actually two beaches here, the state beach and the city beach. Both have gently sloping sand massaged by usually mild waves.

Summerland is dominated by cliffside terrain mostly owned by the financially elite. Lookout County Park is the exception, providing a big, sandy cove beneath the cliffs. It also has a playground and picnic area.

Montecito's sandy shores are accessed at Miramar Beach, Hammonds Beach, and via stairways that drop to the coast from Channel Drive. Bluffs that jut up from the shore occasionally break up the beach here. Due to parking troubles, the crowds tend to be small.

Santa Barbara offers a diverse range of coastal experiences. East Beach, West Beach, Leadbetter Beach, and Arroyo Burro Beach County Park are the most popular places to play. Each location offers a full-range of modern amenities, as well as a healthy helping of people. While not as crowded as the Los Angeles and San Diego beaches, locals definitely make use of their coastal parks.

Access

Hwy 101 is the main access road for the entire region. Carpinteria Ave. is the southern border and Las Palmas bounds the region on the north. All beach access is given from Hwy 101.

For Santa Barbara Airport, contact your airline or travel agent or www.flysba.com. Air service is available to many U.S. cities, and international flights frequently connect through Los Angeles or San Francisco. The Santa Barbara Airport is also popular with private planes.

Beaches

Rincon Beach County Park

Carpinteria State Beach

Carpinteria City Beach

Santa Claus Lane

CARPINTERIA TO SANTA BARBARA

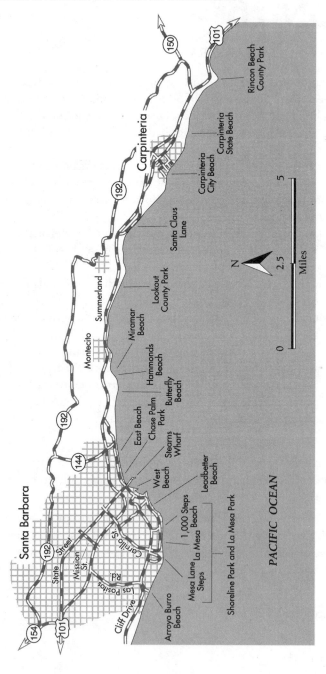

Lookout County Park

Miramar Beach

Hammonds Beach

East Beach and Chase Palm Park

West Beach

Leadbetter Beach

Shoreline Park and La Mesa Park

Arroyo Burro Beach

Camping

Carpinteria State Beach—805-684-2811.

Reservations—800-444-7275, cal-parks.ca.gov/RESERVE/resindex.htm. 260 sites for RVs and tents, showers, restrooms, picnic tables with barbecue grill.

Other points of interest

Santa Barbara Visitor Center—805-965-3021.

Santa Barbara Convention/Visitors Bureau—805-966-9222.

Santa Barbara residents, Santa Barbarians, pride themselves on being cultured. Theatrical, musical, and other artistic events are frequently held here. These numbers will have the schedules.

Scenic Drive—From Hwy 101, take Cabrillo Blvd., (Hwy 225, not Carillo St.) toward the ocean (left if northbound). Follow the signs, which point out a route that connects all of Santa Barbara's coastal offerings. Cabrillo Blvd. becomes Shoreline Dr., which becomes Meigs Rd. Take a left from Meigs Rd. onto Cliff Dr., which becomes Marina Dr., which becomes Roble Dr., which becomes Las Palmas Dr. and returns through the Hope Ranch to Hwy 101.

Santa Barbara Maritime Museum—805-962-8404. An exhibit hall touting the rich maritime history of the Santa Barbara Channel.

Stearns Wharf—805-963-2633. A fire in the winter of 1998 caused severe damage here at the oldest working pier of the West Coast, which is also home to restaurants, shops, and fishing.

State Street—805-965-3021 or 805-966-9222. Shopping, galleries, historic structures, and museums in friendly, downtown Santa Barbara.

Santa Barbara Zoological Gardens—805-962-6310. More than 500 animals in lush, tropical settings.

Andree Clark Bird Refuge—805-564-5433. Gardens and a saltwater marsh that connect to the Santa Barbara Zoo. Good hiking, biking, and birdwatching along a self-guided interpretive tour.

Ash Avenue Wetland/Salt Marsh Park—805-684-5405. A saltwater-marsh home to numerous migratory birds and sea life. The bat rays can be seen in the marsh's channels, which are prime fishing spots for the egrets, osprey, and herons that frequent the area. Check it out via kayak ($10 to $15) during high tide. It's surreal at sunrise.

Mission Santa Barbara—805-682-4713. Out of twenty-one missions, this one, founded in 1786, is the only one with two towers in its church. A large grassy park, Mission Historical Park (805-564-5418), sits next door with paths to old ruins and waterworks.

Presidio State Historic Park—805-966-9719. Buildings of the last Spanish military compound founded in 1782.

Sea Center Nature Conservancy—805-962-0885. Located on Stearns Wharf. Displays and information on marine life.

Santa Barbara Botanic Garden—805-682-4726. 65 acres of native California plants. Miles of trails wind through a variety of habitat displays. This is where to find out about the Channel Islands' floral past and present.

Santa Barbara Museum of Natural History—805-682-4711. The natural history of California, including the first residents, the Chumash. This is the place to delve into the history of the Channel Islands.

Lawn Bowling—805-965-1773 or 805-563-2143. I say ol' chap, anyone roll a few balls? Santa Barbara has two, neatly groomed lawns on which one can practice the refined game involving a jack and three bowls.

Carrillo Ballroom—805-965-3813. Balls held on Saturday nights to the strains of a live orchestra in this historic ballroom. Lessons offered an hour before the dances. $7 ($10 with a lesson).

Moreton Bay Fig Tree—A really old (117 years) and big (largest tree of its kind in the nation) fig tree. The trunk's circumfrence is 38 feet! Go to the intersection of Montecito St. and Chapala St. You can't miss it.

RINCON BEACH COUNTY PARK

Beneath a tall bluff, a point of land catches ocean swells that reach skyward and pitch to create perfect, peeling waves that skirt the horseshoe cove's shore and race toward Highway 101. This is Rincon, the Queen of the Coast. It's one of the premier surf spots in California and perhaps the world. The point separates the beach into two parts. The eastern cove, mostly cobblestone shoreline that all but disappears during high tide, is where the waves are, but it's private property. There are some pieces of driftwood to sit upon, but stay below the mean high-tide level or near the access trail's mouth. The line-up is always crowded. West of the point lies the county park whose sandy beaches sit at the base of a tall bluff topped with a picnic area. A short walk up the coast from here, things get very secluded, which seems to cause people's swimming costumes to disappear mysteriously. The bluff top makes a good whale-watching platform to view the annual migration of the gray whales.

Even if you're not stopping here, the waves may affect your journey. Skid marks on both sides of the highway here are telltale signs of surfers who have drifted out of their lanes while gazing glassy-eyed at the Queen.

ACCESS: From northbound and southbound Hwy 101, exit at Bates Rd. and head toward the ocean. An immediate choice occurs: right to the picnic area or left to the surfer's parking area. A staircase from the county park's picnic area leads down the bluff's face to the beach. An access trail leaves the south side of the surfer's lot.

PARKING: The park's picnic area lot is usually sufficient, but the surfer's lot often fills up. It's possible to watch the surf action by pulling over on Hwy 101 along the seawall, though it doesn't feel very safe.

HOURS/FEES: East side—Sunrise–sunset. Free. West side (the park proper)—8:00 A.M. to sunset. Free.

AMENITIES: Picnic tables, restrooms, barbecue grill, seasonal lifeguard.

ACTIVITIES: Surfing, picnicking, fishing, unofficially nude sunbathing, swimming, whale watching.

FOR MORE INFORMATION:
Santa Barbara County Parks, Rincon Beach—805-681-5650.

CARPINTERIA STATE BEACH

Carpinteria State Beach, an extremely popular campground, sits seconds away from the breakneck pace of traffic on Highway 101, but it's worlds apart. The wide, sandy beach connects to Carpinteria City Beach (see below) and shares the designation as "safest beach on the coast." Tide pools and protected dunes are like an outdoor science class—complex, yet simple—and watching it can make your eyelids droop. Ah. . . sit back . . . relax. . . .

Carpinteria's Tar Pit Park, down the coast from the state beach, was named after the naturally occurring tar that seeps from the ground. The park has a series of trails that drop off the bluff onto the beach. Following the trail east leads to the newly formed Carpinteria Seal Sanctuary. This hauling-out area is closed from December 1 to May 31 to protect the pups.

The Chumash Indians used to make boats nearby and used the natural tar to seal the vessels. Upon seeing the indigenous people's boatyard, the Spanish explorers called the area Carpinteria, which means "carpenter shop."

Beachgoers up and down the Santa Barbara Channel notice tar stuck to their feet from time to time. It's removable with retail concoctions or just use WD-40 as if it were soap. Read the label and make your own decision.

ACCESS: Exit on Linden Ave. off Hwy 101 and head toward the ocean. Turn left on 8th St., then right on Palm Ave. and enter the park.

PARKING: Park in the park's pay lot or on the streets of Carpinteria and walk.

HOURS/FEES: Daylight hours. $5 day parking. $18 camping.

AMENITIES: Lifeguard, restrooms, showers, picnic area, grills.

ACTIVITIES: Swimming, fishing, surfing, picnicking.

FOR MORE INFORMATION:

Carpinteria State Beach—805-684-2811.

California State Parks, Channel Coast District—805-899-1400.

Camping Reservations—800-444-7275, cal-parks.ca.gove/travel/reserve/index.htm.

CARPINTERIA CITY BEACH

The sand between Ash Street and Linden Street marks "the safest beach on the coast," Carpinteria City Beach. The combination of the Channel Islands and an offshore reef keeps swells small and rip currents from forming. Parking close to the beach is scarce, but walking is the best way to see this mellow beach town. If the small lots at the ends of the streets are filled, park inland and perhaps stop by the Carpinteria Valley Historical Society and Museum at 956 Maple Street.

Another place to see while walking around is the Carpinteria Salt Marsh Park. Put the ocean on your left and head up Sandyland Road for three blocks. The vast variety of life here makes each visit unique. Rental kayaks are available at the boathouse.

ACCESS: Exit Hwy 101 at Linden Ave. and head toward the ocean.

PARKING: Park on the street at the end of Linden Ave., Ash St., or anywhere in between.

HOURS/FEES: Sunup to 11:00 P.M. Free.

AMENITIES: Lifeguards, nearby shops.

ACTIVITIES: Fishing, surfing, sunbathing, swimming.

FOR MORE INFORMATION:

Carpinteria Parks and Recreation Department—805-684-5405, ext. 449.

SANTA CLAUS LANE

A thin ribbon of light tan sand runs along the wet side of Santa Claus Lane separated from the road by a rock berm built from rough, gray boulders. There aren't any facilities to speak of, parking is off the pavement, and you must leave room for others to pass, which limits this beach's use. If there isn't any room, either wait for a space or move on. While waiting, take a snapshot of the huge Santa perched atop the store at the lane's end. It's also possible to send mail from here to get a Santa Claus Lane postmark. (Hint, wink, nudge.)

Star searchers may want to take a stroll down the beach. The coast to the southeast is backed by private property commonly owned by celebrities. Be courteous and remember that you will be officially trespassing unless you're below the mean high-tide line.

ACCESS: Exit Hwy 101 on Santa Claus Ln. and head toward the big Santa Claus bust.

PARKING: Park on the seaside shoulder of Santa Claus Ln.

HOURS/FEES: None.

AMENITIES: None.

ACTIVITIES: Surfing, sunbathing, swimming, sandcastle building.

LOOKOUT COUNTY PARK

Summerland's main beach is reached by taking the path down to the beach from this bluff-top park. Below lies a wide sandy beach beneath high, craggy cliffs. It's hard to imagine, but in the oil-boom days the beach was extremely crowded—crowded with oil wells. The park offers a good vantage point for seeing migrating whales. Look for their spouting spray while scanning the horizon, then zoom in with binoculars. Farther east, down the coast, lies Loon Point, which is also an informal nude beach that has recently donned its clothes.

The town of Summerland likes to play up its "spiritual" past. Many places, including "The Big Yellow House," claim to be haunted. The house-turned-restaurant is visible from the highway.

ACCESS: From the north—Take Hwy 101 South, exit at Summerland (Evan Ave.), and turn toward the ocean on Evans Ave. The road will enter the park.

From the south—Take Hwy 101 North and exit onto Wallace Ave., which runs through a residential area before emerging at Evans Ave. and the park.

PARKING: There's a small lot as well as on-street parking. When it's gone, it's gone.

HOURS: 8:00 A.M. to sunset.

AMENITIES: Restrooms, horseshoe pit, barbecue grills, picnic area, trails, playground, volleyball stands.

ACTIVITIES: Hiking, surfing, sunbathing, whale watching, volleyball, picnicking.

FOR MORE INFORMATION:

Lookout County Park—805-969-1720.

Weather—www.keyt.com/003/003/001.html.

MIRAMAR BEACH

A small parking lot at the top of wide, cement steps leads down to a gray sand beach. People sit on the steps looking seaward, deep in thought. Named after the blue-roofed hotel that faces this strand, Miramar Beach has an exclusive ambiance. Extremely limited parking keeps the crowds away, though for some odd reason there always seems to be one parking space left. The beach proper is frequented by couples who stroll hand in hand along the quiet shore.

ACCESS: From the south—Exit Hwy 101 North at San Ysidro Rd. (Eucalyptus Ln.) and turn left. Follow Eucalyptus Ln. to its terminus, where a ten-car lot is tucked away amidst the shrubbery. Descend the steps to Miramar Beach. A path beneath a vine canopy leads to Hammonds Beach.

From the north—Exit Hwy 101 South at San Ysidro Rd. (Eucalyptus Ln.) and turn right. Follow Eucalyptus Ln. to its terminus, where a ten-car lot is tucked away amidst the shrubbery. Descend the steps to Miramar Beach. A path beneath a vine canopy leads to Hammonds Beach.

HOURS/FEES: Twenty-four hours. Free.

PARKING: Do not block the driveways.

AMENITIES: None.

ACTIVITIES: Surfing, swimming, strolling, meditating.

FOR MORE INFORMATION:

Weather—www.keyt.com/003/003/001.html.

HAMMONDS BEACH

Apparently a man named Hammond had a home on the small hill here. In typical surfer fashion, the spot became known as Hammonds, without an apostrophe. This secluded section of coast has light sand that gives way to a grassy field. A monument testifies to the fact that the Chumash people consider this ground sacred.

The lack of facilities is part of Hammond Beach's charm. Driftwood comes to rest at the high-water mark, making it easy to find an impromptu bench. The tall seawall to the east (left) marks the start of Miramar Beach.

The area near Butterfly Lane is appropriately called Butterfly Beach. It is simply more coastline whose access is limited by scarce parking and private property.

ACCESS: From the south—Exit Hwy 101 North onto Olive Mill Rd. Follow the road toward the ocean. The road turns right and becomes Channel Dr., where you may park. Access is via stairways near the Biltmore Hotel and off Butterfly Ln.

From the north—Exit Hwy 101 South onto Butterfly Ln., follow it seaward to Channel Dr., where you may park.

Another path to the beach—Follow Danielson Rd., which connects Olive Mill Rd. to Eucalyptus Ln. via South Jamson Ln.

From Miramar Beach—Hammonds can be reached by walking from the ten-car lot at Miramar Beach.

PARKING: On-street parking is available along Channel Dr. and Danielson Rd. The Miramar lot has room for ten. Always check the signs for parking legality. I shouldn't have to say this, but parking in someone's yard is trespassing.

HOURS/FEES: Twenty-four hours. Free.

AMENITIES: None.

ACTIVITIES: Surfing, swimming, sunbathing, strolling incognito.

EAST BEACH AND CHASE PALM PARK

From the shadow of Stearns Wharf, Chase Palm Park extends eastward along the coast for about a mile before melding into East Beach. Accenting the wide band of sand that curves slightly seaward around the bay, the park has a grassy strip lined with evenly spaced palms and a busy paved path beside Cabrillo Boulevard that carries traffic of bikes, pedestrians, and in-line skaters. The turf zone is also a common place for "residentially challenged" persons to warm up after a cold night by the sea. Such folks tend to be harmless if respected as you would any other being lying in the sun. During summer Sundays and holidays, the park becomes an open-air art gallery sponsored by the city.

East Beach takes over as Cabrillo Boulevard bends inland. This wide sandbox is volleyball heaven. The county and state often hold competitions here. The ever-expanding Santa Barbara Bike Trail heads inland here and follows along Andree Clark Bird Refuge's lake.

The beach's amenities are found at the East Beach Beachhouse, a city-run facility that rents beach stuff, has lockers and showers, and is in charge of the volleyball courts. The city-run Chase Palm Park Recreation Center has restrooms, rents patio space to groups, and offers classes on marine life.

Continuing down the coast (southeast) from East Beach gets you to Graveyard Beach, named for the cemetery that occupies the bluff above. These thin sands are only reachable during low tides.

ACCESS: From the south—Exit Hwy 101 North on Cabrillo Blvd. Stay on this road for 14 miles. The beach and park are on the left.

From the north—Exit Hwy 101 South on Castillo St. and turn right. Turn left in four blocks onto Cabrillo Blvd. and continue 700 yards, passing West Beach and Stearns Wharf.

PARKING: Cabrillo Blvd. has limited on-street parking. A lot on Stearns Wharf and the lots in downtown Santa Barbara also service the area.

HOURS/FEES: 6:00 A.M. to midnight. Free.

AMENITIES: Picnic area, restrooms, lifeguard, showers, barbecue grills, volleyball, bike path.

ACTIVITIES: Biking, volleyball, picnicking, swimming.

FOR MORE INFORMATION:

East Beach Bathhouse—805-965-0509.

Chase Palm Park Recreation Center—805-962-8956.

Santa Barbara Lifeguard—805-897-2680 or 805-965-0509.

Santa Barbara Parks and Recreation—805-564-5418.

Santa Barbara City Info—www.ci.santa-barbara.ca.us/local.html.

Weather—www.keyt.com/003/003/001.html.

WEST BEACH

West Beach is a wide, uncrowded parcel of sand with views of Stearns Wharf and Santa Barbara Harbor from which to watch ships sail by leisurely. Throngs of Santa Barbarians bike, blade, or stroll the coastal bike path to this beach from overflowing Chase Palm Park and East Beach to the south. Or perhaps it's West Beach that flows into the others. Whichever the case, the water here is calm, making the area a popular swimming hole. Wharf pedestrians get a bird's-eye view of the volleyball games and any other active or sedentary activities taking place on the sand.

When conditions are right, a wave will break off the breakwater's sandbar. This rare break, called Sandspit, has fast, hollow waves that draw crowds of talented wave riders when it's "going off." The Coast Guard frowns on surfing into the harbor mouth.

ACCESS: From the south—Exit Hwy 101 North at Cabrillo Blvd. Stay on this road, passing East Beach, Chase Palm Park, and Stearns Wharf. West Beach is immediately after the wharf.

From the north—Exit Hwy 101 South at Castillo St. and turn right. Turn left in four blocks onto Cabrillo Blvd. and look for a parking space.

PARKING: Spaces are available on Cabrillo Blvd. to early risers and the lucky. Shoreline Dr. and side streets are an iffy proposition. If all else fails, parking garages are downtown within walking distance of the beach.

HOURS/FEES: Always free and always open.

AMENITIES: Bike path, sand, Stearns Wharf, volleyball, protected by breakwater.

ACTIVITIES: Swimming, kayaking, sunbathing, volleyball, surfing.

FOR MORE INFORMATION:

Santa Barbara Department of Parks and Recreation—805-564-5418.

Santa Barbara Lifeguard—805-897-2680 or 805-965-0509.

West Beach Wading Pool—805-966-6110.

Santa Barbara City Info—www.ci.santa-barbara.ca.us/local.html.

Weather—www.keyt.com/003/003/001.html.

LEADBETTER BEACH

Leadbetter Beach occupies the sandy cove between Santa Barbara Harbor and the cliff whose rocky base is accessed at 1,000 Steps. The beach is wide and slopes gently, making for a vast visual contrast between high and low tides. It's usually possible to stroll in the water here without fear of being surprised by a thigh-high wave. A busy snack shop sits by the parking area, which is also used by harbor visitors. Nearby Plaza del Mar eases the picnicking population pressure with its grassy area. In summertime, the plaza's band shell reverberates with evening concerts.

ACCESS: From the south—Exit Hwy 101 North at Cabrillo Blvd. Stay on this road, passing East Beach, Chase Palm Park, Stearns Wharf, and West Beach. The road becomes Shoreline Dr. as it bends to the left. The beach's parking lot is on the right at 1000 Shoreline Dr., shortly after Loma Alta Dr. and before climbing the hill.

From the north—Exit Hwy 101 South at Castillo St. and turn right. Turn right again in four blocks onto Shoreline Dr. The parking lot is just past the bend in the road.

Parking: The lot at the beach fills up early. A few streetside spaces are available along Shoreline Dr.

Hours/fees: Twenty-four hours a day, seven days a week. Free.

Amenities: Restrooms, lifeguard, picnic tables with grills.

Activities: Swimming, surfing, sunbathing, picnicking.

For more information:

Santa Barbara Lifeguard—805-897-2680 or 805-965-0509.

Santa Barbara Department of Parks and Recreation—805-564-5418.

Santa Barbara City Info—www.ci.santa-barbara.ca.us/local.html.

Weather—www.keyt.com/003/003/001.html.

Shoreline Park and La Mesa Park

Shoreline Park and La Mesa Park sit atop an oceanside bluff that affords panoramic vistas of the Channel Islands and possibly migrating whales. Sit and contemplate the meaning of the ocean's song or just take a load off your feet on one of the park benches. A stroll on the beach requires a walk down one of three staircases. Mesa Lane's stairs drop to a sandy beach beneath this towering bluff, and the stairs at Shoreline Park drop onto Leadbetter Beach. Halfway between La Mesa Park and Shoreline Park at the terminus of Santa Cruz Boulevard are the infamous 1,000 Steps, which lead to a rocky shore filled with tide pools. The staircase doesn't have 1,000 steps, though, I must admit, I lost count.

Access: From the south—Exit Hwy 101 North at Cabrillo Blvd. Stay on this road, passing East Beach, Chase Palm Park, Stearns Wharf, West Beach, and Leadbetter Beach. The road becomes Shoreline Dr. and heads up the hill. Shoreline Park is at the top of the hill. About 0.5 mile farther is 1,000 Steps. It's another 0.5 mile to La Mesa Park.

From the north—Exit Hwy 101 South at Las Positas Rd. and turn left, following the road for 2 miles. Turn left onto Cliff Dr. In 0.5 mile, Mesa Ln. passes by to the right. Turn on Mesa Ln. to access its staircase. For the parks, continue another 0.5 mile to Meigs Rd. and turn right. This road becomes Shoreline Dr. as it immediately bends to the left at La Mesa Park.

PARKING: Parking is entirely the on-street variety. Pull-over room exists on most of Shoreline Dr.

HOURS/FEES: City parks are open sunrise to sunset and the beach is always open. However, check the sign for legal parking hours.

AMENITIES: Shoreline Park—picnic area, barbecue grills, benches, stairs to beach. La Mesa Park—picnic tables with grills, playground, restrooms.

ACTIVITIES: Shoreline Park—picnicking, kite flying, whale watching. La Mesa Park—picnicking, frolicking in the playground.

FOR MORE INFORMATION:

Santa Barbara Department of Parks and Recreation—805-564-5418.

Santa Barbara City Info—www.ci.santa-barbara.ca.us/local.html.

Weather—www.keyt.com/003/003/001.html.

ARROYO BURRO BEACH

A reed-lined stream meanders seaward alongside the parking lot to this secluded beach. A quiet crowd of sunbathers stretches out on soft sands beneath tall, eroding cliffs topped with luxurious homes. Rogue rocks poke through the sand at irregular intervals on the shore. The stream, Arroyo Burro, offers wildlife a small refuge from civilization.

Arroyo Burro Beach is a nice place to soak up some rays, snorkel, or grab lunch at The Brown Pelican restaurant or in the picnic area that snuggles up to the sand. The trail up the bluff leads to a Chumash ruin, which adds a sense of history to the scene and provides a perch for whale watching. Speaking of scenes, this is the place to be seen during summer weekends, which causes the parking lot to overflow. Come early or plan on walking.

Speaking of walking, heading up the coast leads to the sandy shores of Hope Ranch. If you go, keep in mind that the ranch is privately owned.

ACCESS: From Hwy 101, exit onto Las Positas Rd. (left if northbound) and head toward the ocean. Turn right onto Cliff Dr., which enters the park and ends at the parking lot.

PARKING: The free parking lot at the beach has seventy-three spaces.

HOURS/FEES: Seven days a week from 8:00 A.M. to sunset. Free.

AMENITIES: Picnic tables, barbecues, restrooms, seasonal lifeguard, historical site, snack shack.

ACTIVITIES: Sunbathing, snorkeling, surfing, swimming, volleyball, birding, whale watching.

FOR MORE INFORMATION:

Arroyo Burro Beach—805-687-3714.

Santa Barbara Department of Parks and Recreation—805-564-5418.

Santa Barbara City Info—www.ci.santa-barbara.ca.us/local.html.

Weather—www.keyt.com/003/003/001.html.

PADDLE TO THE SEA

The soft-pink sky of the dawning day is mirrored on the undulating surface of the sea. Stillness hangs over the earth as I wait expectantly for the sunrise. Suddenly a ray of light pierces the horizon and immediately I feel the warm glow that it grants. I smile and take in a deep breath of humid ocean air. Dipping my paddle back into the water, I give a strong pull, really putting my back into the stroke, which causes the bow of my bright yellow plastic kayak to alter its lazily drifting course. Now I dig the other end of my twin-bladed paddle into the water toward the stern on the side opposite my last stroke and leverage the paddle forward for a firm backstroke. The kayak continues the course correction, faster now, and the distant point of land I'm using to guide me comes into line with the bow. I begin a paddling rhythm and head up the coast with the sun at my back.

Kayaking is fast becoming the sport of those who want to experience the ocean shoreline cheaply, easily, and quickly without being glued to the beach. Modern molding techniques allow manufacturers to create diverse kayak designs with plenty of uses. It's also possible to get a dependable kayak and the necessary accessories, like a paddle, for under $500. Of course, like all modern sports, you could spend a lot more as well. However, it's usually money well spent as this sport's enthusiasts definitely reap high returns on their investments. Rentals average $15 for a session at sea.

It doesn't take long to get to a point of relative proficiency. In a short time neophytes are using their boats to explore, to fish, and even to dive and snorkel. Surfing in these crafts takes longer to learn, but with the sit-on-top design, it takes only a short time to regroup from a wipeout.

The modern designs run from about 9 feet in length to more than 17. Which model to choose depends upon what you want the boat to do. A short boat with a rounded underside, or rocker, will be much more maneuverable than a long boat with a flat bottom or very little rocker. Wider is better if you're looking for stability. Depth of the cockpit also figures heavily into how stable a boat is. What does all this translate to? Well, no one design will be perfect for all uses. If you plan learning to surf the boat, a model about 11 feet long with some rocker should give you sufficient turning ability and still be big enough to use for short tours. If you only want to surf the boat, get an even shorter kayak with as much rocker as you can handle.

New surfing designs are constantly being tested. Some models are made just for surf and have fins that protrude from the hull. If long-distance touring or speed is your desire, a long, narrow boat is what you'll require. These are more like traditional sea kayaks, except they are made from impact-resistant plastic and are even self-bailing. Their flat hull and rudder assemblies allow them to hold a straight-line course, which is requisite for navigation.

All the boats from 9 feet up have a cargo capacity of more than 200 pounds and some up to 600 pounds. Places for hatches as well as specially molded compartments for air tanks and coolers make these things extremely versatile. Fishing from these platforms is quite popular, as they require little time to get into the water and can tote along all the gear. Kayaks and fishing were meant to be together, but bring along gear that doesn't suffer from being submerged.

Many beaches in Southern California have locations from which to rent kayaks. You'll see racks full of neon-colored boats near launch points.

Remember to wear your PFD (personal flotation device). If you're a midnight kayaker, don't forget your VDS (visual distress signal); it could save your life, and it's required between sunrise and sunset.

REGION 17

GOLETA TO POINT CONCEPTION

Civilization recedes rapidly in the rearview mirror while driving through the region from Goleta, giving way to rolling hills whose golden grasses overlook an increasingly rocky shoreline. Following the coast actually entails a westward journey as the coastal communities give way to large, private ranches and a few state parks: El Capitan, Refugio, and Gaviota. All three offer camping and plenty of Pacific recreation.

High cliffs separate the shore from the encroachment of civilization, casting an air of seclusion onto the sand below. Goleta and Isla Vista house much of the University of California at Santa Barbara student body, which makes for a diverse population and equally eclectic beach crowd. Playgrounds and picnic areas are provided at Goleta Beach County Park for group gatherings. Coal Oil Point Reserve gives bird watchers a good look into coastal lagoon habitats.

El Capitan, Refugio, and Gaviota all offer a full range of amenities, including camping. The beaches are actually pretty small. However, the rocky tide pools make up for the limited lengths of sand. Refugio and El Capitan both have small shops from which to fill hungry stomachs or empty cameras. Gaviota's pier provides a self-operated crane for small-boat aficionados and is popular with anglers.

As the coastline continues westward toward California's dogleg at Point Conception, the land essentially becomes inaccessible. It's a region of bluffs, secluded cove beaches, and arguments over access rights. The area is composed of the Hollister and Bixby Ranches. Off these shores are some of California's best waves.

Access

The eastern boundary is marked by Hwy 217's exit on Hwy 101. The junction of Hwy 1 and Hwy 101 marks the western border. Use Hwy 101 to access the entire region.

Santa Barbara Airport—Contact your airline or travel agent or www.flysba.com. Air service is available to many U.S. cities and international flights connect through Los Angeles and San Francisco. Santa Barbara Airport is also popular with private planes.

Beaches

More Mesa Beach

Goleta Beach County Park

Isla Vista Beach

El Capitan State Beach

GOLETA TO POINT CONCEPTION

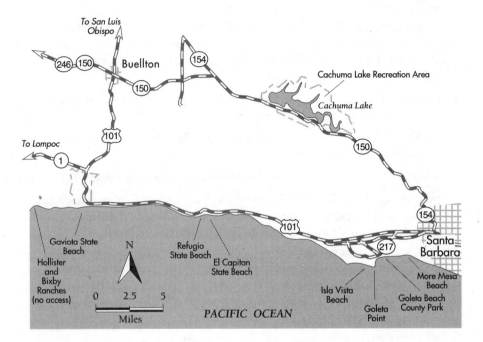

Refugio State Beach

Gaviota State Beach

Hollister and Bixby Ranches

Camping

Refugio State Beach—805-968-3294. Reservations, 800-444-7275.

El Capitan State Beach—805-968-3294. Reservations, 800-444-7275, cal-parks.ca.gov/RESERVE/resindex.htm. 142 sites plus RV en-route camping, showers, restrooms, general store, picnic tables, and campfire programs.

El Capitan Canyon Resort—805-968-2214 or 805-685-3887, www.el-capitancanyon.com. 235 sites for RVs and tents, restrooms, showers, store, nature trails.

Gaviota State Beach—805-968-3294 or 805-444-7275 (reservations), cal-parks.ca.gov/RESERVE/resindex.htm. 52 sites, restrooms, showers, general store.

Cachuma Lake Recreation Area—805-688-4658. 850 sites for RVs and tents.

Other points of interest

South Coast Railroad Museum—805-984-3540. Housed in a restored Southern Pacific Railroad Company station, this place offers everything you want to know about Southern California's railroads but were afraid to ask. 1:00 P.M. to 4:00 P.M. daily. $1 donation.

Stow House, Sexton Memorial Museum—805-964-4407. A Victorian home (Stow House), vintage farming equipment, and even a cannon that washed up on the beach are on these grounds. Tours on Saturday or Sunday 2:00 P.M. to 4:00 P.M. Donation asked for but never required.

Goleta Valley Historical Soceity—805-964-4407 or 805-967-4618. This group publishes literature that allows self-guided tours of the area's historic sites and buildings.

Cachuma Lake Recreation Area—805-686-5054. An inland water playground with fishing, boating, and camping.

Air Heritage Museum—805-683-8936. The history of humanity in this region's sky.

Nojoqui Falls County Park—805-934-6123. A big park with playgrounds, barbecue grills, ball fields, and a trail to a 164-foot waterfall. It's 1.5 miles east of Hwy 101. Take Old Coast Rd. to Alisal Rd. Open daily dawn to dusk.

Mission Santa Ines—805-688-4815. Known as the "Mission of the Passes," its purpose was to link the Santa Barbara mission with the one in Lompoc. It was also meant to create a buffer zone of sorts between an uncooperative group of Native Americans, the Tulares, and the Chumash tribes that the missionaries deemed favorably disposed to Christianity conversion. The garden is quite pleasant and sports a nifty group of hedges in a Celtic cross design.

Elverhoj Museum—805-686-1211. Danish art and artifacts in a Danish-style home. The museum displays Solvang's Danish connections. Free.

More Mesa Beach

After crossing a grassy, privately owned mesa top, the ocean reveals itself lapping the sandy shore below. Stairs, maintained by beachgoers like you, descend to the beach where revelers often are dressed only epidermically. In other words, people go nude. While it's not formally allowed, violation tickets are rarely given here for nudity. Don't use the area to practice behaviors that involve lots of contact and heavy breathing, as this angers those who own the mesa. When those who own the mesa get angry, the police write tickets. They'll also issue tickets to those drooling fools who stay on the mesa top with binoculars and zoom lenses.

Low tide is the time to be here. Otherwise, the ocean will be lapping at the mesa's legs.

ACCESS: From Hwy 101, exit at Turnpike Rd. and turn toward the ocean (left if northbound). Continue to Hollister Ave., turn left, travel two blocks to Puente

Dr., and turn right. Keep right both times that Puente Dr. forks, and you'll be on Vieja Dr. The first left, in 150 yards, is Mockingbird Ln. A dirt path to the beach leaves from Mockingbird Ln. and reaches the stairs about a half-mile later. However, there isn't any parking there.

PARKING: Streetside parking near the access trail. Obey all parking signs. The city will tow.

HOURS/FEES: None posted. Free unless your car is towed.

AMENITIES: Stairway.

ACTIVITIES: Swimming nude.

GOLETA BEACH COUNTY PARK

A long, wide swath of sand extends seaward from a grass knoll where children play, students read, and picnickers fight the gulls. A group picnic area to the west is available for large gatherings and is reserved through the county. There is a fishing pier, snack shack, playground, and volleyball nets at this popular family-oriented beach. Goleta Valley Historical Society has five sites marked here, too.

ACCESS: From Hwy 101, exit onto Clarence Ward Memorial Blvd. (Hwy 217) southbound, then take the Sand Spit Exit. There's a sign for Goleta Beach County Park. Turn left on Sand Spit, then turn right into the park

PARKING: Large parking lot. If full, look along Sand Spit Rd.

HOURS/FEES: 8:00 A.M. to sunset. Free.

AMENITIES: Bike path, volleyball, lifeguard, playground, picnic tables, barbecue grills, restrooms, art sculpture, wildlife area, pier, historical sites.

ACTIVITIES: Birding, whale watching, swimming, surfing, volleyball, picnicking, fishing, sunbathing, snack shack, *no* kites.

FOR MORE INFORMATION:

Goleta Beach Pier—805-967-1300.

Santa Barbara County Parks Administration, South County—805-568-2461.

Weather—www.keyt.com/003/003/001.html.

ISLA VISTA BEACH

Isla Vista Beach has clear-day Channel Islands views for the University of California at Santa Barbara (UCSB) coeds who call this beach home. The beach rounds Goleta Point to the east (left), where views of Santa Barbara are revealed. High cliffs line the beach, with access down stairs or a paved ramp. Two parks, Isla Vista and Window to the Sea, sit atop the cliffs, with benches for those students who don't have time to hit the beach.

Coal Oil Point Reserve (Devereaux Point) lies westward and is a quiet place to observe wildlife. The beach below it, Sands Beach, is reached by walking north from Isla Vista Beach. The area gets its name from the natural tar that often coats watergoers. Onshore winds seem to correlate with the sticky globs. Mineral oil or WD-40 are often used to rid the flesh of this mess. Scuba divers and snorkelers enjoy the spot on clear-water days.

ACCESS: Take the Storke Rd. Exit from Hwy 101 and head toward UCSB and the ocean. Turn left on El Collegio Rd. and right on Camino Corto, which runs into Del Playa Dr., which connects the three stairwells at the ends of Camino Majorca, Camino del Sur, and Camino Pescadero.

PARKING: Be sure to check the signs for regulations before parking on the street. The college's parking areas have some permitted spaces. The pay lot on Ocean Dr. is reached by continuing on El Collegio Rd., then turning right onto Ocean Dr.

HOURS/FEES: Sunrise to sunset. Free.

AMENITIES: Volleyball nets, picnic tables, bluff-top sun decks, hiking trails.

ACTIVITIES: Surfing, volleyball, sunbathing, hiking, birding, whale watching.

FOR MORE INFORMATION:

Isla Vista Beach County Park—805-681-5650.

Weather—www.keyt.com/003/003/001.html.

EL CAPITAN STATE BEACH

El Capitan State Beach's campground feels fairly secluded despite the many campers who frequent the area on any given day. A bait shop/snack house is the only store before Goleta, so it does a brisk business. A pair of paths lead to the bluff-backed beach. The southern end of the shoreline has a grassy platform and rocky shore that are popular with picnickers and fishermen. There's also a self-guided nature trail, which informs hikers as the path winds atop the coastal bluff. Bicyclists will enjoy the 2.5-mile trail connecting El Capitan to Refugio State Beach.

ACCESS: Take Hwy 101 to the El Capitan State Beach Exit, pay the fee, and park your car in the lot.

PARKING: In the day-use lot.

HOURS/FEES: Sunrise to sunset. $5.

AMENITIES: Snack shack, restrooms, trails, campground, picnic ground, grills, lifeguard.

ACTIVITIES: Surfing, swimming, hiking, fishing, scuba diving, biking.

FOR MORE INFORMATION:

Lifeguard Headquarters—805-963-3834.

California State Parks, Channel Coast District, Dispatch Office—805-968-3294.

California State Parks, Channel Coast District—805-899-1400.

REFUGIO STATE BEACH

Refugio, the little sister of El Capitan, is an oasis in a coastal canyon. The tall palms are evenly spaced and the campground neatly laid out, giving a feeling of order. Surfers like the north end of the beach, where a nice wave sets up near the rocks beneath the cove's cliff border. Rocks also bound the beach to the south, but without the dramatic cliff. The beach sands connect the two rocky borders in a classic horseshoe shape. The green, grassy park lying inland of the sand creates a cooling effect on hot summer days, making the campground here a winner. A 2.5-mile bike trail connects Refugio to El Capitan State Beach.

ACCESS: On Hwy 101, drive north from Santa Barbara or south from San Luis Obispo. The park is on the ocean side of the highway.

PARKING: Day-use lot in the park.

HOURS/FEES: Sunrise to sunset. $5.

AMENITIES: Snack shack, restrooms, trails, campground, picnic ground, barbecue grills, lifeguard, playground.

ACTIVITIES: Surfing, swimming, hiking, fishing, scuba diving, biking.

FOR MORE INFORMATION:

Lifeguard Headquarters—805-963-3834.

California State Parks, Channel Coast District, Dispatch Office—805-968-3294.

California State Parks, Channel Coast District, Gaviota Sector—805-968-1711.

California State Parks, Channel Coast District—805-899-1400.

Gaviota State Beach

A short wooden pier juts away from a tilted slab of tan rock to form the northern border of the covelike strand of sand. A towering railroad bridge forms an entrance arch between the beach and the parking lot and campground. Fishing and camping are the main attractions here, along with a dip in the ocean when the sheltered cove gets too hot. This is also a popular place with underwater enthusiasts. The coastline continues westward toward Point Conception. However, this is the last public access point.

East of the state beach is a secluded beach commonly called Gaviota Beach. Its access point is east of the oil tanks visible on Highway 101 between Gaviota State Beach and Refugio State Beach. The pull-out parking area is accessible from southbound Highway 101, which in turn can be reached by making a U-turn at a crossover located at the oil tanks. Look for a "San Onofre State Beach" sign that often marks the trail.

Access: On Hwy 101, drive 30 miles north from Santa Barbara or 70 miles south from San Luis Obispo. The park is on the ocean side of the highway about 12 miles west of El Capitan State Beach.

Parking: Inside the park is a huge parking lot.

Hours/fees: Sunrise to sunset. Day use is $5.

Amenities: Restrooms, showers, pier, picnic tables, barbecue grills, trails, boat launch, lifeguards.

Activities: Swimming, fishing, scuba diving, kayaking, hiking, picnicking.

A railroad trestle marks the entrance to Gaviota State Beach, which is popular with scuba divers.

FOR MORE INFORMATION:

Lifeguard Headquarters—805-963-3834.

California State Parks, Channel Coast District, Dispatch Office—805-968-3294.

California State Parks, Channel Coast District, Gaviota Sector—805-968-1711.

California State Parks, Channel Coast District—805-899-1400.

HOLLISTER AND BIXBY RANCHES

There is a place in California where world-class waves break daily, where the line-up is uncrowded and the shore isn't littered with hotels. It's a place that surfers dream of and few others have ever heard of: Hollister and Bixby Ranches, which occupy the greater portion of Point Conception. Access is extremely limited between Highway 101 and Jalama. For those of us without connections, it's sure to remain an unknown, though there are rumors that Bixby Ranch and the California Coastal Commision are talking deal. You never know.

To gain access, people used to buy "surfer parcels," which were 8.3-acre bits that allowed a person access to the coast. That practice has stopped. Reports of vandalism and threats of violence, along with fences, keep the area empty. Legally, access to the land below the mean high-tide line is allowed. However, getting there requires a boat, trespassing, or the scenario mentioned in the access section below.

Those who boat in are rewarded with waves aplenty, though the locals may make you feel unwelcome. This is true explorers' country. It is the forbidden promised land.

It seems odd that a sport like surfing, whose practitioners pride themselves on being free and open, can be so closed-minded when it comes to access rights. Yet many of these surfers claim they are simply trying to keep their sport pure. Where I get confused is when I consider that surfing's early days are reputed to have been days of togetherness. Many feel that this camaraderie has been lost. I disagree. Surfers still share a special bond. I feel it's those who have decided to own the ocean who have lost contact with surfing's touchstone.

Meanwhile, the ocean continues to lap at the area's bluffs and cove beaches, oblivious to the pettiness of humankind.

ACCESS: You need to know someone who knows someone whose brother's wife has a friend who knows a guy with a key to one of the ranch's gates, and while he'd get in trouble if he brought along a guest, your sister-in-law's friend said he knows where the guy keeps the key. It is also possible to boat in from the north or south. From the north requires crossing through Vandenberg Air Force Base's missile range, which requires checking in with the base. Information on the proper procedures can be found at Santa Barbara Harbor and Port San Luis. A hotline (800-648-3019) lists which danger zones are open in the region.

AMENITIES: None.

ACTIVITIES: Surfing. (If I knew *and* I told you, I'd have to kill you.)

FOR MORE INFORMATION: My friend's second-cousin-twice-removed's sister's friend has changed his number. Sorry.

RIDE THE WIND!

The day's dawn has a delicate breeze that keeps the heat from building. It's not windy by any stretch of the imagination. Yet, unseen by those on land, there is wind approaching from offshore. As noon approaches, whitecaps are visible and by 12:30 the ocean has that familiar victory-at-sea look. This is when the windsurfers hit the water. They constantly shift their weight to counteract the force of Mother Nature's breath, then subtly release pressure from the boom to ease into a wave. As the wave's energy ceases to drive the vessel, the sailor pumps the sail by pulling on the boom, gains speed, tacks, and heads out for another run, like a bee skittering from flower to flower and gathering waves of pollen to create sweet memories.

Ocean windsurfers use shortboards, which allow skilled sailors to use the waves as launching pads for aerial maneuvers. When the ocean serves up a big swell paired with a strong breeze, watch out!

GOOD PLACES TO SURF THE WIND (NORTH TO SOUTH):

North of San Simeon (the rugged coast south of the Elephant Seal observation points near Point Piedras Blancas)

Surf Beach

Jalama

Seaside Park

Malibu

Will Rogers State Beach

Dana Point

Oceanside

Tamarack Surfing Park

Tourmaline Surfing Park

Ocean Beach

Imperial Beach

REGION 18

POINT CONCEPTION TO PORT SAN LUIS

From the whine of ATVs playing on the Oceano Dunes adjacent to the flying migrants in Oso Flaco Lakes, from the roar of a Vandenberg rocket's rapid ascent to the stars to the silent beating of a butterfly's wings in jittery flight near its euca-lyptus home and the silent opening of a feeding Pismo clam beneath the like-named beach, extremes seem the norm of this region.

Sea captains know Point Conception as the graveyard of the Pacific, a place where rough seas and rocky shores can send ships to watery deaths. The land here makes a 90-degree turn to form California's dogleg and the central coast. Government and private land make a good deal of this coast all but inaccessible, but the few exceptions are spectacular. Those making the effort will be awarded with lots of sand and plenty of Pacific.

Jalama, the first access point north of Point Conception and a gem in the Santa Barbara Parks and Recreation system, is very popular with campers and surf-ers alike. Surf Beach allows easy access to the folks of Lompoc, Santa Maria, and surrounding communities. Jalama Beach is the jewel of the Santa Barbara system, offering a modern campground in a very secluded environment. The pillow-soft sand is laid beneath eroded, tan-colored cliffs with the blue-green Pacific covering the rest of the scene.

Point Sal, visited by a few hardy souls who brave the journey, is a secluded portion of pristine Pacific. The access road to Point Sal State Beach slipped off the mountain in 1998 and the "powers that be" (Vandenberg Air Force Base, Bureau of Land Management, California State Parks) state that reopening land-based access is not in the cards. If you can manage to get there, you'll find a sandy, cliff-backed beach with nary a soul upon it. Harbor seals hang out at the point while surfing visitors hang out at the beach.

Lompoc offers its mural-filled town for coastal visitors as a base location. Though landlocked, the town boasts a long California history, along with the nearby Vandenberg base and its space camp. Surf Beach is the next easily accessible point of shore. This long, wide swath of sand is the playground of Vandenberg AFB, Lompoc, and the endangered snowy plover. Surf Beach offers lots of room to spread out and a fickle beach break for waveriders. Every June the town holds a flower festival with tours of more than 1,400 acres of flowering fields.

The Oceano Dunes portion of coastline offers diversity typical of California. The Oso Flaco Lakes, a protected region, delivers some views into what wetlands were like before human machines. On the other side of the fence lies the Oceano Dunes State Vehicular Recreational Area, California's only coastal dunes available for vehicular use. The sand here is naked to the wind, a stark contrast to the wetlands.

POINT CONCEPTION TO PORT SAN LUIS

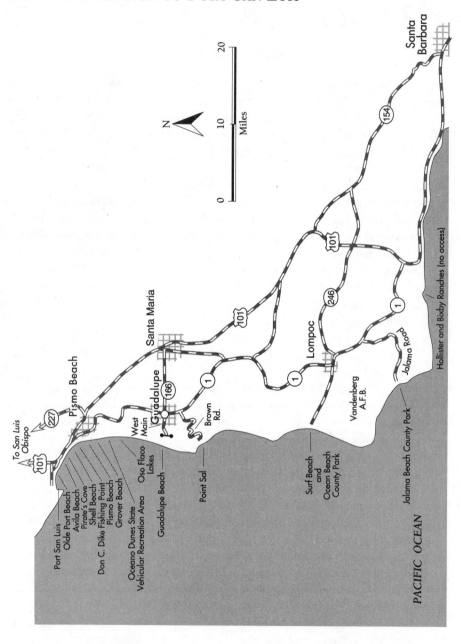

Civilization returns with Grover Beach, Pismo Beach, Shell Beach, and Avila Beach, which all still lean toward the natural experience with sand, sun, and surf the main offerings. Pismo Beach throws in some volleyball courts and a pier to complement the nature trails in the state beach's campground. The trails visit the Monarch butterfly's wintering grounds, a must-see between November and February. Shell Beach offers secluded coarse-sand coves accessed by metal staircases. It's common to see kayaks gliding among the large waterbound rocks that give seabirds a perching point.

Avila Beach is a throwback to the days when sea people owned the oceanfront stores that border the beach. The sand is soft, the pier is weathered, and the parking is right at the beach. Summer weekends bring crowds, making this the place to be if you're into being seen.

Port San Luis also has a beach. This skinny sand ribbon reaches Avila on the left and the port's breakwater on the right. The view is of the port's moorings and an oil-company pier. This beach acts as a relief valve for crowded Avila. The port offers docktop dining and guided fishing trips and is a put-in spot for large boats. The lighthouse is accessible via a guided hike.

The coast north of the port is home to the Diablo Canyon nuclear generating facility and is off-limits. This is the reason for all the cryptic signs describing warning sirens. Upon hearing three warning blasts, tune your radio to 920 AM, 1400 AM, or 98.1 FM and listen to how much radiation you've just been exposed to. If you're at sea, tune to VHF channel 16.

Access

Hwy 1 provides the coastal access for the entire region. However, Hwy 101 is the quick route into the region from Los Angeles or San Francisco. Beach access is given from Hwy 101.

Beaches

Jalama Beach County Park

Surf Beach and Ocean Beach County Park

Point Sal State Beach

Guadalupe Beach

Oso Flaco Lakes

Oceano Dunes State Vehicular Recreation Area

Grover Beach

Pismo Beach

Don C. Dike Fishing Point

Shell Beach (Margo Dodd and Ocean Parks)

Pirate's Cove

Avila State Beach

Olde Port Beach

Camping

Jalama Beach County Park—805-736-3504 or 805-736-6316. Sites for tents and RVs, snack shack, restrooms, showers, picnic area, grills, trails, playground. $21 with hookups, $15 without.

Pismo State Beach North—805-489-2684 or 805-549-3312. Reservations, 800-444-7275, cal-parks.ca.gov/RESERVE/resindex.htm. 103 sites for tents and RVs, restrooms, water, picnic tables with barbecue grills. Wintering ground for thousands of Monarch butterflys.

Pismo State Beach Oceano Campground—805-489-1869 or 805-489-2684. 80 sites in the southern portion of the park (42 with hookups), beach camping available, pay showers and restrooms.

Oceano Memorial County Park—805-781-5930 (County Parks Office), 805-781-5219 (Group Picnic Reservations). 64 sites in a park surrounding a small lake.

Avila Hot Springs Spa and RV Resort—805-595-2359. 75 sites for tents and RVs, recreation center, toilets, showers, picnic tables with barbecue grills, pool, television.

Le Sage Riviera—805-489-5506, 319 Hwy 1, Grover Beach.

Pismo Coast Village Recreation Vehicle Resort—888-RVBEACH or 805-773-181, www.rvbeach.com. 400 RV sites with everything imaginable, including satellite TV and miniature golf.

Pismo Sands RV Park—805-481-3225, 2220 Cienega, Oceano.

Sand and Surf RV Park—805-489-2384, Hwy 1, Oceano.

Silver Spur RV Park—805-489-7787, 1207 Silver Spur Pl., Oceano.

Other points of interest

Port San Luis Lighthouse—805-541-8735. While you can't go in, the Pecho Coast Trail heads up past the Port San Luis Lighthouse on a 4-mile journey. The trail is only accessible via a naturalist-guided tour, which requires that participants be over twelve years old, in good shape, and wearing hiking shoes. Two trips are offered: a 4-hour trip to the lighthouse and an 8-hour trip to Rattlesnake Point. Reservations are required for this free tour.

Port San Luis Harbor—805-595-5400. Fishing report—805-595-2803. Steeped in history, the Hartford Pier (Pier 3) provides fishing, a restaurant, and a fish market. This is also a self-service boatyard with a massive mobile hoist, a big crane for boats.

Diablo Canyon Nuclear Power Plant—805-546-5280. Free tours of the plant and its accompanying marine biology lab. The power plant uses seawater to cool its core, then returns the heated water to the ocean. The lab studies the effects on sea life in the area. Visitors are treated to views of sea creatures in aquariums.

Dunes Discovery Center—805-343-2455, in the town of Guadalupe on Hwy 1. A free look at the Guadalupe and Nipomo Dunes' colorful histories and info on the local flora and fauna. Open weekends from noon to 4:00 P.M. and Friday from 2:00 P.M. to 4:00 P.M.

Santa Maria Museum of Flight—805-922-8758. From satellites to a replica of a Wright brothers model, this museum has a wide variety of aeronautical displays. Friday to Sunday from 9:00 A.M. to 5:00 P.M. or by appointment.

The Parks-Janeway Carriage House—805-688-7889. Native American artifacts, ranching history, and lots of things that horses used to pull are on display thanks to the Santa Ynez Historical Society. The house is open 10:00 A.M. to 4:00 P.M. every day. The museum is open Friday to Sunday from 1:00 P.M. to 4:00 P.M. It's all free.

Arroyo Grande Walking Tour—805-489-7242 or 805-473-2250. A self-guided tour through a town that time seems to be passing by.

La Purisima Mission State Historic Park—805-733-3713. Known as the most restored of the state's missions, Misión la Purísima Concepción de Maria Santísima often hosts re-creations with participants in traditional dress doing traditional tasks. Hiking trails are also accessible here.

Lopez Lake, Arroyo Grande—805-489-1222. Waterskiing, boating, fishing, picnicking, swimming, hiking, and some camping at scenic lakes.

Vandenberg Air Force Base—805-734-8232, ext. 63595. This is the Cape Canaveral of the West. Located on a vast wildlife sanctuary, tours here are a mind-provoking mix of human capacity for destruction and nature's ability to adapt. The area is also used to send up commercial packages, in other words, they launch satellites here.

See Canyon Road—Apples and other produce are available from the growers along See Canyon Rd. This rough dirt road twists through an impressive forest, then climbs to deliver views of Morro Rock and San Luis Obispo.

Wintering Grounds of the Monarch Butterfly—805-489-2684 or 805-773-1661. Every winter the eucalyptus trees grow living, orange leaves that bend branches toward the ground. They are the monarch butterflies that migrate to these groves to mate. Count on getting a sore neck from looking up in fascination.

Jalama Beach County Park

As hard as this beach is to reach, you'd think it'd be less crowded. Actually the beach has ample space for the hordes—it's the campground that gets full. The beach consists of light sands leisurely sloping away from the campground and its snack shack. Bluffs rise at either end of the beach. A famous secret surf spot, Tarantulas, lies out here. It's really not secret—it just takes a lot of time to get to it. The beach lies at the end of a 14-mile access road. Luckily for campers, a (no) vacancy sign shows the status of the first-come-first-served campground in the road's first mile.

Access: Exit Hwy 1 and go northbound to Lompoc. After 14 miles on this scenic road, turn left onto Jalama Rd. A small sign for Jalama Beach should be visible. Follow this narrow road 14 miles on a roller-coasterlike ride filled with sharp, blind corners. Jalama Rd. is 8 miles south of Lompoc on Hwy 1.

Parking: The parking lot/campground has a sufficient lot.

Hours/Fees: Day use is 6:00 A.M. to 8:00 P.M. $5 for day use, $15 for camping. An annual pass is available for $50 or $45, the latter for Santa Barbara County residents.

Amenities: Snack shack, campground, restrooms, showers, picnic area, grills, trails, playground.

Although Jalama Beach is relatively secluded, its modern campground is very popular and often full.

ACTIVITIES: Windsurfing, surfing, camping, wildlife watching, tide pooling, picnicking, kite flying, hiking, boating, fishing, whale watching.

FOR MORE INFORMATION:

Jalama Beach County Park—805-736-6316 or 805-736-3504.

SURF BEACH AND OCEAN BEACH COUNTY PARK

This wide beach is Lompoc's easiest access to the ocean. The park provides ample parking along with a playground and some shelter from the wind. The beach is reached by following the sidewalk and passing under the railroad bridge to Surf Beach. The area provides bird watchers with plenty to see in its marshlike flats. The snowy plover is known to nest in the dunes. Please observe the intent of the signs marking closed areas.

ACCESS: From Hwy 101, take either Hwy 246 or Hwy 1 to Lompoc. The two roads meet east of the town. Stay on Hwy 246 (Ocean Ave.) when Hwy 1 heads north. Hwy 246 leads straight to the beach. Before the road climbs the last dunes to the beach, turn right on Ocean Park Rd. and enter the park. From the north side of the park, a path leads under the railroad bridge to the beach.

PARKING: Park in the large lot in the county park. A small dirt lot is available seaward of the park's entrance road. However, the train crossing there is dangerous.

HOURS/FEES: Daylight hours.

AMENITIES: Playground, restrooms, picnic tables, barbecue grills, wildlife information.

ACTIVITIES: Surfing, birding, whale watching, fishing, sunbathing, kite flying.

FOR MORE INFORMATION:

Santa Barbara County Parks and Recreation—805-934-6123.

POINT SAL STATE BEACH

Point Sal is a lonely piece of land sheltering a series of sandy coves where seals and surfers hang out, neither ever in great numbers. The road, when open, is a hair-raising drive down a hillside on a one-car-wide slumping slab of asphalt that leans precariously toward the sea. The reward is usually solitude and a reminder of what California once was. Don't forget to pack out what you pack in.

ACCESS: *The beach was officially closed in 1998 when Brown Rd./Point Sal Rd. slid from the hill. The official word is that "It is unkown when or if this road will be repaired." If they repair it, here are the directions.*

From Hwy 101 in Santa Maria—Take Hwy 166 west to Guadalupe. Turn left onto Hwy 1 southbound, continue 1.8 miles, and turn right on Brown Rd. (Point Sal Rd.). There should be a small sign. Follow the road for 4 miles. Turn right and follow the road as it turns back on itself and begins to climb the hill while Brown Rd. heads to a ranch house. The remainder of the road is intermittently dirt. It's another 6 miles to Point Sal. Keep left at mile 2.8

PARKING: Park where the road ends.

HOURS/FEES: *The beach is closed. Call the contact numbers below for information.*

AMENITIES: None.

ACTIVITIES: Surfing, camping, wildlife and whale watching.

FOR MORE INFORMATION:

Bureau of Land Management—805-391-6000, 3801 Pegasus Dr., Bakersfield, CA 93308.

California Parks, Channel Coast District, La Purisima Sector—805-733-3713, 2295 Purisima Rd., Lompoc, CA 93436.

GUADALUPE BEACH

Guadalupe Beach is actually the southern entrance to the Nipomo Dunes Preserve. When the road is open, it's possible to drive close to the beach. However, count on a mile hike as the road is usually closed due to dunes forming upon it. It's a nice enough hike, but the first portion is on a road that you drive down in hopes that it is open to the sea. If there are cars in the small day-use lot, it's a good bet that the road is closed.

The beach itself is wide, sandy, and definitely uncrowded, delivering views of the central coast up to Port San Luis. The Dunes Discovery Center (in the town of Guadalupe on Hwy 1) offers visitors a free look at the area's colorful history and info on the flora and fauna. It's open Saturday and Sunday from noon to 4:00 P.M. and Friday from 2:00 P.M. to 4:00 P.M.

ACCESS: From Hwy 101, take Hwy 166 west to Guadalupe. At the intersection of Hwy 1 and Hwy 166, cross Hwy 1 and continue straight toward the ocean. The road becomes West Main St. It's 3 miles to the gate and 4.7 miles to beach parking when the road is open.

PARKING: Either park in the lot by the beach or in the small lot next to the entrance gate.

HOURS/FEES: Sunrise to sunset. $4 for day use.

AMENITIES: Restrooms, wildlife, hiking, biking, and horseback trails.

ACTIVITIES: Bird-watching, fishing, hiking, biking.

FOR MORE INFORMATION:

Santa Barbara County Parks and Recreation—805-934-6123.

Dunes Discovery Center—805-343-2455.

OSO FLACO LAKES

This is possibly the most deserted beach in this book, with the exception, maybe, of Point Sal. The trail to the ocean from the northern entrance passes a pair of pristine lakes that are home to local and migratory birds. A boardwalk keeps footfalls from harming the fragile dunes habitat, which is as natural as any left on the West Coast. Looking toward Pismo Beach, it's striking to notice the diffence between the preserved side of the fence and the motor-vehicle side. There is a stark void of life over the fence.

Once at the beach, stay off the dunes to keep from disturbing the snowy plovers, which nest between March 15 and September 15. The only amenity here, other than the boardwalk, is a friendly ranger who informs visitors while patrolling the area. This is a must-see during the winter. The morning fog clings to the glassy lake surface as thousands of birds wake up and start their day.

ACCESS: From Hwy 101, take Hwy 166 west to Guadalupe. At the intersection of Hwy 1 and Hwy 166, turn right on Hwy 1 and travel 3.75 miles. Turn left on Oso Flaco Lakes Rd. and follow it another 3 miles to its end.

PARKING: A small lot next to the entrance gate.

HOURS/FEES: Sunrise, closing time varies. Check with the ranger. $4 for day use.

AMENITIES: None.

ACTIVITIES: Bird-watching, hiking.

FOR MORE INFORMATION:

Dunes Discovery Center—805-343-2455.

Oceano Dunes SRVA Ranger—805-473-7220.

Oceano Dunes State Vehicular Recreation Area

This is the only place in the state where it's legal to drive on the beach and surrounding dunes. Camping on the dunes is also popular and inexpensive, though the neighbors tend to be up early and they have loud toys. Regulations for dune vehicles are extensive and available at the entrance gate. A few of the basics for noncycles include the following: mandatory helmets, adequate muffler, an 8-foot whip with an orange or red flag, and roll bars (or sufficient roof structure).

Access: From Hwy 101, exit on Old Park Rd. and head toward the ocean. Turn right on Grand Ave. and continue, crossing Hwy 1, all the way to the beach. From Hwy 1, turn seaward on Grand Ave.

Parking: Anywhere that is open to off-road use. The whole idea is that you don't have to park.

Hours/Fees: 6:00 a.m. to 8:00 p.m. $8.

Amenities: Porta Potties, camping allowed.

Activities: Off-road driving with dune vehicles such as sand buggies and motorcycles, horses allowed.

For more information:

Conditions, Warnings, and General Information—805-473-7223.

Camping Reservations—800-444-7275.

Ranger Station (tide information)—805-473-7220.

Weather—805-541-3322.

California Parks, OHMVR Division—916-324-4442, www.calohv.ca.gov.

San Luis Obispo County Visitors Bureau—800-634-1414.

Grover Beach

This beach even has a golf course! Grover Beach, the southern continuation of Pismo Beach, is also characterized by wide sand and established dunes. Leeward of the dunes lays a nine-hole, state-run golf course. A large, free parking lot serves the beach and a restaurant with plenty of spaces left over. The seaward side of the parking area has a large cement picnic area and a wooden boardwalk that traverses the dunes and provides access to the beach. Surfers can be seen catching the beach break early in the morning before the winds pick up.

ACCESS: From Highway 101—Exit on Old Park Rd. and head toward the ocean. Turn right on Grand Ave. and continue, crossing Hwy 1, all the way to the beach. From Hwy 1, turn seaward on Grand Ave.

PARKING: A large lot at the end of Grand Ave.

HOURS/FEES: 8:00 A.M. to 8:00 P.M. Free.

AMENITIES: Restrooms, picnic area, snack shack, golf course.

ACTIVITIES: Fishing, surfing, strolling, picnicking, golfing.

FOR MORE INFORMATION:

Grover Beach Parks and Recreation—805-473-4580.

Golf Course—805-481-5215.

Grover Beach Chamber of Commerce—805-489-9091.

San Luis Obispo County Visitors Bureau—800-634-1414.

PISMO BEACH

This expansive field of bright sand subtly sloping into the sea is a perfect home for clams. Hence the Pismo clam. Beachgoers do no harm to the bivalve mollusk. However, in the recent past these clams were depleted by extensive harvesting. They are making a comeback after regulations regarding size and limits were created.

Surfing is popular next to the pier, which is often busy with fishermen and strolling couples. Located next to Pismo's downtown shops, the pier offers a place to walk off the evening meal. It also has coin-operated binoculars for watching wildlife and beach life.

The north end of the beach remains wide until disappearing into the cliffside beneath a row of hotels. These hotels provide access to the shore via long stairways that drop away from a walkway that makes its way along the bluff.

Tall eucalyptus trees and dunes separate the south and north portions of Pismo Beach. During the winter months, thousands of monarch butterflies mate in these trees. An information kiosk stands outside a dense grove of trees in which a trail meanders, affording glimpses of the green leaves and orange wings that make up the forest's winter canopy.

ACCESS: From Hwy 101 northbound, exit on Price St., turn left on Pomroy, and head toward the ocean. After crossing Dolliver St. (Hwy 1) it's two blocks to the large parking lot at the pier. The beach is accessible beside the pier and via stairways located at the end of Wadsworth Ave. and Addie St. The campground, Pismo State Beach North, is located south of the pier on Dolliver St. From Hwy 101 south-bound exit on Pierce St., turn right and follow the above directions.

PARKING: If the lot at Pomroy is full, there's another lot that often has spaces. Leave the Pomroy lot on Hinds (the only choice) and turn right on Cypress St. Follow this road to Addie St. and turn right to the lot. Downtown Pismo has three-hour parking spaces on side streets such as Cypress St. and Wadsworth Ave. Day-use parking in the campground is well signed.

HOURS/FEES: Daylight hours. Free. Parking at the state beach campground costs $5 for day use.

AMENITIES: Restrooms, pier, snack shack, volleyball nets, swings, trails, campground.

ACTIVITIES: Surfing, hiking, volleyball, sunbathing, butterfly watching, fishing.

FOR MORE INFORMATION:

Recorded Info—805-489-2684.

Pismo State Beach North—805-549-3312.

Camping Reservations—800-444-7275, cal-parks.ca.gov/RESERVE/resindex.htm.

Pismo Beach Visitors Bureau—805-773-4382.

San Luis Obispo County Visitors Bureau—800-634-1414.

DON C. DIKE FISHING POINT

A bronze mermaid watches the ocean from atop a bluff where a plaque reads, "Don C. Dike carved the pathway from solid rock, making this inaccessible area safely useable by countless thousands." Well, it's only relatively safe. Plenty of "at your own risk" signs remind you of the crumbling cliffs beyond the fence. A small park where shrub-lined paths wind behind ragged boulders serves as the gate to this public coastal access. A dirt trail leaves the sidewalk from behind the Shelter Cove Best Western Hotel and heads into the tiny lookout-point park. The path splits to guide visitors to three different places: a bluff-top vista, a window on the sea between two monolithic rocks, and a large platform protected from the Pacific by cement walls. The latter also grants access to a cove with a pebbly beach.

ACCESS: From Hwy 101, take the Price St. Exit onto Shell Beach Rd. Head toward the town of Shell Beach (put the ocean on your left). A parking lot will be on the right immediately after the Shore Cliff Restaurant next to some tennis courts. Put the ocean on your left and walk along the road to the Shelter Cove Best Western. The public access is behind the hotel. Parking is also available farther down Shell Beach Rd., past the hotel. Turn left on Cliff Dr. and park adjacent to the field. Walk back to the hotel with the ocean on your right.

PARKING: Park in the dirt parking area on the undeveloped side of the road on Cliff Dr. or next to the tennis courts.

HOURS/FEES: Sunrise to sunset. Free.

AMENITIES: Gazebo, staircase, benches.

ACTIVITIES: Fishing, tide pool.

SHELL BEACH (MARGO DODD AND OCEAN PARKS)

Stairs bring visitors on a switchbacked descent to thin, cove beaches with coarse golden sand. Eroded, undercut cliffs create an auditorium effect when in the right place. Kayakers are also spotted in the area, having paddled over from Pismo Beach. Margo Dodd Park, named for a civic and community leader, has eighty-seven steps to descend before reaching the shore. Rocks that seem like remnants of an old coastline lie just offshore. Birds have frosted these preferred perches with a thick layer of guano. Ocean Park has fewer stairs, as the cliffs backing it are lower. Four picnic tables and three grills are situated in a small area of turf to afford views of the rock-filled bay. These parks are like oil paintings come to life.

ACCESS: Exit Hwy 101 onto Shell Beach Rd. Turn left onto Cliff Dr. and follow it as it bears right along the bluff's edge and becomes Ocean Blvd. This is Margo Dodd Park. To reach Ocean Park, continue past Cliff Dr. on Shell Beach Rd. and turn left onto Vista del Mar Ave., which leads directly to the park.

PARKING: Pull-over areas are available all along Ocean Blvd. In the event the spaces are filled, look on the residential streets, taking care to respect driveways.

HOURS/FEES: No overnight camping. Free.

AMENITIES: Stairs, picnic tables, barbecue grills, walking path.

ACTIVITIES: Tide pools, bird-watching, private sunbathing at low tide.

FOR MORE INFORMATION:

Pismo Beach Recreation Division—805-773-7040.

San Luis Obispo County Visitors Bureau—800-634-1414.

PIRATE'S COVE

At the base of a rapidly eroding cliff on a loose-pebble beach lie those who like privacy when they sunbathe. The "clothing challenged" have found that this secluded cove is situated away from the prying eyes of those who can't help but stare and then complain about what they were forced to see. Pirate's Cove probably remains a haven for the au-natural bather because those who lodge complaints must admit to their peeping tendencies to gaze on this beach.

ACCESS: From Hwy 101, exit onto Avila Rd. heading toward the town of Avila Beach. After 2 miles, turn left onto Cave Landing Rd. It splits off from Avila Rd. and heads up a steep hill. The road is marked with a yellow "Not a Through Road" sign. If you're watching the golfers on your right, you may miss the turn. Follow Cave Landing Rd. to a big dirt parking area. Beach access is via a steep, sometimes slippery, dirt path from the south side of the parking area.

PARKING: The dirt lot can be rough and rutted. If your car can't handle it, there are a few spaces on the paved terminus of Cave Landing Rd.

HOURS/FEES: The beach has no set hours. However, no overnight camping is allowed. Free.

AMENITIES: None.

ACTIVITIES: Sunbathing, strolling, tide pools.

AVILA STATE BEACH

Avila Beach starts at the rocky base of a tall cliff line, which diminishes in height as the sands of the beach below expand seaward. The strand is split by a wooden pier used primarily for fishing, though there is a public boat lift. The town of Avila forms just inland along Front Street with a clustering of buildings that seem to grow out of each other. By San Luis Obispo Creek's mouth is a bridge that keeps the beach beneath it from plain view. Use care when crossing the small river channel as the emptying lagoon can create quite a current. A fringe benefit provided here is the healthy prescence of Cal Poly coeds who frequent this beach in late spring and late summer. I watched bemused as an older gentleman with binoculars climbed up the beach's cement then sneaked glances of a thong-clad coed.

The area to the right of the pier has all the playground equipment and room to play, while the left side focuses on tanning and socializing. Tide pools are located beneath the cliff among the rocks.

AVILA STATE BEACH IS SCHEDULED TO REOPEN IN THE SUMMER OF 2000, FOLLOWING THE YEARLONG CLEANUP OF AN ENVIRONMENTAL HAZARD.

This beach was plagued by an environmental hazard caused by the local oil biz. The beach was closed for all of 1999 to be reopened in summer 2000 with a "clean" bill of health, though the cleanup methods are suspect to some. The oil folks, prior to cleanup, had the place tested and deemed that "human safety is not believed to be compromised." The public decided otherwise, which led to the controversial cleanup.

ACCESS: From Hwy 101, exit on Avila Beach Dr. and head toward the ocean. (That's a left-hand turn for northbound traffic.) Travel 2.75 miles down the road and turn left on San Miguel St., which runs straight into Avila and ends at the beach.

PARKING: A large parking lot at San Miguel St. and First St. and another lot at the north end of Front St. on San Juan St. provide most of the parking. A lucky few get to park on Front St. along the beach.

HOURS/FEES: Sunup to 10:00 P.M. Free.

AMENITIES: Kayak rental, beach equipment, restrooms, playground, pier, picnic area with barbecue grill, seasonal lifeguard.

ACTIVITIES: Swimming, surfing, kayaking, sunbathing, gawking at sunbathers.

FOR MORE INFORMATION:

Avila Beach Lifeguard Headquarters—805-595-5425.

San Luis Obispo County Visitors Bureau—800-634-1414.

Olde Port Beach

Olde Port Beach is a slightly curving, golden-sand beach, which looks out upon the boats moored in San Luis Bay and at Hartford Pier (Pier 3). On clear days the expansive sands of the Nipomo Dunes are visible far down the central coast. This little beach takes some of the population pressure off Avila Beach and serves as a small, public boat launch.

The nearby Port San Luis Harbor District Boat Launching and Fueling Facility has one of the coast's few self-service boatyards to go with a restaurant, fish market, bait sales, and Nobie Point, which is an RV camp for three or four vehicles. Fishing is popular off the end of the pier. The entrance to Diablo Canyon Nuclear Power Plant is between Pier 3 and Olde Port Beach.

ACCESS: From Hwy 101, exit on Avila Beach Dr. and head toward the ocean. (That's a left-hand turn for northbound traffic.) Follow the road past Avila Beach (first pier), over the bridge, and past a second pier. The beach is located between this second pier and the Port San Luis Pier.

PARKING: Pull over on the bay side of the road.

HOURS/FEES: Sunrise to sunset. Free.

AMENITIES: Restrooms, boat launch, pier.

ACTIVITIES: Boating, sunbathing, swimming.

FOR MORE INFORMATION:

Avila Beach Lifeguard Headquarters—805-595-5425.

San Luis Obispo County Visitors Bureau—800-634-1414.

Port San Luis Harbor Fishing Report—805-595-2803.

Pinnipeds

The Marine Mammal Protection Act makes it a violation of federal law to interfere in any way with the natural behavior of marine mammals. If your actions cause the animals to alter their behavior, you may be found in violation of this law. To report violations, advise the on-duty lifeguard or call the National Marine Fisheries at 619-557-5994 or 310-980-4049.

"Pinniped" is the scientific name for seals and sea lions. The word is Latin for "fin foot" and is meant to describe the creature's use of its fins as feet. The name actually represents two similar animals with distinctly different ancestry and is an example of evolutionary convergence. In other words, the "true" seals and sea lions aren't related. However, they have developed similar characteristics, possibly from living in the same environment. It gets even more confusing. Some seals aren't true seals. Rather, they are related to sea lions. These animals are called the eared seals. To oversimplify, if it doesn't have ears and can't turn its hind flippers toward the front, then it's a true seal.

Pinnipeds often "haul out" (get out of the water) onto Southern California's beaches. They were once quite common up and down the coast. Now, with human settlement of the coast, they tend to stay in secluded areas. The harbor seal and the California sea lion are the most commonly sighted pinnipeds in Southern California. The northern elephant seal, Steller's sea lion, northern fur seal, and Guadalupe fur seal can be found in certain nooks and crannies covered by this book.

San Miguel Island's Point Bennett is famous for being frequented by all six species of these mammals. A ranger-guided trip is possible and requires a call to Channel Islands National Park. The trip requires a 14-mile round-trip hike that starts with a steep climb. It also requires getting to San Miguel Island. The other Channel Islands are also good bets for seeing pinnipeds.

For those who stick to mainland viewing, harbor seals are common in the southern regions and are often seen lounging in the sun on the beach or near-shore buoys. La Jolla Cove has become a popular place for viewing these creatures. The beach is at the south end of the San Diego-La Jolla Ecological Reserve, which protects the seals' food source, making it a nice place to hang out if you're a seal. These animals are common to harbors and secluded sections of shore as well.

For a unique glimpse into the lives of the gargantuan northern elephant seal, there are two viewing areas between San Simeon and Ragged Point. During the winter months the elephant seals use the area to find mates. The state has provided two large parking areas for visitors. Unfortunately, many people seem unable to resist pulling over on the highway rather than using the parking areas. Use caution when driving here—and please use the parking lots.

When viewing wildlife, whether at a special site as noted above or simply at a popular beach, please keep your distance. When these creatures are out of the water they are conserving their energy and resting from their ocean excursions. It uses up a lot of energy to have to shuffle back to the ocean and its exhausting currents, which the animal will do if approached. If it doesn't flee, it is probably due to exhaustion, illness, or injury. In that case it still would like space. Imagine if you were exhausted from swimming and were trying to get warm on the beach when a large group of alien beings surrounded you. Too tired to move, you sit there, terrified. The pinnipeds' big eyes cry to rid them of sand, not because the animal is sad. Compassion is appreciated, but remember that often the best thing to do is nothing. Humans love to help. However, we often do the wrong thing. Give the animal its space and continue to enjoy the beach. Just because everyone else is gathering around an animal doesn't mean it's a good thing to do. Please move along and tell others to do the same.

True Seals

Harbor Seal—*Phoca vitulina*

The harbor seal comes in a variety of colors ranging from black or dark brown to light gray and usually have spots that contrast their main fur color, which gives them the alternative name of leopard seal. These are "true" seals that often haul out on the beaches near bays, river mouths, and harbors. They are 5 to 6 feet long and appear to lack a neck. One reason for this animal's prevalence is its small size, which makes it undesirable to commercial operations.

Northern Elephant Seal—*Mirounga angustirostris*

The northern elephant seal is a breathtaking sight. Large males are more than 15 feet long, weigh more than 1,800 kilograms, and can dive more than 200 meters and remain underwater for up to eighty minutes. The name comes from the large, inflatable trunklike nose that hangs on the male's face. These pendulous snouts are used to make deep, snorelike sounds. The females are *only* 10 feet long and lack the inflatable nasal appendage. The males are very territorial as they assemble harems in the winter and while the females give birth around January. Despite their size, these mammals can be quite fast. Keep this in mind when viewing and give them room. These animals have seen their population shrink as they are hunted for their oil.

Sea Lions and "Eared" Seals

California Sea Lion—*Zalophus Californianus*

These black to dark brown animals are the trained "seals" seen in acts at aquatic shows. In fact, these often playful animals aren't seals at all. They have short, pointed ears, are 6 to 7 feet long, and have a distinct voice. They bark. This bark is often heard before the sea lion slips into the water at a secluded beach. The males have a pronounced forehead and the females are lighter in color.

Steller's Sea Lion—*Eumetopias jubatus*

The Steller's sea lion (or northern sea lion) is large (up to 10 feet long) and has straw-yellow or yellow-brown fur that can seem white when underwater. Though found mostly up north, this species is also seen at the Channel Islands. The Steller's sea lion is also distinguishable by its enlarged forequarters and neck, along with its voice that roars rather than barks.

Northern Fur Seal—*Callorhinus ursinus*

This "eared seal" has especially long rear flippers and toenails on the top side of its flippers. Dark brown in color, the northern fur seal has a large neck visible as it perches on its front flippers. This animal has a tendency to stick one flipper out of the water as it swims, giving the appearance of waving. The species is making a comeback after being hunted indiscriminately. It has recently increased its range and is now seen at San Miguel Island.

Guadalupe Fur Seal—*Arctocephalus townsendi*

Another mammal making a comeback, the Guadalupe fur seal was almost extinct in 1950. Its range is increasing northward from Baja California and can occasionally be seen on the Channel Islands. These "eared seals" have grayish fur when dry that looks dark brown when wet. They are fairly small with the males reaching 6 feet in length. They are recognizable by their long, narrow snouts and long front flippers.

REGION 19

Montaña de Oro to Ragged Point

The final region of this book boasts some of the most picturesque locations in California with the golden poppy-covered hills of Moñtana de Oro, the bay and estuary guarded by stately Morro Rock, and a coastline where sand begins mixing with jagged rocks while otters and elephant seals play in the surf beneath the vertigo-inducing vistas of Ragged Point.

"Montaña de Oro" means "mountains of gold." However, it doesn't refer to the metal. The golden California poppy that covers the hills in spring lends its image to the park of the same name. This may be the best coastal park in the state.

Morro Rock, the Gibraltar of the Pacific, reflects in the glassy water of the bay while the multihued hulls cast their color upon a looking-glass bay front lined with shops, restaurants, and a busy wharf. Morro Bay, while still commercially active, was a busy fishing port for abalone fishermen before the decimation of the species. The bay and adjacent sandspit now teem with nature's variety, affording biology lessons to all who choose to watch.

The coast progresses from sand to rock as it heads north to Ragged Point. Cayucos, Cambria, and San Simeon all lie in this zone. Cayucos, with its mom 'n pop shops, is a beach town that lacks the tourism push of its southern cousins. Cambria's roads to nowhere twist among expensive homes, giving it an elitist feel. Yet, the town begs for tourist dollars on its two-sectioned Main Street. San Simeon sits beside Pacific Coast Highway atop a dusty, windblown bluff, seeming to exist solely as a place for travelers to stay and play while visiting William Randolph Hearst's world-renowned castle. The Hearst Castle's intriguing architecture, gardens, and landscaping are definitely worthy of a look.

San Luis Obispo County is wine country. Harmony, a tiny art community, and Cambria offer three wineries for coastal connoisseurs near Pacific Coast Highway. Paso Robles and Templeton, north of San Luis Obispo (shortened to SLO by locals) along Highway 101, is the nucleus of the county's northern wineries. The area south of SLO, on Hwy 227, also puts out its share of vino.

The Charles Paddock Zoo and the region's lakes (Santa Margarita Lake, Atascadero Lake, and Whale Rock Reservoir) add to the area's recreation options.

The city of San Luis Obispo has its share of historical sites, including the Misión San Luis Obispo de Tolosa. Also home to California Polytechnic State University, SLO has a charming Thursday night farmers' market. The streets fill with pedestrians as barbecue smoke, music, and laughter filter up into the city's canopy of trees.

MONTAÑA DE ORO TO RAGGED POINT

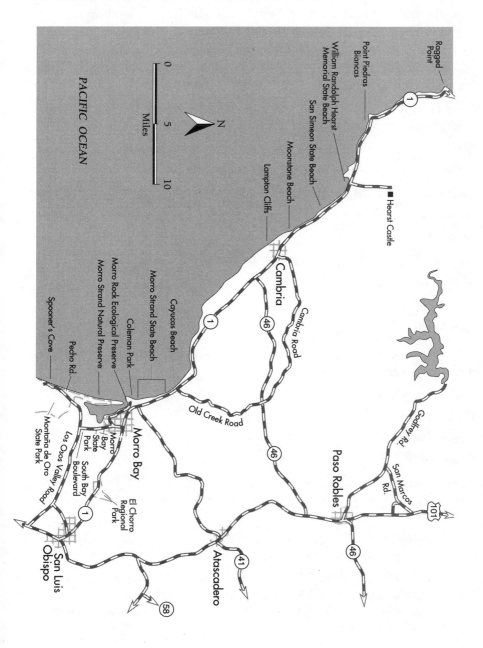

Access

From the south—Travel north on Hwy 101 to reach the area's southern border at Los Osos Valley Rd., just shy of San Luis Obispo.

From the north—The area is reached via the scenic Pacific Coast Hwy (Hwy 1) or Hwy 101. Take either thoroughfare south to reach the county's border, which marks the region's northern limit.

From Hwy 101—Take Hwy 1 north from San Luis Obispo to reach the ocean. Hwy 1 is the main access for the beaches of Morro Bay and northward.

Beaches

Spooner's Cove (Moñtana de Oro State Park).

Morro Strand Natural Preserve

Morro Bay State Park

Morro Bay

Coleman Park and Morro Rock Ecological Preserve

Morro Strand State Beach

Cayucos Beach

Lampton Cliffs

Moonstone Beach

San Simeon State Beach

William Randolph Hearst Memorial State Beach

Point Piedras Blancas

Ragged Point

Camping

Montaña de Oro State Park—805-528-0513 or 805-549-3312. 54 tent sites for RVs under 24 feet long, pit toilets, seasonal water, primitive and group sites available. $10 to $11.

El Chorro Regional Park—805-781-5219. 75 tent or RV sites, flush toilets, water, playground, near San Luis Obispo. $13 to $25.

Morro Bay State Park—805-772-2560 or 805-549-3312. Reservations, 800-444-7275, cal-parks.ca.gov/RESERVE/resindex.htm. 135 sites, 20 with hookups, for tents and RVs under 31 feet, grills, tables, water, toilets, showers, dump station, near Morro Bay. $17 to $23.

Morro Dunes Trailer Park and Camp—805-772-2722. 180 sites, 43 suitable for tents, many with hookups. $15 to $25.

Morro Strand State Beach—805-772-2560 or 805-549-3312. 81 sites for RVs under 31 feet and 22 sites for tents, grills, tables, toilets, beach shower. $17 to $20.

Rancho Colina RV Park—805-772-8420.

San Simeon State Park, San Simeon Creek —805-927-2035 or 805-927-2020. 135 sites for tents or RVs, grills, tables, water, toilets, showers, dump station. $17 to $22.

San Simeon State Park, Washburn—805-927-2035 or 805-927-2020. 70 sites for tents or RVs, grills, tables, water, toilets, showers, dump station. $17 to $22.

Santa Margarita KOA—805-438-5618.

North and South Shore on San Antonio—805-472-2311.

Nimpo RV Parking—4 spaces between Avila and Port San Luis. First come, first served. $20.

Other points of interest

Downtown San Luis Obispo—Every Thursday night the city holds its farmer's market on Monterey Street. A variety of musical bands take position among the carts that sell produce, incense, jewelry, food, and other neat stuff. It feels like you're walking into times past when markets were friendly and trust was the rule rather than the exception.

Hearst Castle—800-444-4445 or 805-927-2020. Tours are offered of this elaborate erection of William Randolph Hearst. Without reservations one may be limited to viewing the IMAX film in the state-run monument's visitor center. Special sunset tours are offered in spring and fall. $25 for adults, $13 for children.

Centennial Park—805-772-6278. A small park with a giant chessboard in downtown Morro Bay. Play chess with 3-foot-tall pieces or use the smaller ones on the surrounding boards.

Mission San Luis Obispo de Tolosa—805-543-6850; Mission San Miguel Arcangel—805-467-3256. The fifth and sixteenth in the chain of twenty-one "Alta" California missions. The former has a variety of exhibits to accompany the grounds. The latter's well-preserved murals, painted more than 200 years ago using natural paints, are still quite vibrant. Art thieves have forced "management" to hide some of the portable art.

Charles Paddock Zoo—805-461-5080; Atascadero Lake Park—805-461-5000. From alligators to wallabies, these five acres of animals are located at Atascadero Lake Park, which has jogging paths, picnic tables, a fishing pier, and paddleboat rentals. The zoo opens at 10:00 A.M. and closes at 6:00 P.M. in the summer and 4:00 P.M. in the fall.

Morro Bay Aquarium—805-772-7647. A place where it's okay to feed the seals (with food purchased here). Other exhibits include the abalone, which was hunted (to the verge of extinction) then processed in the area.

Edna Valley Arroyo Grande Appellation—805-541-5868; Paso Robles Vintners and Growers Association—805-239-8463. For more than 200 years they've grown grapes here, and there are forty wineries to help one enjoy it. Take a tasting room tour and designate a driver.

Laguna Lake—805-781-7300, San Luis Obispo.

Santa Margarita Lake—805-438-5845.

Lake Nacimiento—805-238-3256, Paso Robles.

Waterskiing, boating, fishing, picnicking, swimming, hiking, and some camping at these scenic lakes.

Lampton Cliffs City Park—A quiet, bluff-top park in coastal Cambria with stairway access to tide pools.

Morro Bay State Park Museum—805-772-2694. Exhibits portraying natural history and indigenous culture in a building that looks out over the Morro Bay Estuary. There's also a good bookstore/gift shop. 10:00 A.M. to 5:00 P.M. daily.

SPOONER'S COVE (MONTAÑA DE ORO STATE PARK)

The clinking of faint musical tones is heard in Spooner's Cove as the ocean shuffles the flat, dominolike stones lining the shore. A small stream meanders through the cozy cove's northern edge. Many visitors here simply stand and absorb the scene. The tide pools and rocks are provided by nature; the park service provides pit toilets and primitive camping nearby.

ACCESS: From Hwy 101 in San Luis Obispo (SLO)—Take Los Osos Valley Rd. west toward the ocean. This road will pass through the town of Los Osos and bend south to enter Montaña de Oro State Park. The parking lot at Spooner's Cove's is 4 miles from the park entrance.

From Morro Bay Blvd. in Morro Bay—Take Hwy 1 east toward SLO. Take the first exit, South Bay Blvd., and follow it south more than 4 miles to Los Osos Valley Rd. and turn right. This road will pass through the town of Los Osos and bend south to enter Montaña de Oro State Park. The parking lot at Spooner's Cove is 4 miles from the park's entrance.

PARKING: Parking is available on a dirt pull-out beside the cove.

HOURS/FEES: Sunrise to sunset, seven days a week. No fee, yet.

AMENITIES: Pit toilets, campground, trails.

ACTIVITIES: Tide pools, hiking, horseback riding, mountain biking, fishing, and surfing.

FOR MORE INFORMATION:

Montaña de Oro State Park—805-528-0513 or 805-772-2560.

San Luis Obispo County Visitors Bureau—800-634-1414.

MORRO DUNES NATURAL PRESERVE

Stretching from Hazard Canyon to the mouth of Morro Bay, this 7-mile strand is perhaps the most pristine beach described in this book. Sanderlings, one type of shorebird, dart dexterously in the shore break while digging for dinner in front of a Morro Rock backdrop. The beach, part of Morro Bay State Park, takes some effort to reach, and there are no amenities except a parking lot and a platform trail. This keeps the crowds small and the scene serene.

ACCESS: From Hwy 101 in San Luis Obispo (SLO)—Take Los Osos Valley Rd. west toward the ocean. This road will pass through the town of Los Osos and bend south to enter Montaña de Oro State Park.

From Morro Bay Blvd. in Morro Bay—Take Hwy 1 east toward SLO. Take the first exit, South Bay Blvd. and follow it southward more than 4 miles to Los Osos Valley Rd. and turn right. This road will pass through the town of Los Osos and bend south to enter Montaña de Oro State Park. Continue on this road, which is now called Pecho Rd., as it winds through the park. Turn right at Sand Spit Rd. and descend to the parking lot. The beach lies at the end of a dirt walkway, 0.5 mile from the lot.

HOURS: Sunrise to sunset. No fee, yet.

PARKING: Parking for thirty cars is available in the free lot.

AMENITIES: Wooden plank walkway to beach, parking lot, trails.

ACTIVITIES: Surfing, hiking, bird-watching, paragliding, and hang gliding.

FOR MORE INFORMATION:

Montaña de Oro State Park—805-528-0513 or 805-772-2560.

San Luis Obispo County Visitors Bureau—800-634-1414.

Morro Bay State Park

One of the better bird-watching locales on the coast, Morro Bay State Park provides camping and an informative museum to complement its natural endowments. A rookery for blue herons nestles alongside the bay, affording a glimpse into the lives of the long-necked birds. It's on Lower State Park Road across from the golf course. Black Mountain offers scenic vistas into the bay area.

Access: From Hwy 101 in San Luis Obispo—Take Hwy 1 north 11.2 miles toward Morro Bay and exit on South Bay Blvd. at the sign for Morro Bay State Park. Continue on this road for 0.7 mile to State Park Rd., turn right, and enter the park. The museum lies past park headquarters and the marina.

From the City of Morro Bay—Follow Main St. south into the park.

Hours: Sunrise to sunset. Free.

Parking: Roadside parking is available throughout the park.

Amenities: Campground, museum, rookery, golf course, trails.

Activities: Bird-watching, kayaking, golfing, camping, hiking, biking.

For more information:

Morro Bay State Park (recorded info)—805-772-2560.

Morro Bay State Park—805-772-7434.

Camping Reservations—800-444-7275, cal-parks.ca.gov/RESERVE/res-index.htm.

Museum of Natural History—805-772-2694.

San Luis Obispo County Visitors Bureau—800-634-1414.

Morro Bay

Tidelands Park connects to the bayside promenade overlooking the active fishing harbor of Morro Bay as Morro Rock and the Morro Bay Power Plant seem to face off across the still waters. The park's playground has dolphins and seals upon which the kids can climb and informative displays on the harbor's history. Feeding culinary appetites are the restaurants along Embarcadero, which compete for patronage by offering low-priced fish and chips. Kayaks, available for rent along the promenade, grant access to the sand spit across the bay. Bayshore Bluffs, with views of Morro Rock and the bay, offers quiet picnic sites.

A WATERFRONT PROMENADE OVERLOOKS THE ACTIVE FISHING HARBOR AT MORRO BAY.

The giant chessboard in Centennial Park is another of the eclectic sights in this sleepy bayside town. The chess club has the pieces out on Saturdays and encourages the public to participate. The pieces can also be obtained with a permit, $16, and a driver's license.

ACCESS: From Hwy 1, take the Main St. Exit. Follow Main St. into town and turn right on Beach St., Harbor St., Pacific St., or Marina St. to reach the Embarcadero, which provides access to the bayside. Tidelands Park is at the south end of the Embarcadero, Centennial Park is on the Embarcadero between Pacific and Harbor, Bayshore Bluffs overlooks the Embarcadero. The park entrance, marked with a "Coastal Access" sign, is off Main St. near the entrance to Morro Bay State Park.

HOURS: The sidewalks are rolled up around 10:00 P.M.

PARKING: Parking is free along the Embarcadero. Additional free parking is available at the north end of the Embarcadero in the shadow of the electrical plant and in the boat-launch parking lot next to Tidelands Park.

AMENITIES: Tidelands Park—restrooms, barbecue grill, promenade, playground, boat launch, and parking. Bayshore Bluffs—Gazebo, restrooms, parking. Centennial Park—Giant chessboard, restrooms, parking.

ACTIVITIES: Kayaking, shopping, dining, fishing, picnicking, strolling, biking, chess.

FOR MORE INFORMATION:

Morro Bay Parks and Recreation (to get chess pieces)—805-772-6278.

Morro Bay Chamber of Commerce—800-231-0592 or 805-772-4467.

San Luis Obispo County Visitors Bureau—800-634-1414.

COLEMAN PARK AND MORRO ROCK ECOLOGICAL PRESERVE

The Morro Rock Ecological Preserve has a small sandy cove that looks out upon the Morro Dunes. The beach sits behind a breakwater at the bay's entrance, giving a feeling of safety. However, the Pacific has swept unsuspecting people from the breakwater. Morro Rock is off-limits. The endangered peregrine falcons, which call the rock home, can often be seen from the viewing area.

Within walking distance, Coleman Park lies in the shadow of Morro Rock. The huge dirt parking lot is where surfers suit up to ride the break known as The Rock. An outflow from the Morro Bay Power Plant keeps the water relatively warm compared to the surrounding areas, allowing longer surf sessions. The park also has a skateboard area available to sidewalk surfers.

The smaller, jagged rocks that surround Morro Rock appear to be covered with white frosting or possibly fresh ice from the fog that frequently forms there. However, the coating is simply the result of birds perching and, uh—it's from birds perching.

ACCESS: From Hwy 1, take the Main St. Exit and turn right (both north and south). Follow Main St. into town and turn right on Beach St. and continue down to the Embarcadero. Turn right on Embarcadero, which becomes Coleman Dr., and follow it past the power plant and into the park. Coleman Park's parking will be on the right and Morro Rock Ecological Preserve will be at the end of the road.

HOURS/FEES: Always open. However, there is no overnight camping.

PARKING: Coleman Park has room for 100 cars in its dirt lot while the pullover area for the preserve holds roughly 15 cars. Free parking in both areas.

AMENITIES: Bike lane, restroom, parking, skateboard park, playground.

ACTIVITIES: Surfing, skateboarding, bird-watching, kayaking.

FOR MORE INFORMATION:

Morro Bay Parks and Recreation—805-772-6278.

Morro Bay Chamber of Commerce—800-231-0592 or 805-772-4467.

San Luis Obispo County Visitors Bureau—800-634-1414.

Morro Strand State Beach

Morro Strand sees the most overall use of the area's beaches. Luckily, it is also the largest. This equals a lot of room to play on a wide, sandy, dune-backed beach with multiple access points. The crowd tends to keep close to Morro Rock and thins the farther north you go.

Access: Southern Access Point—From Hwy 1 take the Atascadero Rd. Exit (CA 41). Turn toward the ocean and follow the road as it makes a hard left onto Embarcadero, which ends in a dirt parking lot. This access point lies 0.5 mile north of the Main St. Exit in Morro Bay along Hwy 1.

Central 1 Access Point—From Hwy 1, turn toward the ocean on San Jacinto Ave. Take the next left onto Coral Ave., followed by a right on Azure St., which leads to a parking lot.

Central 2 Access Point—From Hwy 1, turn toward the ocean on Yerba Buena St. Turn right onto Beachcomber Ave. and park along the street. Use this access point to reach the campground.

North Access Point—From Hwy 1, turn toward the ocean on Studio Dr. Access points dot this street, which ends in a small parking lot. This access point is 1.8 miles south of the Cayucos Dr. Exit along Hwy 1.

Other Access—Coleman Park also provides access to this beach.

Parking: Free parking is available in the parking lots and along the Embarcadero, Beachcomber Ave., and Studio Dr.

Amenities: Restrooms at Coleman Park, Azure St., and the campground at the junction of Yerba Buena St. and Beachcomber Ave.

Activities: Camping, surfing, tide pools, shell collecting.

For more information:

Morro Strand State Beach—805-772-2560.

San Luis Obispo County Visitors Bureau—800-634-1414.

Cayucos Beach

The town of Cayucos or, more accurately, the mouths of Cayucos Creek and Little Cayucos Creek, provide the last public beach access before Cambria. A bronze sculpture marks the entrance to a weathered pier that juts into the Pacific, affording views back to the small shops that line the beach's dry side. An expansive barbecue area lies north of the pier, sending the smells of summer into the sea breeze

Cayucos Beach features an expansive barbecue area, as well as a snack shack for those not inclined to cook.

and making one's stomach long for nourishment. Luckily, there's a hot dog stand at the pier. Cayucos Beach feels like a real beach town, though the telltale signs of real-estate offices leave cold shadows on the town's friendly steets.

ACCESS: From Hwy 1, take the Cayucos Dr. Exit and follow this road straight through town to Ocean Front Ave. Turn left and find a space to park. A lot at the north end of Ocean Ave. provides additional spots.

HOURS/FEES: Sunrise to sunset.

PARKING: Free, on-street, angled parking is available right beside the beach. Parking is also available in the town proper. Finding parking on busy days, such as when the classic car festival is in town, requires patience.

AMENITIES: Restrooms, showers, pier, barbecue area, snack shack.

ACTIVITIES: Surfing, swimming, fishing, sunbathing, tide pools.

FOR MORE INFORMATION:

San Luis Obispo County Parks and Recreation—805-781-5930.

Cayucos Chamber of Commerce—805-995-1200.

San Luis Obispo County Visitors Bureau—800-634-1414.

LAMPTON CLIFFS

Otters play beneath the rocky cliffs lining this residential area's shore. The park here provides a staircase down to a rough set of tide pools. The benches atop the low bluff provide a quiet place to watch sunsets.

ACCESS: Take Ardath Dr. off Hwy 1. It's a left turn when traveling from the south. Stay on this main road as it weaves through the residential community. It's a bit confusing. Just keep on the main road and when in doubt head downward. Turn right on Marlboro Ln., then left onto Lampton St. The park is on the left where the road turns to the right to become Sherwood Dr.

HOURS/FEES: Sunrise to sunset.

PARKING: Free parking for five or six cars is provided via a pull-out at the park. Additional parking is available on the road, heeding private driveways, of course.

AMENITIES: Benches, stairs to beach, short trail.

ACTIVITIES: Wildlife viewing, tide pools.

FOR MORE INFORMATION:

Cambria Chamber of Commerce—805-927-3624.

San Luis Obispo County Visitors Bureau—800-634-1414.

San Luis Obispo County Parks and Recreation—805-781-5930.

MOONSTONE BEACH

Moonstone Beach, which is actually the southern end of San Simeon State Beach, is named after the milky-white stones that seem to glow with moonlight as they lay on the coarse, dark sand. Most of the white stones here are simply white quartz, but moonstones are found by patient rock hounds. A narrow trail runs along Moonstone Drive, connecting the access points.

ACCESS: Shamel County Park, Leffingwell Landing, Santa Rosa Creek Access, and Moonstone Dr. Vista all access the beach. Shamel County Park is reached by turning onto Windsor Blvd. from Hwy 1 and is at the northernmost traffic light in Cambria. Keep left past Moonstone Dr. and continue on Windsor Blvd. about 0.3 mile to the park. The other access points all lie on Moonstone Dr. Simply turn onto Moonstone from Windsor or, north of town, from Hwy 1. The sites are well signed.

HOURS/FEES: Sunup to sundown.

PARKING: Free parking is available in lots at each location.

AMENITIES: Shamel Park—pool, barbecue grill, picnic tables, horseshoe pits, grassy playground, volleyball. Leffingwell Landing—restrooms, benches. Santa Rosa Creek Access—restrooms. Moonstone Dr. Vista—picnic area, benches.

ACTIVITIES: Rock collecting, surfing, swimming, picnicking.

FOR MORE INFORMATION:

Cambria Chamber of Commerce—805-927-3624.

San Luis Obispo County Visitors Bureau—800-634-1414.

San Luis Obispo County Parks and Recreation—805-781-5930.

SAN SIMEON STATE BEACH

The majority of usage at this strand is from campers traveling up and down Pacific Coast Highway and birds traveling up and down the coast on their migratory routes. The campground access is also home to a lagoonlike wetland, which provides an excellent habitat for birds and bird watchers alike. Driftwood lies strewn on the pepperlike dark sands of the lagoon's pathway to the sea. Surfer's search for beach breaks here to satisfy their wave craves.

ACCESS: To reach the campground, turn at the well-signed San Simeon Creek Rd. and follow it to the entrance station. The San Simeon Creek day-use site is reached by pulling off the highway about 0.3 mile from the campground entrance.

HOURS: Sunrise to sunset.

PARKING: Campers only at the campground, $20 a night. The rest of the parking is free with an 8-hour limit.

AMENITIES: Camping, restrooms, showers, picnic tables, barbecue grill, and a dump station.

ACTIVITIES: Bird-watching, surfing, rock collecting, driftwood collecting.

FOR MORE INFORMATION:

San Simeon State Park—805-927-2035 or 805-927-2068.

Camping Reservations—800-444-7275, cal-parks.ca.gov/RESERVE/res-index.htm.

San Luis Obispo County Visitors Bureau—800-634-1414.

WILLIAM RANDOLPH HEARST MEMORIAL STATE BEACH

This is an excellent place to picnic before or after visiting the Hearst Castle. The pier used by Hearst during his castle's construction bisects a cove beach framed by low cliffs to the north and rocky shore to the south. A split-level barbecue area allows bluff-top or beachside picnicking. An on-site store provides extra film or snacks in addition to guided fishing trips. Sebastian's General Store, the oldest store in the state, lies a few yards north on San Simeon Road.

A variety of undeveloped sites exists in the area. A small place to park at the end of Ruta Lane, just north of the Cavalier Hotel in the hotel-filled town of Simeon Acres, marks a stairway to a long, sandy cove beach. Overlooks with small parking areas can be found all along Pacific Coast Highway (Highway 1). There are also places where pulling over is specifically forbidden. Check the signs. If white markers fill the road's shoulder, wait for an established overlook to pull over.

ACCESS: From Hwy 1, turn onto San Simeon Rd. The road is about 50 yards north of the entrance to the Hearst San Simeon State Historical Monument (Hearst Castle). Turn left into the beach entrance station, pay the fee, and park.

HOURS: 8:00 A.M. to sunset. Longer hours are held during the summer.

PARKING: A paved lot provides space for paying customers ($4). Limited free parking is available on the roadside outside the day-use area.

AMENITIES: Pier, guided fishing, barbecue grill, picnic area, bait shop, snack shack.

ACTIVITIES: Fishing, swimming, picnicking, surfing, tide pools, and whale watching.

FOR MORE INFORMATION:

Hearst San Simeon State Historical Monument—805-927-2020. Tour reservations, 800-444-4445. IMAX Theater, 805-927-6811.

State Beach—805-927-2068.

Fishing Report—805-927-4676 or 800-ROCKCOD.

San Simeon Chamber of Commerce—805-927-3500 or 800-342-5613.

San Luis Obispo County Visitors Bureau—800-634-1414.

POINT PIEDRAS BLANCAS

The beacon of the lighthouse at Point Piedras Blancas bathes the low, rocky shore where northern elephant seals spend the winter. Viewing these pinnipeds is so popular that parking areas have been provided. Unfortunately, many people still pull off onto the highway shoulder, creating hazardous driving conditions on winter weekends. When the gates are open, so are the trails that lead to vistas of kelp-covered rocks and tide pools. The area is privately owned, but visitation rights have been secured by the Marine Mammal Center. Members of a local group, Friends of the Elephant Seals, open the area on winter weekends and provide information on the giant mammals that breed there. The picturesque lighthouse is not available for visits.

ACCESS: Turn into one of the two parking lots located 5 miles north of William Randolph Hearst Memorial State Beach and 10 miles south of the Ragged Point Inn.

HOURS: No overnight camping.

PARKING: There is room for about 50 cars at the paved, north lot. The south lot is gravel and holds about a hundred cars.

AMENITIES: Parking area, informational signs, trails.

ACTIVITIES: Wildlife viewing, lighthouse viewing.

FOR MORE INFORMATION:

Friends of the Elephant Seals—805-927-4274.

Marine Mammal Center—415-289-SEAL.

San Luis Obispo County Visitors Bureau—800-634-1414.

Ragged Point

A stream cascades down a towering, eroded cliffside and under a trail bridge as the Pacific Ocean grinds away at the rocky cove just north of Ragged Point. The cove is visible from a breathtaking, bluff-top vista at the trailhead behind the Ragged Point Inn. Coffee, food, lodging, and gas are also available.

ACCESS: 15 miles north of William Randolph Hearst Memorial State Beach and 23 miles south of Lucia on Pacific Coast Hwy (Hwy 1) lies the Ragged Point Inn. The trail starts between the buildings in an exotic garden complete with koi fish.

PARKING: Limited parking is available between the lodge and gas station.

HOURS/FEES: No official hours posted. As this is private property, hours can vary. Sunrise to sunset is a good rule of thumb. No fee is charged. However, guilt tends to steer you toward buying a hot chocolate at the snack shack.

AMENITIES: Gas station, snack shop, restaurant, lodging, restroom for customers.

ACTIVITIES: Tide pools, wave watching, photography, rock hunting, hiking.

FOR MORE INFORMATION: Ragged Point Inn—805-927-4502.

WEATHER OR NOT

Normal weather in Southern California is like most other "normal" things in the Golden State: nonexistent. The climate is officially labeled Mediterranean for its mild temperatures and cyclic wet and dry seasons. However, the climate is such that extremes tend to be common.

Everywhere you go in the world people say, "If you don't like the weather, wait a minute. It'll change." Well, in SoCal you usually have to wait a couple of days for the often foreseeable changes. These short-term changes are often predicted accurately. It's the long-term trends that the weather forecasters seem to miss.

The Pacific Ocean buffers Southern California with an area of high pressure, called the Pacific high, which acts like a shield pushing storms toward the north. When it breaks down or moves south for winter, Southern California sees storm activity. Of course, it's much more complex than that—or much simpler, depending upon where you stand. It's complicated by such phenomena as El Niño, La Niña, Santa Ana winds, offshore eddies, tropical storm patterns, the Pineapple express—the list goes on and on. Yet, it's really quite simple. Sometimes it's really dry for a long time and sometimes it rains a lot.

Californians were all weathermen in past lives, and so you'll hear this phrase used everywhere: "It's never been this _____. We haven't seen _____ in a month!" Replace the blanks with one of these pairs: foggy/sun, sunny/fog, rainy/sun, dry/mudslide, smoggy/breathable air, clear/smog, stable/a quake, flat/wave. Basically, it's never how it usually is and it was always perfect yesterday. This comes from the surf culture's practice of telling someone who wasn't here yesterday that yesterday was the best day ever to have been here.

All that said, there are some generalities that I'm willing to stake someone else's reputation on.

Southern California is famous for lots of sun and very little rain. The spring and early summer are known for fog. Sunny days and clear nights dominate most of the summer, and winter is the rainy season, though usually the storms are few and the weather is generally mild.

The northern reaches of this book, namely San Luis Obispo County, have the most seasonal weather, meaning the weather changes as the year progresses. San Diego remains mostly sunny and warm year-round. Of course, terms like warm are relative. Appendix A lists the actual numbers gathered by the U.S. Weather Service. Of course, these are averages. Actual temperatures may vary. For those entering the water, Appendix B lists the average water temperatures on a month-by-month basis.

Mornings and evenings are dependably cool. As the fog, known as the marine layer in politically correct households, burns off, things heat up, giving way to peak tanning hours between 11:00 A.M. and 3:00 P.M. (This is when the sun's rays do the most damage to the skin.) The marine layer usually settles back in late in the day, hopefully after sunset, as things cool off. What this means is that it's a good idea to bring a wool pullover and to dress in layers if planning a full day on the coast.

All this goes out the window when El Niño conditions exist. El Niño is simply the name given to a warm-water event. It wreaks havoc on the normal weather patterns and is linked to wet, stormy seasons. El Niño, Spanish for "the boy child," is named after the Christ child, as the event is first noticeable around Christmas.

A few places exist in each region where you can get weather reports. The phone numbers below, listed by county, provide regionwide information:

San Diego—619-289-1212.

Orange—949-494-6573.

Los Angeles—213-554-1212.

Ventura—805-988-6610.

Santa Barbara—805-988-6610.

San Luis Obispo—805-541-3322.

Internet savvy folks can find out a variety of information, too:

The UV Report—nic.fb4.noaa.gov/products/stratosphere/uv_index/uvi_map.gif.

The Pacific Satellite Picture—asp1.sbs.ohio-state.edu/text/wximages/sat/ir/00LATEST.gif.

Satellite Picture (wind and pressure shown)— lumahai.soest.hawaii.edu/gifs/models/AVN/pac_AVNgoes.gif.

Weather Forecsts—seaboard.ndbc.noaa.gov/data/Forecasts/FZUS6.KLAX.html.

If you're wondering whether or not to go to the beach and the forecast looks bleak, remember this: The best way to check out the weather is by heading to the beach. Go on! So what if it rains! You won't melt! Any day at the beach is, well, a day at the beach!

Appendix A

IMPERIAL BEACH

Average Maximum Temperature

	Jan	Feb	Mar	Apr	May	Jun	Jul	Aug	Sep	Oct	Nov	Dec	Year
°C	17.3	17.6	17.4	18.6	19.3	20.2	22.1	23.4	23.2	21.8	19.9	17.8	19.9
°F	63.1	63.7	63.3	65.5	66.7	68.4	71.8	74.1	73.8	71.2	67.8	64.0	67.8

Average Minimum Temperature

	Jan	Feb	Mar	Apr	May	Jun	Jul	Aug	Sep	Oct	Nov	Dec	Year
°C	7.5	8.4	9.2	10.9	13.1	15.0	17.0	17.9	16.9	13.6	10.2	7.8	12.2
°F	45.5	47.1	48.6	51.6	55.6	59.0	62.6	64.2	62.4	56.5	50.4	46.0	54.0

SAN DIEGO

Average Maximum Temperature

	Jan	Feb	Mar	Apr	May	Jun	Jul	Aug	Sep	Oct	Nov	Dec	Year
°C	18.8	19.1	19.0	20.2	20.6	22.0	24.5	25.4	25.0	23.6	21.0	18.9	21.5
°F	65.8	66.4	66.2	68.4	69.1	71.6	76.1	77.7	77.0	74.5	69.8	66.0	70.7

Average Minimum Temperature

	Jan	Feb	Mar	Apr	May	Jun	Jul	Aug	Sep	Oct	Nov	Dec	Year
°C	9.3	10.3	11.5	13.1	15.0	16.6	18.7	19.6	18.6	16.0	12.1	9.3	14.2
°F	48.7	50.5	52.7	55.6	59.0	61.9	65.7	67.3	65.5	60.8	53.8	48.7	57.6

Average Rainfall

	Jan	Feb	Mar	Apr	May	Jun	Jul	Aug	Sep	Oct	Nov	Dec	Year
in.	2.2	1.6	2.0	0.8	0.2	0.1	0.0	0.1	0.2	0.3	1.2	1.4	10.0

AVALON

Average Maximum Temperature

	Jan	Feb	Mar	Apr	May	Jun	Jul	Aug	Sep	Oct	Nov	Dec	Year
°C	17.7	17.8	18.2	19.4	20.1	21.2	23.0	23.9	23.6	22.6	19.9	17.7	20.4
°F	63.9	64.0	64.8	66.9	68.2	70.2	73.4	75.0	74.5	72.7	67.8	63.9	68.7

Average Minimum Temperature

	Jan	Feb	Mar	Apr	May	Jun	Jul	Aug	Sep	Oct	Nov	Dec	Year
°C	9.0	9.4	9.9	11.1	12.7	14.2	16.0	16.9	16.3	14.2	11.4	9.2	12.5
°F	48.2	48.9	49.8	52.0	54.9	57.6	60.8	62.4	61.3	57.6	52.5	48.6	54.5

Average Rainfall

	Jan	Feb	Mar	Apr	May	Jun	Jul	Aug	Sep	Oct	Nov	Dec	Year
in.	2.4	2.6	1.9	1.0	0.2	0.0	0.0	0.1	0.3	0.4	1.4	2.3	12.7

LONG BEACH

Average Maximum Temperature

	Jan	Feb	Mar	Apr	May	Jun	Jul	Aug	Sep	Oct	Nov	Dec	Year
°C	19.3	19.8	20.0	21.9	22.9	25.0	28.1	28.8	27.8	25.7	22.2	19.4	23.4
°F	66.7	67.6	68.0	71.4	73.2	77.0	82.6	83.8	82.0	78.3	72.0	66.9	74.1

Average Minimum Temperature

	Jan	Feb	Mar	Apr	May	Jun	Jul	Aug	Sep	Oct	Nov	Dec	Year
°C	7.1	8.2	9.4	11.0	13.5	15.4	17.4	18.2	17.0	14.3	10.2	7.2	12.4
°F	44.8	46.8	48.9	51.8	56.3	59.7	63.3	64.8	62.6	57.7	50.4	45.0	54.3

Average Rainfall

	Jan	Feb	Mar	Apr	May	Jun	Jul	Aug	Sep	Oct	Nov	Dec	Year
in.	3.0	3.0	2.4	1.0	0.3	0.1	0.0	0.1	0.2	0.5	1.3	2.4	14.0

TORRANCE

Average Maximum Temperature

	Jan	Feb	Mar	Apr	May	Jun	Jul	Aug	Sep	Oct	Nov	Dec	Year
°C	19.3	19.8	19.8	21.3	22.1	23.7	26.0	26.6	26.2	24.8	21.8	19.3	22.6
°F	66.7	67.6	67.6	70.3	71.8	74.7	78.8	79.9	79.2	76.6	71.2	66.7	72.7

Average Minimum Temperature

	Jan	Feb	Mar	Apr	May	Jun	Jul	Aug	Sep	Oct	Nov	Dec	Year
°C	7.3	8.0	8.6	10.0	12.1	14.0	15.8	16.6	15.8	13.5	10.1	7.5	11.6
°F	45.1	46.4	47.5	50.0	53.8	57.2	60.4	61.9	60.4	56.3	50.2	45.5	52.9

Average Rainfall

	Jan	Feb	Mar	Apr	May	Jun	Jul	Aug	Sep	Oct	Nov	Dec	Year
in.	3.1	2.9	2.2	0.9	0.1	0.0	0.0	0.1	0.2	0.3	1.3	2.2	13.5

LOS ANGELES INTERNATIONAL AIRPORT

Average Maximum Temperature

	Jan	Feb	Mar	Apr	May	Jun	Jul	Aug	Sep	Oct	Nov	Dec	Year
°C	18.7	18.8	18.6	19.6	20.5	22.1	24.0	24.7	24.7	23.5	21.2	18.8	21.3
°F	65.7	65.8	65.5	67.3	68.9	71.8	75.2	76.5	76.5	74.3	70.2	65.8	70.3

Average Minimum Temperature

	Jan	Feb	Mar	Apr	May	Jun	Jul	Aug	Sep	Oct	Nov	Dec	Year
°C	8.7	9.6	10.2	11.5	13.5	15.2	17.1	17.8	17.3	15.1	11.5	8.8	13.0
°F	47.7	49.3	50.4	52.7	56.3	59.4	62.8	64.0	63.1	59.2	52.7	47.8	55.4

Average Rainfall

	Jan	Feb	Mar	Apr	May	Jun	Jul	Aug	Sep	Oct	Nov	Dec	Year
in.	2.8	2.4	2.0	0.8	0.1	0.0	0.0	0.1	0.2	0.3	1.5	1.7	11.9

OXNARD

Average Maximum Temperature

	Jan	Feb	Mar	Apr	May	Jun	Jul	Aug	Sep	Oct	Nov	Dec	Year
°C	19.0	19.2	19.0	20.1	20.5	21.9	23.5	24.3	24.2	23.6	21.2	19.1	21.3
°F	66.2	66.6	66.2	68.2	68.9	71.4	74.3	75.7	75.6	74.5	70.2	66.4	70.3

Average Minimum Temperature

	Jan	Feb	Mar	Apr	May	Jun	Jul	Aug	Sep	Oct	Nov	Dec	Year
°C	6.7	7.2	7.9	9.0	10.9	12.8	14.3	15.0	14.1	11.9	9.1	6.7	10.5
°F	44.1	45.0	46.2	48.2	51.6	55.0	57.7	59.0	57.4	53.4	48.4	44.1	50.9

Average Rainfall

	Jan	Feb	Mar	Apr	May	Jun	Jul	Aug	Sep	Oct	Nov	Dec	Year
in.	3.4	3.0	2.4	1.0	0.1	0.0	0.0	0.1	0.1	0.4	1.6	2.6	14.8

SANTA BARBARA

Average Maximum Temperature

	Jan	Feb	Mar	Apr	May	Jun	Jul	Aug	Sep	Oct	Nov	Dec	Year
°C	18.3	18.7	19.1	20.3	20.7	22.0	24.0	25.0	24.3	23.4	20.6	18.6	21.2
°F	64.9	65.7	66.4	68.5	69.3	71.6	75.2	77.0	75.7	74.1	69.1	65.5	70.2

Average Minimum Temperature

	Jan	Feb	Mar	Apr	May	Jun	Jul	Aug	Sep	Oct	Nov	Dec	Year
°C	6.3	7.4	8.3	9.4	11.0	12.7	14.3	15.1	14.2	12.1	9.1	6.4	10.5
°F	43.3	45.3	46.9	48.9	51.8	54.9	57.7	59.2	57.6	53.8	48.4	43.5	50.9

Average Rainfall

	Jan	Feb	Mar	Apr	May	Jun	Jul	Aug	Sep	Oct	Nov	Dec	Year
in.	4.0	3.8	2.6	1.3	0.3	0.1	0.0	0.0	0.2	0.4	1.8	3.1	17.6

PISMO BEACH

Average Maximum Temperature

	Jan	Feb	Mar	Apr	May	Jun	Jul	Aug	Sep	Oct	Nov	Dec	Year
°C	17.2	18.2	18.3	19.7	20.1	21.0	21.1	21.8	22.2	22.2	19.8	17.5	19.9
°F	63.0	64.8	64.9	67.5	68.2	69.8	70.0	71.2	72.0	72.0	67.6	63.5	67.8

Average Minimum Temperature

	Jan	Feb	Mar	Apr	May	Jun	Jul	Aug	Sep	Oct	Nov	Dec	Year
°C	4.8	6.0	6.2	6.9	8.1	9.9	11.0	11.5	11.2	9.7	7.5	5.1	8.2
°F	40.6	42.8	43.2	44.4	46.6	49.8	51.8	52.7	52.2	49.5	45.5	41.2	46.8

Average Rainfall

	Jan	Feb	Mar	Apr	May	Jun	Jul	Aug	Sep	Oct	Nov	Dec	Year
in.	3.5	3.1	2.5	1.6	0.3	0.1	0.0	0.0	0.2	0.7	2.0	2.6	16.6

SAN LUIS OBISPO

Average Maximum Temperature

	Jan	Feb	Mar	Apr	May	Jun	Jul	Aug	Sep	Oct	Nov	Dec	Year
°C	17.4	18.2	18.3	20.0	21.1	23.5	25.6	26.2	26.0	24.6	20.7	17.8	21.6
°F	63.3	64.8	64.9	68.0	70.0	74.3	78.1	79.2	78.8	76.3	69.3	64.0	70.9

Average Minimum Temperature

	Jan	Feb	Mar	Apr	May	Jun	Jul	Aug	Sep	Oct	Nov	Dec	Year
°C	5.2	6.2	6.3	7.2	8.3	10.1	11.2	11.5	11.3	10.0	7.6	5.2	8.3
°F	41.4	43.2	43.3	45.0	46.9	50.2	52.2	52.7	52.3	50.0	45.7	41.4	46.9

Average Rainfall

	Jan	Feb	Mar	Apr	May	Jun	Jul	Aug	Sep	Oct	Nov	Dec	Year
in.	4.8	4.3	3.7	1.7	0.4	0.1	0.0	0.0	0.2	0.9	2.1	4.3	22.6

MORRO BAY

Average Maximum Temperature

	Jan	Feb	Mar	Apr	May	Jun	Jul	Aug	Sep	Oct	Nov	Dec	Year
°C	16.7	17.1	17.0	17.4	17.0	18.0	18.5	19.1	20.2	20.8	19.0	16.8	18.1
°F	62.1	62.8	62.6	63.3	62.6	64.4	65.3	66.4	68.4	69.4	66.2	62.2	64.6

Average Minimum Temperature

	Jan	Feb	Mar	Apr	May	Jun	Jul	Aug	Sep	Oct	Nov	Dec	Year
°C	5.6	6.4	6.5	7.1	8.3	10.1	11.0	11.6	11.2	10.1	7.9	5.5	8.5
°F	42.1	43.5	43.7	44.8	46.9	50.2	51.8	52.9	52.2	50.2	46.2	41.9	47.3

Average Rainfall

	Jan	Feb	Mar	Apr	May	Jun	Jul	Aug	Sep	Oct	Nov	Dec	Year
in.	3.2	2.9	3.2	1.3	0.3	0.1	0.0	0.1	0.4	0.7	1.9	2.2	16.3

APPENDIX B

AVERAGE WATER TEMPERATURES

WATER TEMPERATURES IN DEGREES FAHRENHEIT

Location	Jan	Feb	Mar	Apr	May	Jun	Jul	Aug	Sep	Oct	Nov	Dec
Scripps Pier	58	57	58	60	63	65	67	68	66	65	61	59
Oceanside	57	57	58	60	62	65	67	69	67	65	61	59
San Clemente	57	57	58	59	61	63	66	68	66	65	61	58
Avalon	58	57	58	59	62	64	67	70	69	68	63	60
Dana Point	57	57	59	62	63	67	68	68	67	65	61	58
Balboa	57	57	58	59	62	64	66	67	65	65	61	59
Newport Beach	58	60	60	61	64	66	69	70	69	68	64	61
Los Angeles	58	58	60	60	61	64	67	68	67	66	64	60
Santa Monica	57	57	58	59	61	65	67	68	67	65	61	59
Zuma Beach	57	57	57	57	58	60	63	66	65	64	61	58
Point Mugu	57	57	56	55	56	58	60	62	62	62	60	59
Anacapa Island	56	56	56	57	59	61	64	65	65	64	61	59
Port Hueneme	56	56	56	56	57	60	62	62	62	62	60	58
Ventura	55	57	58	59	61	64	65	67	66	65	60	56
Santa Barbara	56	57	57	58	60	62	63	65	64	64	60	57
Gaviota	57	57	56	57	58	60	63	64	64	62	61	58
Avila Beach	55	56	55	54	55	57	60	60	60	59	57	55
Morro Bay	54	54	54	54	55	57	58	58	58	57	56	55

WEBSITES FOR CURRENT TEMPERATURES

Los Angeles   http://www.olld.nos.noaa.gov/station_plots/9410660w.html
(46045)
Santa Monica   http://www.olld.nos.noaa.gov/station_plots/9410840w.html
Santa Barbara   http://www.olld.nos.noaa.gov/station_plots/9411340w.html

APPENDIX C

RULES AND REGULATIONS

You go to the beach to enjoy yourself and the company of those with you or those you meet. That's why everyone else is there as well. Not everyone likes the same things. Okay, that's no surprise, but now I'm going to ruffle some feathers. Some people are so opposed to what some others may want to do that certain activities have been banned. Others may be banned to help keep order and safety in a crowded environment. Though nobody likes to be told what to do, rules and regulations are a fact of life. If you don't like one, work to get it changed.

While different beaches' rules are as different as grains of sand, some generalities can be made. If you are planning an activity that has been regulated elsewhere in society, chances are it's regulated on the beach. Before getting your heart set on bungee jumping naked with your personal watercraft and a speargun, call the phone numbers given in the beach descriptions in this book. The most common categories of regulation are listed below.

Glass: Most people who go to the beach like to feel the sand between their toes. Slicing a foot open because someone without the blessing of forethought brought a beer bottle is a real drag. Thanks to modern technology, Jimmy Buffett's Margaritaville ailment (stepped on a pop-top) is no longer a problem. However, any litter should be brought home or put in trash cans. If you like to litter, do us all a favor and go hang out at the landfill.

Fires: There's nothing quite like a barbecue at the beach—the sights, sounds, and sand in the buns. Bonfires are pretty neat too, slowly spinning to keep you warm while someone bangs away on a guitar. There's also nothing quite like walking barefoot on the beach and stepping on sand that has been heated to over 400 degrees by somebody who buried their coals. Basically, fire are outlawed unless containers for them have been provided. Some places allow portable grills. However, *never, never, never* bury your coals! If it's legal to use a grill, there will be a place to put your used coals. Third-degree burns are not simply inconvenient: They are crippling.

Dogs: Anyone who has shared in a dog's life knows how much fun they can be at the beach! Everyone loves Fido and Fluffy, right? Those dog regulations are for those with mean dogs or dog owners who don't bring pooper scoopers, right? Wrong! Almost every beach in this book has regulations regarding dogs. Some restrict all usage. Others limit the hours to morning and evening. Still others allow full-time, leashless run of the canines. No matter where you are with a dog, a responsible owner cleans up after it. If you see a dog and owner breaking the rules, it is best to tell a lifeguard. Think about it: A person with a barking, growling dog probably owns it because the person is actually a frightened individual. Such an individual may react defensively to a confrontation, which usually means aggressively, which the animal will pick up on. Not a good mix.

Alcohol: These regulations rival the dog rules for the top spot on the "most complained about" list—and probably the "most not obeyed list," too. Like any regulations, the intentions are good. While not many people really mind others being drunk, the disorderly business that can accompany drunkenness can be a pain to others. Then there's the safety issue. Mixing drinking and swimming is pretty chancy. Drinking and swimming in the ocean is asking for trouble. So what, you say? It's your life? Well, the lifeguard that has to save a flailing drunk probably values his or her own life, and he or she is required to try to save yours. All that said, many beaches still allow alcohol to be imbibed on site. These places often regulate where and when one can partake in spirits. One reason for these regulations is to help curb the homeless problem: It gives the cops an official reason to hassle the homeless.

Water Activities: A beach's recreation zone extends into the water past the surf zone. When the area is packed with humanity, surfing with a long, hard, piece of fiberglass could kill or maim. Too many people also mess up the ride. To allow everyone an equal chance to play in the Pacific, water activities are often regulated. Sometimes this means mornings and evenings only. Sometimes there's an outright ban. Still other beaches split the surf zone up, allowing surfing on one side and boardless activities on the other. A good rule of thumb is this: If the beach is the wide, sandy variety that is usually crowded, then it's likely to regulate surfing. These regulations are sometimes indicated by flags that are posted at lifeguard towers. Yellow with a black spot (ball) means no surfing. Checkered flags often mean separate areas for surfers and swimmers. If in doubt, ask the lifeguard. They're really nice people. Honest.

Lifeguards: It's illegal to interfere with a lifeguard doing his or her duty. This means you must do whatever lifeguards tell you to and you can't give them false information. It's a misdemeanor, but that's not why you shouldn't do it. It's just wrong. Anyone who injures a lifeguard will be prosecuted for felony battery.

Cliff Diving: It seems like "No Cliff Diving" signs show up everywhere, even where there aren't cliffs. I doubt there are really any patrols looking for people breaking this rule, but its existence means one probably won't win a lawsuit after jumping onto the rocks and smashing one's brains in the tidal pools.

ABOUT THE AUTHOR

This is the third installment of "About the Author" for me. The first two are in *Mountain Biking Colorado Springs* and *Mountain Biking Moab,* both published by Falcon. In those books, I described the path that led me to California, where I was learning to surf.

Now it's two years later and I'm still learning to surf. Riding the ocean is something that can never be perfected but can always be learned from. It teaches one to roll with the flow, be patient, watch for opportunities, and enjoy everything that comes along. These are things that one is always in a state of relearning. However, surfing almost daily does give one a certain amount of proficiency.

After researching and writing this book, I find myself living in Los Osos, California, with my fiancee, Heidi. We share a passion for the outdoors...and I tolerate (read love) her cats.

I'm discovering that I like this writing thing. So I've decided to do more of it. Until next time, remember: "Life is a sandwich...take big bites!"

HEIDI DAVID PHOTO

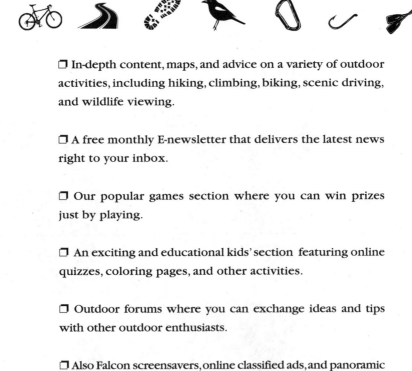

FALCON GUIDES ®Leading the Way™

■ *To order any of these books, check with your local bookseller*
*or call FALCON ® at **1-800-582-2665**.*
Visit us on the world wide web at:
www.FalconOutdoors.com

FALCON®

FALCON GUIDES ® Leading the Way™

WILDLIFE VIEWING GUIDES

Alaska Wildlife Viewing Guide
Arizona Wildlife Viewing Guide
California Wildlife Viewing Guide
Colorado Wildlife Viewing Guide
Florida Wildlife Viewing Guide
Indiana Wildlife Vewing Guide
Iowa Wildlife Viewing Guide
Kentucky Wildlife Viewing Guide
Massachusetts Wildlife Viewing Guide
Montana Wildlife Viewing Guide
Nebraska Wildlife Viewing Guide
Nevada Wildlife Viewing Guide
New Hampshire Wildlife Viewing Guide
New Jersey Wildlife Viewing Guide
New Mexico Wildlife Viewing Guide
New York Wildlife Viewing Guide
North Carolina Wildlife Viewing Guide
North Dakota Wildlife Viewing Guide
Ohio Wildlife Viewing Guide
Oregon Wildlife Viewing Guide
Puerto Rico and the Virgin Islands WVG
Tennessee Wildlife Viewing Guide
Texas Wildlife Viewing Guide
Utah Wildlife Viewing Guide
Vermont Wildlife Viewing Guide
Virginia Wildlife Viewing Guide
Washington Wildlife Viewing Guide
West Virginia Wildlife Viewing Guide
Wisconsin Wildlife Viewing Guide

HISTORIC TRAIL GUIDES

Traveling California's Gold Rush Country
Traveling the Lewis & Clark Trail
Traveling the Oregon Trail
Traveler's Guide to the Pony Express Trail

SCENIC DRIVING GUIDES

Scenic Driving Alaska and the Yukon
Scenic Driving Arizona
Scenic Driving the Beartooth Highway
Scenic Driving California
Scenic Driving Colorado
Scenic Driving Florida
Scenic Driving Georgia
Scenic Driving Hawaii
Scenic Driving Idaho
Scenic Driving Indiana
Scenic Driving Kentucky
Scenic Driving Michigan
Scenic Driving Minnesota
Scenic Driving Montana
Scenic Driving New England
Scenic Driving New Mexico
Scenic Driving North Carolina
Scenic Driving Oregon
Scenic Driving the Ozarks including the
  Ouchita Mountains
Scenic Driving Pennsylvania
Scenic Driving Texas
Scenic Driving Utah
Scenic Driving Virginia
Scenic Driving Washington
Scenic Driving Wisconsin
Scenic Driving Wyoming
Scenic Driving Yellowstone & Grand Teton
  National Parks
Back Country Byways
Scenic Byways East & South
Scenic Byways Far West
Scenic Byways Rocky Mountains

*To order any of these books, check with your local bookseller
or call FALCON ® at **1-800-582-2665**.
Visit us on the world wide web at:
www.FalconOutdoors.com*

FALCON®

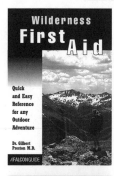

WILDERNESS FIRST AID

By Dr. Gilbert Preston M.D.

Enjoy the outdoors and face the inherent risks with confidence. By reading this easy-to-follow first-aid text, all outdoor enthusiasts can pack a little extra peace of mind on their next adventure. *Wilderness First Aid* offers expert medical advice for dealing with outdoor emergencies beyond the reach of 911. It easily fits in most backcountry first-aid kits.

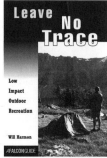

LEAVE NO TRACE

By Will Harmon

The concept of "leave no trace" seems simple, but it actually gets fairly complicated. This handy quick-reference guidebook includes all the newest information on this growing and all-important subject. This book is written to help the outdoor enthusiast make the hundreds of decisions necessary to protect the natural landscape and still have an enjoyable wilderness experience. Part of the proceeds from the sale of this book go to continue leave-no-trace education efforts. The Official Manual of American Hiking Society.

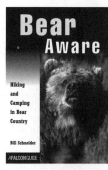

BEAR AWARE

By Bill Schneider

Hiking in bear country can be very safe if hikers follow the guidelines summarized in this small, "packable" book. Extensively reviewed by bear experts, the book contains the latest information on the intriguing science of bear-human interactions. *Bear Aware* can not only make your hike safer, but it can help you avoid the fear of bears that can take the edge off your trip.

MOUNTAIN LION ALERT

By Steve Torres

Recent mountain lion attacks have received national attention. Although infrequent, lion attacks raise concern for public safety. *Mountain Lion Alert* contains helpful advice for mountain bikers, trail runners, horse riders, pet owners, and suburban landowners on how to reduce the chances of mountain lion-human conflicts.

Also Available

Wilderness Survival • Reading Weather • Backpacking Tips • Climbing Safely • Avalanche Aware • Desert Hiking Tips • Hiking with Dogs • Using GPS • Route Finding • Wild Country Companion

To order check with your local bookseller or call FALCON® at **1-800-582-2665.**
www.FalconOutdoors.com